Why should we wait to teach our children the beautiful truths of Scripture? Brian Dembowczyk has made it simple for us to communicate the most important doctrines of the Christian faith to the next generation. With this resource, parents and children alike will grow in their knowledge and understanding of who God is, what he is like, and what he has done to save us.

—Trevin Wax, Bible and Reference publisher at LifeWay Christian Resources, general editor of The Gospel Project, author of *This Is Our Time: Everyday Myths in Light of the Gospel* and *Gospel-Centered Teaching*

The task to take the gospel to the nations, for Christian parents, begins in the living room. But many parents feel overwhelmed. Where to begin? *Cornerstones*, by Brian Dembowczyk, is a great help. These questions and answers are a useful tool for teaching children the core truths of Christianity, and the parent guide gives parents the knowledge they need to confidently teach their children. I strongly recommend this book!

—Ed Stetzer, Billy Graham Distinguished Chair, Wheaton College

As a mom of three and children's ministry champion, I need a book like *Cornerstones* to help me cover the fundamentals of doctrine and truth in a systematic way. Knowing that haphazard discipleship can lead to confusion, I'm grateful for Brian's carefully crafted questions that make it easy to have age-appropriate gospel conversations.

—Jana Magruder, director, LifeWay Kids, author of *Nothing Less: Engaging Kids in a Lifetime of Faith* and *Kids Ministry that Nourishes*

I love anything that makes theology accessible, especially to children. This book is not only accessible, but it is beautiful. It will prove to be a real asset to you and your family as you help your children grow in the knowledge of God and his character.

—Micah Fries, pastor, Brainerd Baptist Church

The *Cornerstones* resources are easy and effective tools for discipling our kids. Created from the ministry and personal experience of trusted leader Brian Dembowczyk, every parent will feel empowered by these books.

—Philip Nation, pastor and author of *Habits for Our Holiness*

D0111821

Cornerstones is tremendous. Brian Dembowczyk offers a systematic theology for parents and children. Easily accessible, yet its simplicity does not minimize its effect. His work comes from a heart deeply concerned about the future of families and the church. *Cornerstones* has the capacity to change significantly the way you do family worship and children's ministry. Anyone involved with the spiritual development of children will find the book useful. Paul states in 1 Corinthians 1:18 (NIV), "For the message of the cross is foolishness to those who are perishing, but to us who are being saved it is the power of God." *Cornerstones* displays and teaches the power of God.

—Dr. Kevin M. Jones, associate dean of Academic Innovation and professor of Teacher Education, Boyce College

Cornerstones is remarkably understandable and theologically comprehensive, making it a resource that will help parents and kids from all walks of life grasp the central truths of the Christian faith. This well-rounded guide provides categories that are essential, questions that are accessible, and support for parents in the most important conversations they will ever have with their children. There is potential for this resource to make waves for generations to come in families and churches who embrace its potential. Take the long view and utilize this resource from cover to cover, and I assure you it will be a blessing to you and your children.

—Steven Ackley, NextGen pastor, LifePoint Church

In my role as LifeWay's leader of ministry to men, one of the biggest frustrations I observe is the lack of knowledge and tools they need to lead their families spiritually. These incredible resources alleviate that hurdle. This is a must-have!

—Kris Dolberry, LifeWay Men leader

As a parent and a kids minister, I am grateful for a resource that not only refuses to shy away from teaching kids the deep truths of theology but also provides practical answers for parents to pass on these truths to their children. *Cornerstones* is a must-have for every ministry leader and every parent's library, because this is one resource that you will find yourself using over and over again.

—Danielle Bell, minister to children, Dawson Family of Faith; national KidMin speaker, curriculum writer, and blogger

CORNERSTONES

PARENT GUIDE

200
QUESTIONS & ANSWERS
TO TEACH TRUTH

BRIAN DEMBOWCZYK

PUBLISHING GROUP

NASHVILLE, TENNESSEE

To Joshua, Hannah, and Caleb. You are a blessing!
I am grateful for God's kindness in choosing me to be your father.
I pray that I may be a faithful steward of the amazing gift
God has given me. I love you!

Contents

CREATION

SIN

JESUS

SALVATION

DISCIPLESHIP

THE CHURCH AND LAST THINGS

Acknowledgments

This book began about fifteen years ago when, as a family pastor, I grappled with how to help parents teach the key doctrines of our faith to their children. I didn't just want to teach theology to parents—I wanted to teach parents *how* to teach theology to their kids. Over the years, I would play with a resource to do just that.

Enter the B&H Publishing team.

When I shared a proposal for a book of questions and answers with brief explanations of each that parents could read with their kids and feel empowered to have meaningful conversations about God, I held my breath; hoping the B&H team could at least see the vision for such a resource. But they didn't just see it; they ran forward with it and took this project to a place I couldn't dream of.

Thank you for your partnership. You have a reputation for being a joy to work with and for valuing your authors and going above and beyond for them. You are amazing and surpassed that well-earned reputation. It has been a privilege and an honor to work with you, and I am deeply humbled by this experience.

One person from B&H needs to be singled out for a special thank-you. Taylor Combs, this book is leaps and bounds better because of your work on it. I owe you my deepest gratitude for the feedback, suggestions, and direction you provided. You not only helped me beyond measure, but you also were an amazing encouragement. Thank you for your patience and understanding.

Thanks also goes to Paul Enns and Russell Moore, my theology professors in seminary, as well as the rest of my masters and doctoral professors at The Southern Baptist Theological Seminary and New Orleans Baptist Theological Seminary. You helped instill a deep love and appreciation of theology within me.

Thank you to you, the parents who are reading this book. I am grateful that you value one of the greatest gifts God gives us—our children—by discipling them. May God bless your efforts to share the gospel with your children.

Finally, thank you to my wife, Tara. I did not earn or deserve your patience, understanding, and grace during the evening after evening and weekend after weekend while I wrote this book, but you gave it to me anyway. You are the rock of our family—you keep things going, and you keep us thriving even in the seasons when I am not walking alongside you, or in front of you, as I should be. You are an amazing mother and wife. I love you.

Soli Deo gloria!

Introduction

I recently built a wood deck that wraps around two sides of the concrete patio in the back of our house. The dirt where we live in middle Tennessee is a hard, rocky clay, and our builder didn't do us any favors by putting just a slight dusting of topsoil on it. It took all I had to dig holes for the roughly thirty concrete deck blocks I needed; and once they were all in place, I began the tedious process of leveling them, row by row.

To my surprise, the first row was close to being level, and after just a few minutes of removing dirt, adding dirt, and repeating that a few more times, I managed to get it level. I swung around to the other side of the patio to level a row there next. If I leveled a row on both sides and if they were level with each other, I would be in great shape to level the rest. After about thirty minutes, the row was leveled. Everything looked like it was in good shape. The first row was level with the patio, and this second row was too. But when I dropped the level on both rows, I saw the one thing I didn't want to see—a bubble floating away from the center circle on the level. The two rows were not level.

I double-checked that both rows were level with the patio. I triple-checked. And then I sat down to ponder where my fledgling deck project had gone awry. Both rows were level with the patio. Why weren't they level with each other? And then it hit me. I placed the level on the patio itself and looked at the bubble. It was out of the circle. The patio was not level.

The patio was built sloping away from the house to pull water away from the house and foundation when it rained. That hadn't occurred to me before. I had just assumed it was level, which is why, while both of the rows were level with it, they were not level with each other. The standard I was using was off, and so my first two rows were off as well.

Jesus *the* Cornerstone

Paul's favorite metaphor of the church was the human body, with Jesus being the head and each person in the church being a different body part. He used this picture in Romans, 1 Corinthians, Ephesians, and Colossians. But this wasn't the only way Paul described the church. He also pictured the church as the bride of Christ (2 Corinthians, Ephesians), a family (2 Corinthians, Galatians, Ephesians, 1 Timothy), and a building (1 Corinthians, Ephesians). It is this last metaphor of the church as a building where we see Jesus called the cornerstone:

> So then you are no longer foreigners and strangers, but fellow citizens with the saints, and members of God's household, built on the foundation of the apostles and prophets, with Christ Jesus himself as the cornerstone. In him the whole building, being put together, grows into a holy temple in the Lord. (Eph. 2:19–21)

Jesus is the cornerstone, and the apostles and prophets are the foundation upon which the church is built. It's a great image of the church, especially if we think back to building projects in Paul's day.

We have to think back to a time before computers and precision power tools and equipment, when building stones were hewn by hand. The cornerstone was the most important stone because it determined if the entire structure was going to be square and level. If the cornerstone were off, the entire structure would be off too. Kind of like my deck. My cornerstone, the patio, was not level, and had I built my deck with that standard, it would have been all off. That is why a builder in Paul's day would choose the best stone—the perfect one—to be the cornerstone. If the cornerstone were perfect, the rest of the foundation and the structure that stood above it would be right. The cornerstone was the most important part of a building—by far.

That is why Paul's image in Ephesians 2 is so powerful. It reminds us that Jesus is our perfect standard of truth and life. Everything we believe and everything we do is based on who Jesus is and what he has done. The reason we can believe and live with confidence is because Jesus is indeed the perfect cornerstone. But Paul wasn't the first to call Jesus the cornerstone. Here is what Isaiah wrote about the Messiah hundreds of years before:

> Therefore the Lord GOD said:
> "Look, I have laid a stone in Zion,
> a tested stone,
> a precious cornerstone, a sure foundation;
> the one who believes will be unshakable.

And I will make justice the measuring line
and righteousness the mason's level."
Hail will sweep away the false refuge,
and water will flood your hiding place. (Isa. 28:16–17)

Jesus is the precious cornerstone who was tested and proved to be perfect. The church, then, is built on a solid foundation of the teachings of the apostles and prophets because their teachings were based on Jesus. Our foundation is secure and unshakable.

Peter picked up on this image too and quoted Isaiah in 1 Peter 2:6, but notice what he called us in the verse before:

> You yourselves, as living stones, a spiritual house, are being
> built to be a holy priesthood to offer spiritual sacrifices accept-
> able to God through Jesus Christ. (1 Pet. 2:5)

Jesus is the cornerstone; and we are living stones, bricks in the house of faith we call the church, standing on the foundation that Jesus has made square and level. Think about that for a minute. While the cornerstone is essential, each stone or brick of the structure is important in its own right too. Each one needs to be square and level as well, or the building will still be off. Square and level stones standing on top of a square and level foundation anchored on the square and level cornerstone—that is how a strong structure is built. That is how the church is built.

Cornerstones of Theology

So what does this have to do with us as parents? Well, on the most basic level, it matters to us because as followers of Jesus we need to have a solid theology based on who Jesus is and what he has done.

I know what you're thinking. *Theology* is an intimidating word. When many of us think of theology, we picture seminary professors in tweed jackets with elbow patches discussing the hypostatic union or the peccability of Jesus.[1] Those are theologians; we are not. While those deep discussions have a place in theology and the church, at its core, theology is simply what you understand about God. That's what *theology* means—the study of God. That means that everyone is a theologian—including you and me. We all have an understanding of God. The only question is if we are good theologians or poor theologians.

And that is where we come back around to Jesus being the cornerstone. While we all have beliefs about God, the problem is that we often develop our understanding of God—our theology—from the wrong sources—places other than God's Word—or that we don't quite understand what we read in God's Word. That is what leads to a poor and sometimes even an incorrect view of God. If Jesus is the cornerstone—the standard for all that we believe and do as his followers—and if the Bible bears witness to him (Luke 24:27), then the way we can be sure to develop a proper theology is by spending time in God's Word. That is how we can ensure that we are the square and level living stones that Peter talked about.

And that takes us to the deeper level of why Jesus' being the cornerstone matters to us as parents—because we are parents. Our kids need to develop a solid theology as well; they need to be square and level stones. While Jesus is *the* cornerstone, in a sense, as parents, we are cornerstones for our children, helping to give their budding faith shape and direction. This isn't working against Christ or apart from him, but according to God's plan for us in the home. Here is what we see in Deuteronomy 6:4–9 in a passage known as the Shema:

> "Listen, Israel: The Lord our God, the Lord is one. Love the Lord your God with all your heart, with all your soul, and with all your strength. These words that I am giving you today are to be in your heart. Repeat them to your children. Talk about them when you sit in your house and when you walk along the road, when you lie down and when you get up. Bind them as a sign on your hand and let them be a symbol on your forehead. Write them on the doorposts of your house and on your city gates."

God's design is for parents, not the church, to be the primary disciplers of their children. Sure, the church matters—it matters quite a bit—but the responsibility, and privilege, of discipling children rests on parents. The home is to be the primary laboratory where faith is worked out. The gospel is to be lived out and talked about as a normal rhythm of a family's life. The church's role is to come alongside and around families and encourage, equip, and support them in their primary calling. That's why we need to be good theologians who are helping our kids become good theologians too—it is our primary ministry as parents.

OK, so how do we do that? It starts by picturing theology as an intricate tapestry of dozens or hundreds of fine threads woven tightly together. Or as an elaborate stained glass window with hundreds of small pieces of colored glass fitted tightly and perfectly together. If one thread or one piece of glass, no matter how small, is off, the entire project will be off too. Each of our beliefs about God impacts other beliefs about him. And for that reason, each one is like a little cornerstone in itself.

And that brings us to the *Cornerstones* books. *Cornerstones: 200 Questions and Answers to Learn Truth* provides 200 questions and answers that work together to provide a broad and deep understanding of who God is and what he has done for us in Christ. By learning the questions and answers with your kids and then having conversations together about them, you will find yourself exploring the wonders and marvels of the gospel and coming to a deeper understanding and love of God. And that is where this book comes into play. The *Cornerstones Parent Guide* is designed to help you come to a better understanding of the theology behind each question and answer so that you will be better able to talk about it with your child. The more you understand each question and answer, the more confidence you will have in talking with your child and guiding them to truth. This book isn't meant to be read to your kid; it is meant for you to read on your own. Think of this as your commentary on the questions and answers to read in preparation for having those life-changing conversations with your kids in your normal rhythms of life.

Cornerstones in Practice

Why questions? Why are the cornerstones in question-and-answer format and not just statements? It's a good question that deserves an answer.

Questions engage us on a much deeper level than statements. Questions pique our curiosity, stir our imaginations, and invite us in. Questions and answers are also easier for kids to memorize. Kids have amazing memories, but even they need some help jarring them at times. The questions do just that, which is also why many of the questions are repeated in the answers. In this way, the questions themselves become memory pegs, giving your child an opportunity to reach back into his or her memory for the right answer as the question part of the answer is being repeated.

This is why the question-and-answer format has been used to teach children, and even adults, theology for so long. From the time of the Protestant Reformation in the 1500s when Martin Luther developed a resource of structured questions and answers to teach children, theology has been taught in this manner in Lutheran, Methodist, Pentecostal, Reformed, Baptist, and other churches. The famed and beloved Baptist pastor Charles H. Spurgeon even wrote a resource of questions and answers in the 1800s.

So how does it work best? How do you use *Cornerstones* most effectively? It's not as hard as you might think. That's the beauty of it.

The questions are grouped into eight categories covering major areas of theology:

+ **God:** 30 questions on who God is and what he is like.
+ **Creation:** 20 questions on what, why, and how God created.
+ **Sin:** 20 questions on Adam and Eve's first sin, how it impacted everything, and what sin is.
+ **Jesus:** 20 questions on who Jesus is and what he has done.
+ **Salvation:** 20 questions on how people are saved and the key terms of the salvation process.
+ **The Bible:** 30 questions on what the Bible is, how it is structured, and some of its key teachings.
+ **Discipleship:** 40 questions on how people grow in their faith and live each day for Christ.
+ **The Church and Last Things:** 20 questions on what the church is, its role, and what will happen when Jesus returns for his church.

As you thumb through the questions, you will notice that many of the questions in each category progressively build on the previous ones, so you may want to ask them in order so they make the most sense. At the same time, you might want to bounce around from category to category to add variety, especially when your child really begins to learn them.

Once you feel comfortable with the questions and answers and are ready to begin teaching them to your child, you will want to start by setting aside regular time each week for memorizing and discussing them. This might be a night or two a week at dinnertime, Sundays at lunch, or Saturday mornings. Pick the time or times that work best for your family, are easiest to protect from hectic schedules, and allow your child to focus and engage with you. Establishing a rhythm right away is important because this is a pretty long process. There is a lot to learn and discuss, and a routine will help make sure you stick with it instead of watching it fall by the wayside.

But here's the thing: while you want to structure time each week to go over *Cornerstones*, you don't want to make the time itself too structured. You want your child to enjoy this time and not come to see it as a boring chore during the week. So if your schedule is one night a week at dinner, always have a fun dinner your child enjoys that night. Or do it right after dinner while you eat ice cream sundaes. Or better yet, as you eat ice cream sundaes for dinner! If it is Saturday mornings, make it a tradition that you always have banana pancakes while you learn the questions and answers. Do what you can to make this memorable in a good way!

As you begin, take your time and ask just a few questions each time. Don't worry about trying to cover all 200 questions and answers in any certain time frame. If it takes a year, that's great. If it takes four years of a question a week, that's fantastic. If you are still calling your kid up in college to finish the last few questions, that works too! Just don't pressure yourself to complete the questions in an artificial time frame. The goal is not necessarily to finish, but to learn.

As you ask new questions, read the question and see if your child can answer it in his or her own words. Then read the answer in the book and talk about it. Ask questions like:

- Does that make sense to you?
- How does that make you feel?
- Does that make you think of any other questions you might have?
- Is there anything more you would like to know about that?

Your goal here is to get below the surface and have a meaningful discussion about God. Draw from what you read in this book or what you have learned as you have grown in your faith. If you are asked a follow-up question you can't answer, research the answer together. You can make a great impact on your kid by acknowledging without any shame that you are still learning about God yourself and then rolling up your sleeves to learn together. If a meaningful conversation happens after one question and that is all you get to that time, consider it a major win! Remember, the key here is quality, not quantity.

The next time you go over the questions, start by asking the ones you went over the last time. Try to help your child memorize these as close to verbatim as possible—not necessarily because the exact wording of each answer is essential, but because it helps in the memorization process. And memorization is important, because while your child may not fully understand the theology of the question and the answer at this time, the words will stick with him or her until the time when he or she is able to understand.

Once you have reviewed the questions and answers you have covered, work in new ones. Kids learn best by repetition, so don't be afraid to ask the same questions over and over again. As you progress further into the questions, you won't be able to repeat all of the questions you have asked to that point, so ask a sampling of questions and then add new ones.

That takes care of your structured times to go over *Cornerstones*, but that is not the only time you want to talk with your child about the questions and answers. Remember that God wants us to talk with our kids about him as a normal part of our day. Take the opportunities you have each day to ask a question or two—even if it is just for a couple of minutes. The great thing about these questions is that they don't need much time to ask and answer. You can knock out a handful while waiting in a long fast-food line.

Think about the normal rhythm of your days. When can you weave some questions and answers into what you are already doing? During meals. While driving to school, church, or practice. At bedtime. During chores. During commercials. While playing outside, riding bikes, or going for a walk. There doesn't have to be any structure at all to this. Just ask a question. That's all it will take. You might be surprised what can happen just by asking a question.

The Win of *Cornerstones*

As you read through the four Gospels, you will come across Jesus using the phrase "Truly I tell you" at times. Some translations use "truly, truly" or "verily, verily" instead. This doesn't mean what he says after is true and everything else isn't. This was Jesus' way of getting people's attention. You can almost think of it as "Listen up now. Lean in and pay close attention to what I am about to say."

Truly I tell you that what I am about to say is important. OK, are you leaning in now? Good. Here goes.

Don't measure the win of using *Cornerstones* by how much your kids know. Without a doubt, it is important that they learn the questions and answers, and it would be great if they were to memorize all two hundred. But that is not the win. The win you want to pursue is if they come to know the God behind the questions. We want to spend the time learning and talking about these questions, not so our kids have more knowledge for the sake of knowledge, but so that they get to know God more, and as a result, love him more. It's loving God that we are after. We want our kids to love who God is and what he has done. That is the win. Learning the questions and answers is just a tool—an important one, but just a tool all the same. We are after the heart, because that is what God is after.

Do you remember Jesus' encounter with the two disciples traveling on the road to Emmaus on Easter Sunday? We read about it in Luke 24.

Two disciples were walking back to Emmaus talking about what had happened in Jerusalem the prior week when Jesus approached them. Jesus' identity was hidden from them, and he asked what they were talking about. The two stopped dead in their tracks and looked sad. They then shared about what had happened to Jesus, ending with the report of some of the other disciples saying that Jesus was alive. But the two disciples couldn't get there themselves. They just hadn't embraced the resurrection at that point. They mostly had the facts right about what had happened, but they just couldn't put it all together.

Jesus responded by walking them through the Old Testament, showing how all of Scripture pointed to him. Soon after, he disappeared from their sight, and this is how they summed up their experience:

> They said to each other, "Weren't our hearts burning within
> us while he was talking with us on the road and explaining the
> Scriptures to us?" (Luke 24:32)

What was it that stirred their affections? It wasn't the facts themselves—as important as they were. It was seeing how those facts fit together to reveal Jesus that moved them. That is what they were missing—or, more precisely, *he* is who they were missing. And once they found him, their hearts were moved and their lives were surely never the same.

That is what we want for our kids. We want them to know the questions and answers—to learn theology—as a step toward meeting the God behind that theology. We want them to get to know Jesus, trust in him, and have their lives changed forevermore. The gospel changes hearts, which, in turn, changes lives. We can't forget that is our goal.

The Choice We Must Make

Once the children of Israel had completed the conquest of the promised land, their leader Joshua gathered the people to share a final charge much like Moses had done years before. Joshua called on the people to choose whom they would worship—God or the pagan gods of the people who had lived in the land before them. The people said they would worship and obey God. They promised they would.

But they didn't.

Joshua's generation slowly died off one by one, and then we read this:

> That whole generation was also gathered to their ancestors. After them another generation rose up who did not know the LORD or the works he had done for Israel. (Judg. 2:10)

Do you see it? The generation that had conquered the promised land failed to live out God's instructions in Deuteronomy 6. An entire generation of parents failed to teach their kids about God. That next generation didn't know what God had done for their parents, their grandparents, and all of their ancestors back to Abraham, Isaac, and Jacob. And when you read the rest of the book of Judges, you see the disastrous results and great cost as this generation and the following ones rebelled against God over and over again.

But then we flip over and see what Paul wrote to Timothy hundreds of years later:

> Remembering your tears, I long to see you so that I may be filled with joy. I recall your sincere faith that first lived in your grandmother Lois and in your mother Eunice and now, I am convinced, is in you also. (2 Tim. 1:4–5)

Three generations of faithfulness. Three generations of teaching God's Word to the next.

And that is the choice we each must make.

Will we be like the children of Israel who entered the promised land, or will we be like a faithful grandmother and mother?

Because you're reading this book, I presume you have chosen the latter. May God bless you as you teach your kids about God and point them to the beauty of the gospel and a life of seeking to bring Christ Jesus glory.

GOD

Q. What is God?

A. God is creator and ruler of everything.

When you stop and think about it, answering the question of what God is can be pretty challenging. Most of us are so familiar with God that we have forgotten what it was like not to know him. We can't remember when we asked that very question ourselves. That's why our immediate response to this question might be, "Well, God is just . . . God." It's about the same response we give when our kids ask us what a food they have never had tastes like. "Well, pork tastes like . . . pork." Or why the sky is blue. "It just is."

But when it comes to helping our kids understand what, or who, God is, they will want more than that. They'll need more than that. So where do we begin?

We could answer the question by sharing some of God's attributes—his love, glory, mercy, power, and so forth. But we would quickly realize that there are so many important characteristics of God that our definition would be way too long. It would feel like a laundry list of amazing attributes. Besides, many of God's attributes are pretty complicated themselves and thus would require definitions within our definition. We'll address God's attributes later because they are extremely important to knowing God, but for now, we'll set them aside in answering this fundamental question of what God is.

Perhaps a better approach in answering this question is to focus on one overarching description that is unique to God—a description that provides glimpses of his other important characteristics but that is simple enough for our kids to get their arms around. A description like this: *God is creator of everything*. After all, that is how God introduced himself to us:

In the beginning God created the heavens and the earth. (Gen. 1:1)

Now, that's a pretty simple definition, but when you think about it, it's packed full of helpful jumping-off points to talk over with our kids.

First, it hints at God's power. God created *everything*! The mountains, the oceans, every grain of sand on every beach in the world, all the animals, trees and plants, people, planets, the sun and moon, all of the stars—all billions and billions of them—everything. This is a God of whom we should be in awe!

Second, it sets God apart as being the only uncreated thing in existence. Everything else has a beginning, but not God. God is unique and special.

Third, it establishes that God has absolute authority over everything—including us. If God is creator, then he owns everything. And if God owns everything, then he gets to make up the rules and be in charge. That idea is critical, and the sooner we help imbed it in our kids' hearts, the better. That's why it is a good idea to add it to our definition.

What is God? God is creator and ruler of everything.

Short and sweet, but foundational truth for our kids.

Genesis 1:1; Hebrews 11:3

2

Q. Can we know that God exists?

A. Yes, we can know that God exists from evidence in nature and in the Bible and from an inner sense that tells us he does.

Believing in God takes faith, but not blind faith. There's a difference, and it's an incredibly important one. Blind faith says that we have to believe in something without any evidence. We believe it just because we believe it. But faith in God isn't like that. While we cannot point to evidence that completely proves God's existence, he has given us ample proof that makes our faith in God reasonable—rational:

> Now without faith it is impossible to please God, since the one who draws near to him must believe that he exists and that he rewards those who seek him. (Heb. 11:6)

Much of that evidence is all around us for everyone to see—creation itself. Let's start by talking about something we are all familiar with—cause and effect. We know that everything has a cause. If you were to walk into the living room and see a broken lamp on the end table, a football on the floor, and your son standing with his hands over his mouth, you might ask, "What happened?" all the while having a pretty good idea of the answer. That's your intuitive awareness of cause and effect. The lamp just didn't fall over broken. There was a cause. And in this case, there is a pretty good chance the cause was your son playing ball in the house.

We see the same law of cause and effect in nature all around us. Trees grow where they are because an acorn once fell on the soil where they stand.

Rivers flow into the ocean and don't run out because rain falls in the mountains to replenish them. A chicken is hatched because a hen laid an egg. Everything has a cause. A beginning. The same is true of the world as a whole. The world has a cause and that cause is God, who can be called the uncaused cause because he alone has no cause. This evidence for the existence of God was developed by philosophers centuries ago and is called the *cosmological argument for the existence of God.*

Nature gives us another helpful piece of evidence for God's existence in its complex design. From the intricate and precise orbit of the planets, to the finely tuned balance of the food chain, to the inner workings of the human body, to the cellular composition of a plant, nature shouts design. And where there is design, there is a designer. Just as we would look at a wristwatch and know there is a watchmaker behind it, we can look at creation and know there is a creator behind it. This is known as the *teleological argument for the existence of God.*

But we can see God's fingerprints in creation all around us even more plainly. The majesty of a mountain range stirs our hearts, and we just know there is an even more majestic Creator behind them. The mind-boggling size of the universe hints at the infinite size of the Creator who spoke it all into existence. The beauty of a field of wild flowers hints at the unmatched beauty of their Creator.

Nature gives us a good start in knowing God exists, but the Bible provides even more. The Bible was written by more than forty authors who wrote over a span of fifteen hundred years, on three continents, in two main languages. And yet the Bible records one cohesive story of God without contradiction or error. History and archaeology support what the Bible records, and there is greater manuscript evidence for the Bible than any other widely accepted work of antiquity. We can know God exists because the Bible is his story and it is amazingly reliable.

And that takes us to the third type of evidence for the existence of God—our inner sense that he exists. While some may not want to count this as viable evidence for God, it should not be dismissed. First, almost every culture in the world has some awareness of a supreme being or power behind creation. While not everyone knows who God is, almost everyone has an awareness that there is a God. Second, our personal experience with God matters. Skeptics may be able to poke holes in the philosophical evidences of God and rationalize creation with natural causes, but a person's experiences with God cannot be discounted or disproven.

When we put all of this together, we are left with a compelling argument that it is more rational to believe that God exists than to believe he does not.

Romans 1:20; Hebrews 11:6

Q. How many gods are there?

A. There is one true God, and only he deserves worship.

One of the most important passages for the Jewish people in the Bible is known as the Shema. *Shema* is the Hebrew word for "listen" or "hear," the first word of Deuteronomy 6:4 which begins the passage:

> "Listen, Israel: The LORD our God, the LORD is one."

The Shema is part of the Law that God gave to Israel after he delivered them out of slavery in Egypt. For hundreds of years before that, God's people had lived among a people who worshiped many different gods, and God wanted to set the record straight that there is one and only one true God who is to be worshiped.

It shouldn't be surprising, then, that the Ten Commandments begin with, "Do not have other gods besides me" (Exod. 20:3). God knew that one of the most important truths his people needed to grasp was that all the other gods that people believed in were false. The gods of the Egyptians. The gods of the Hittites, Assyrians, and Babylonians. The gods of the Greeks and Romans. All of the gods that his people would encounter were to be rejected.

Unfortunately, they didn't take this to heart. God's people fell into idolatry over and over again, even creating some of their own false gods, such as the golden calf while Moses was receiving the Law from God (see Exod. 32).

We are no different from the people of Israel in needing to remember that there is one true God who alone deserves worship. There are still religions that worship false gods all around us: Hinduism with its multitude of gods, Buddhism, Islam, and New Age religions, to name a few. It is common today to suggest that all of these religions, and Christianity as well, worship the

18

same god just by different names. But that is not what the one true God says. He is the one true God alone. Every other god is not simply another way to know him; they are all false gods that drive people away from him. But those are not the only gods we need to avoid turning to. Sometimes we worship gods that don't take the form of a physical idol. Money. Possessions. Sports. Family. Friends. Work. School. Entertainment. Happiness. Ourselves. We are worshipers by nature. We will worship something, whether that is the one true God or the false gods that we find or create. This is why the Shema and the first commandment are so important for our kids to understand. They will be tempted to worship plenty of other things besides God, just like us. But there is only one true God who deserves their worship and our worship. And he is glorious and easy to worship when we know him.

Deuteronomy 6:4; Exodus 20:3

Q. In how many Persons does God exist?

A. God is one God in three Persons.

God is one. We have seen how this truth is clearly taught in Scripture and how important it is. If only it were that easy! God is one, all right, but he is one *in three Persons*, a teaching often called the Trinity, or the triune nature of God.

So what does the Trinity mean exactly? What does God being one God in three Persons look like? Let's start with what we know:

+ There is one God, not three.
+ Each of the three Persons of the Trinity is fully God.
+ Each of the three Persons of the Trinity is distinct; God is not one person in different roles.
+ The three Persons of the Trinity perform different acts in time, and even though each of these acts is ultimately done by one God, the Bible distinguishes among the Persons in their actions toward us.

That's about it. If it still isn't clear, that's OK. This is one of the most baffling mysteries of the Christian faith that theologians have been trying to understand for centuries. Books have been written on it. Councils have met to debate it. And yet, we still don't understand much about it at all. And again, that's OK. If we knew all the answers to the questions about God—if we fully knew him—he wouldn't be that amazing, would he? He'd be rather ordinary. So while not having satisfying answers to questions like this one may be frustrating, we can also be grateful for them because they remind us of how much greater God is than us! Our kids don't need us to give them an answer for every question they have; they need us to give them the right answers to their questions when we know them, and they need us to help them wonder in awe at God when we simply don't know them.

You may have heard someone try to explain the Trinity with an analogy such as water and perhaps tried to explain it to your kids the same way. Water, it is said, can be a solid, a liquid, or a gas—three states but one substance. Or the Trinity is like a man who can be a husband, a father, and a son. Or the Trinity is like an egg with the shell, the white, and the yolk. While these illustrations can certainly be appealing, we need to be careful with all of them because they end up teaching something incorrect about the Trinity.

In the water analogy, water takes one form at a time, but the Trinity is three Persons at the same time, all the time. The man is one person who has three different roles in life, but the Trinity is three Persons. And none of the three parts of the egg is completely an egg, but each Person of the Trinity is fully God. In an effort to make the Trinity clearer, we may accidently give our kids the wrong understanding about it, so it's probably best not to try to explain the Trinity with an analogy. Instead we should be content to wrestle with what the Bible teaches us, knowing the Trinity will remain a mystery that we must accept in faith.

But just because we cannot fully understand the mystery of the Trinity doesn't mean we shouldn't try. Some have made that mistake, but it's important that we grow in our understanding of the Trinity as best as we can because it provides us with safeguards for understanding God properly. Remembering that God is one protects us from worshiping false gods, as we have seen. But remembering that God is one in three Persons is critical for recognizing the Holy Spirit and Jesus Christ as God. If God were not one in three Persons, then our very salvation itself would unravel.

The Trinity also reveals something fundamentally important about God—that he is relational in his essence! From eternity past, God the Father, God the Son, and God the Holy Spirit have enjoyed a perfectly fulfilling and satisfying relationship—a relationship of complete love, harmony, and unity. God did not create people because he was lonely and craved relationship. He already had perfect relationship within his triune nature! Instead, he created us—at least in part—so that we would be invited into that relationship and experience it ourselves.

That's why the doctrine of the Trinity matters—because it reminds us of God's kindness to create us to be in relationship with him and then to rescue us from sin and death to restore that relationship when we broke it. The Trinity reveals the heart of the gospel to us—the heart that we pray connects with our kids' hearts.

2 Corinthians 13:13; John 14:26

5

Q. Who are the three Persons of God?

A. The three Persons of God are God the Father, God the Son, and God the Holy Spirit.

The three Persons of God are the Father, the Son, and the Holy Spirit. But how do we *know* that? Or to be more precise, because God the Father being God isn't really in question, how can we know that the Son and Holy Spirit are God? Well, to be quite simple about it, we can know the Son and Holy Spirit are God by observing that they both demonstrate the qualities of being God.

First, here are some of the divine qualities we see in the Son. Jesus demonstrated omniscience, or knowing all things, when he knew the thoughts of others (Mark 2:8). He claimed to be able to forgive sins, which only God can do (Mark 2:9–11). He received worship, which is only appropriate for God to do (Matt. 14:33; 21:9; 28:9; Rev. 5:8–10). He is described as being eternal (John 1:1–2), the creator of everything (John 1:3; Col. 1:16), and the One who holds all things together (Col. 1:17). These are all qualities only God possesses, so if Jesus possesses them, he is God.

And now here are some of the Holy Spirit's divine qualities. The Spirit is eternal (John 14:16). He is omnipresent, or not confined to being in one place at a time (Ps. 139:7–8), and he is omniscient (1 Cor. 2:10). And like Jesus, the Holy Spirit is recognized as God (Acts 5:3–4). Again, the Holy Spirit possesses qualities that reveal he is God.

So we can see that there is plenty of evidence for the Son and Holy Spirit being God. But actually, we could have just turned to one verse to verify that the Son and Holy Spirit are God—Matthew 28:19. These are the final words of instruction Jesus gave his disciples, that we call the Great Commission:

> "Go, therefore, and make disciples of all nations, baptizing them in the name of the Father and of the Son and of the Holy Spirit."

As Christians, we are instructed to make disciples and baptize them in the name of the Father, the Son, and the Holy Spirit—placing them as equals while at the same time reminding us that these three Persons are different.

Knowing that Jesus is God is, of course, essential for salvation. If Jesus were not God, he would not have been able to live a life of total obedience to the Father and pay the penalty of sin for others in his death. But we cannot look past the importance of the Holy Spirit being God too. Because the Holy Spirit is God, he is able to be with all Christians permanently and encourage, comfort, and guide us as we, and our kids, so desperately need.

God the Father is God. God the Son is God. God the Holy Spirit is God. Fully and in perfect harmony.

Matthew 28:19; Ephesians 4:4–6

6

Q. Can we know the one true God?

A. Yes, we can know the one true God because he has revealed himself to us and he wants us to know him.

As creator, God is outside and above his creation. This is known as the *transcendence* of God. If this were the only way God related with his creation, then we would not be able to know him. He would be beyond our reach. Thankfully though, this is not the only way God relates with his creation. God has chosen to be active in his creation, not detached from it. In fact, creation itself depends on God to continue to exist and function. Without him, everything would come to a crashing halt. God's interaction with his creation is known as the *immanence* of God. So God is set apart from his creation (transcendence), but he has chosen to step into it and reveal himself and be known (immanence).

The greatest example of God stepping into his creation to reveal himself to us is his provision of Jesus. God did not have to provide Jesus. He chose to so that we could have a way to know him. Look at how the apostle John put it in 1 John 5:20.

> And we know that the Son of God has come and has given us understanding so that we may know the true one. We are in the true one—that is, in his Son Jesus Christ. He is the true God and eternal life.

Jesus came so that we might know what we could not know without him—the one true God. If we know Jesus, we know the one true God because he is God himself.

Some people think that God is distant—a far-off, detached, authoritative ruler of the cosmos—almost like a king or leader you don't know and cannot even approach. Our kids might be tempted to see God that way because that is how they tend to see authority figures around them every day. God is certainly the ruler of all, and he certainly has authority, but he is not far off and detached. He has chosen to come to us—to step into his own creation and provide a way we can know him and have a personal relationship with him as mighty King *and* as loving Father. God stepped into creation by wrapping himself in a human body, living a perfect life, being unjustly condemned, and suffering and dying in our place. God then walked out of the grave, leaving death and sin as defeated foes behind him so that we too can escape them and have eternal life in him. But as amazing as that is, that wasn't all! Jesus didn't just bring God to us; he brought us to him. Hebrews 4:16 tells us that when we trust in Christ, we can approach God with boldness. While our sin once drove a wedge between us and God, making it impossible for us to be with him, Jesus crossed the divide and removed it. We were once torn apart as enemies; in Jesus we are brought back to God as his children.

That is not a distant God! That is a God who is near, who wants to be known, and who wants us to draw near to him. That is the God our kids need to meet.

1 John 5:20; Psalm 46:10

7

Q. How can we know God?

A. God has revealed himself to us through general revelation and special revelation.

———————

There are two ways through which God has revealed himself to us. The first is known as *general revelation,* which is available to everyone—that's why it is called "general." Through general revelation we can know that there is a God and can even know a good amount about him. However, we cannot know what we must do to be in relationship with God and how to live a life that pleases him through general revelation alone. We need another way to know God—a way that is more specific.

That is where the second way God has revealed himself comes into play—*special revelation.* Special revelation focuses on God's direct communication to explain how we can know him and how to live in a way that pleases him. General revelation is broad and can be unclear, while special revelation is narrow and clear.

God designed general revelation and special revelation to work hand-in-hand creating an awareness of God and stirring a desire to know him. General revelation comes first and hands the baton to special revelation, which identifies who God is and how we can know him. Once we know God, we are not done with general revelation though. General revelation reminds us of God's presence all around us each day and can often trigger worship, awe, and appreciation of who God is and what he has done for us.

Psalm 19:1–11; Hebrews 1:1

Q. What is general revelation?

A. General revelation is God revealing himself to everyone through his creation.

The universe calls out to us that there is a God and he is amazing! This is how David put it in Psalm 19:1–6.

> The heavens declare the glory of God,
> and the expanse proclaims the work of his hands.
> Day after day they pour out speech;
> night after night they communicate knowledge.
> There is no speech; there are no words;
> their voice is not heard.
> Their message has gone out to the whole earth,
> and their words to the ends of the world.
> In the heavens he has pitched a tent for the sun.
> It is like a bridegroom coming from his home;
> it rejoices like an athlete running a course.
> It rises from one end of the heavens
> and circles to their other end;
> nothing is hidden from its heat.

Have you have ever looked up into the sky on a clear night, seen countless stars, and wondered about how big the universe is? It is estimated that there are between 100 and 200 billion (yes, *billion* with a *b*) stars in our galaxy alone, and there could be 10 trillion galaxies or more in the universe![2] Multiplying those numbers together results in a huge, mind-boggling number of total stars in the universe! Then think of how many planets circle them! To think that

God created each, spread them across the heavens, and controls the orbits and movements of each and every one tells us that God is amazing beyond description.

But then we can go the other direction and think about the intricate design and beauty of a butterfly and reflect on the amazing process of transformation the butterfly went through after starting life as a caterpillar and we end up being equally in awe of God. He is a God of unmatched creativity and design. Walking on a beach, hiking through a park, gazing upon a full moon, and holding a newborn baby all are designed to make us keenly aware of God and how good he truly is.

The great thing about general revelation is that it is all around us. The problem with general revelation is that it is all around us. It's too easy for us to take it for granted much of the time. We become immune to the beauty of a sunset, or we miss seeing it because we are too fixated on a smartphone. It is too easy for us to purchase food in a supermarket, so we fail to appreciate what God has done to provide the food for us—all that goes into growing a single grain of wheat. God is loudly and boldly declaring himself to us. The trick is, we have to listen.

Psalm 19:1–6; Romans 1:20

9

Q. What is special revelation?

A. Special revelation is God revealing himself directly to people through the Bible.

Psalm 19 begins by describing how we can experience God through general revelation, but then it switches gears and shares how we can know God through special revelation, the Bible. Here is how David described God's Word in Psalm 19:7–11.

> The instruction of the LORD is perfect,
> renewing one's life;
> the testimony of the LORD is trustworthy,
> making the inexperienced wise.
> The precepts of the LORD are right,
> making the heart glad;
> the command of the LORD is radiant,
> making the eyes light up.
> The fear of the LORD is pure,
> enduring forever;
> the ordinances of the LORD are reliable
> and altogether righteous.
> They are more desirable than gold—
> than an abundance of pure gold;
> and sweeter than honey
> dripping from a honeycomb.
> In addition, your servant is warned by them,
> and in keeping them there is an abundant reward.

Now that is a glowing review! Perfect. Trustworthy. Right. Radiant. Reliable. And notice that David is even talking about God's *commands* in Scripture, not just his promises! Many people see reading the Bible as a chore, or at best a tolerable task; so how was David able to see it as being so wonderful? Because David understood that it is only through reading the Bible that we can know its Author. And that Author is perfect, trustworthy, right, radiant, and reliable. That is why David considered the Bible to be more valuable than pure gold and sweeter than honey straight off the honeycomb. Because each word we read in Scripture is given to us by God so that we can know him, love him, and find perfect contentment in him.

The question we need to ask ourselves, then, is this: *How are we reading the Bible and how are we teaching our kids to read it?* Are we reading the Bible to say we did and check off a box? Are we reading the Bible to make sure we do what is right and stay out of trouble with God? Are we reading the Bible because we think it makes us better people? If any of those are our reasons, then we probably won't be too excited to read it.

But, if we read the Bible to know the one true living God and see his beauty, we will taste the sweetness that David savored. We will hold our Bibles dearly as our most beloved possession, because in them, we find words of life.

Psalm 19:7–11; 2 Timothy 3:16

10

Q. What can we know about God?

A. We can know what God is like, what he wants, and how we can have a relationship with him.

God's attributes describe what he is like in his essence. These are not just characteristics or qualities he demonstrates at times like we do. We can be kind one minute and mean the very next minute. God is not like that—he is constant in all his attributes. But these aren't even qualities God demonstrates all the time. It goes deeper than that. God displays his attributes because they are naturally born from who he is. Perhaps some examples will help.

One of God's attributes is love (1 John 4:8). Now, this doesn't simply mean that God acts lovingly, although he certainly does. This means that God in his very essence is love, so it is natural that he will act lovingly because loving actions are the overflow of who he truly is. Love is not something he expresses at times or something he has acquired. He *is* love, and he *is* the source and standard of all love.

God is also truth (John 14:6–7). Again, this means that everything God does and says is true, because truth is who he *is*. God is truth, and he is the source and standard of all truth.

God is love and truth fully, completely, and always. He is 100 percent love and he is 100 percent truth. All of God's attributes are perfect, which is why sometimes they are called his "perfections," and all of his attributes work together to best describe him. In other words, no one attribute is more or less important or more or less defining, and God does not demonstrate any one more or less than the others. To know God best is to understand him through *all* of his attributes.

So we can know God's attributes; now, let's turn our attention to knowing God's will. When we speak of knowing God's will, we have two things in mind. First, God's will is what he wants us to do, such as always giving thanks (1 Thess. 5:18). This is probably what most people think of when they think of God's will. While there are times when it is difficult to know God's will for our lives, the Bible shares a great deal about his will, and we can know it in many, perhaps even most, situations we encounter.

The second way we speak of God's will is what he has chosen to do. We can look back and see what God's will has been, and we are to look forward praying for his will to be done (Matt. 6:10).

Knowing God's attributes and will is fantastic. However, there is even another layer in how we can know God. We can know quite a bit *about* someone, such as a celebrity or an athlete, but not really *know* him. You know *of* him, but you don't know him. God doesn't just invite us to know of him—such as knowing about his attributes and will. He invites us to know him. And he does this by revealing how we can have a relationship with him through Jesus Christ and how we can enjoy and foster that relationship through prayer and worship.

The more we know God's perfect attributes, the more we will love and trust him. The more we love and trust him, the more we will want to follow his will for our lives. And the more we follow his will for our lives and experience his goodness and kindness, the more we will want to spend time with him in prayer and worship. And the more we spend time in prayer and worship, the more we will understand his attributes. And so the beautiful cycle goes, over and over again.

Romans 12:2; Acts 17:27

Q. Can we fully know God?

A. No, we can know much about God, but we cannot fully know him because of our limited minds.

Can you imagine what a year feels like? Sure you can. Not too hard, right? OK, how about a decade? No problem. A century? Getting a little harder. A millennium? Pretty challenging. How about eternity? That's a tough one, isn't it? One last one. How about timelessness? Can't do it, can you? Timelessness, or eternality, is one of God's attributes. He has always existed and always will exist. While we can understand this to a degree, we can't fully understand it, because our minds are trapped in time. We are used to things beginning and ending—not having either is beyond what we can comprehend. We get the concept, but not the fullness of the reality. It's too hard to fathom.

Or how about being in two places at once? Ten places? A hundred places? A million? Everywhere in the universe at once? This is called omnipresence, meaning God is everywhere at once, because he is not confined to a physical body. Again, we can understand the concept to a degree, but we cannot really process it fully in our minds, because we are fixed in one place at a time.

What about knowing everything there is to know about a single subject, say baseball? Knowing every rule, every statistic, every pitch that has ever been thrown, every player who has ever played and what make of glove and bat they each used. Every baseball stadium, and every person who has sat in each seat for every game. Too much to process, isn't it! There's no way someone can know all of that. And baseball is just one small area of knowledge in the universe. But God knows everything about baseball, and every star and planet, and how many grains of sand are on every beach in the world. He knows everything that has ever happened, and everything that will ever happen, and even everything that could have happened. Hard to wrap your arms around God's omniscience, isn't it? Those are all examples of how we cannot fully know God because our minds cannot grasp him in his entirety. He is too big. Too glorious. Too different from us in so many ways. Though our failure to get our arms around God can be frustrating, it is actually a good thing. Our inability to know him fully reminds us that he is so much higher than we are, and leads us to worship (Isa. 55:8–9). He is a great God who came down to us and communicates with us in ways we can somewhat understand. Why he did even that for sinners like us is hard to understand in the first place. But aren't you glad he did?

Isaiah 55:8–9; Job 36:26

Q. What does it mean that God is eternal?

A. *God is eternal* means he has always existed and always will exist.

Many people don't realize that Moses wrote one of the Psalms—Psalm 90. Here is part of it, Psalm 90:2:

> Before the mountains were born,
> before you gave birth to the earth and the world,
> from eternity to eternity, you are God.

God has eternally existed. Before anything else existed, God did. He is the creator of everything, including matter and time itself. Even time has a beginning, but God does not.

Not only has God always existed, he always will exist. He exists timelessly. This is what Jesus had in mind when he was in the middle of a heated debate with some religious leaders in John 8. At one point, Jesus told them that anyone who keeps his word would not see death. This infuriated the Jewish leaders who responded that even Abraham died, and surely Jesus wasn't claiming to be greater than he. Jesus replied that he is more concerned with the Father's glory and that Abraham rejoiced to see his day. The leaders retorted that Jesus wasn't even fifty years old (which was being generous because he was in his early thirties), so how could Abraham have seen him? And here is the part that should catch our attention. Jesus responded, "Truly I tell you, before Abraham was, I am" (John 8:58).

When you read that, it sounds odd. Didn't Jesus mean to say, "I was"? While that might be better grammar, Jesus wasn't worried about verb tenses in that moment—he was thinking about theology. Theology found in Exodus 3:14 to be exact.

Exodus 3 records God calling Moses to bring his people out of Egypt. Moses pushes back and asks who he is to do this for God. God answers Moses that he would be with him. So Moses takes another approach. Who should he say sent him?

God replied to Moses, "I AM WHO I AM. This is what you are to say to the Israelites: I AM has sent me to you." (Exod. 3:14)

Sound familiar? This is where God shared with us what is considered to be his most holy name—*Yahweh*. While we don't fully understand the meaning of this most holy name for God, it seems that God wants us to understand that a fundamental aspect of his identity is existence. God just *is*. All the other gods are not. But God *is*.

So when Jesus told the Jewish leaders "I am," he was making a direct claim to be God—to be *Yahweh*. That is why we read in the next verse that the Jews picked up stones to stone him. Remember, just a minute before this, they were basically laughing at Jesus for claiming to be old enough for Abraham to have seen him. So that wasn't what made them so angry. Instead, they understood Jesus' claim to be God and considered that blasphemy.

John 8:58 is an important verse affirming that Jesus claimed to be God based on eternality. The Jews that day didn't believe him and wanted to kill him. Thankfully, in God's kindness, he has revealed the truth to us that Jesus is indeed God and in him, we have eternal life too. Not an eternal life that has no beginning like God, but an eternal life that has no ending—an eternal life we hope and pray that our kids receive through Christ.

Psalm 90:2; Exodus 3:14

Q. What does it mean that God is a Person?

A. *God is a Person* means he demonstrates intellect, emotion, and will.

When we think of a person, we usually think first of their physical form. So if someone were to say the name Taylor to you, you would probably picture in your mind a Taylor you know. You would see that Taylor's face and physical form. That's understandable, but that's not who Taylor really is. Taylor is actually a person of intellect, emotion, and will within that picture of Taylor in your mind. Taylor thinks, feels, and decides. That's really who Taylor is—that's a person.

So where do we see intellect, emotion, and will demonstrated by God? Well, plenty of places, but here are a few.

Isaiah 55:8–9 shows us a glimpse of God's intellect:

"For my thoughts are not your thoughts,
and your ways are not my ways."
This is the Lord's declaration.
"For as heaven is higher than earth,
so my ways are higher than your ways,
and my thoughts than your thoughts."

Not only do these verses tell us that God thinks, but they remind us once again that we cannot fully know God. His thoughts are so far greater than our thoughts. We can't possibly understand them in their fullness.

Psalm 78:40–41 gives us a glimpse at the emotions of God:

How often they rebelled against him
in the wilderness

and grieved him in the desert.
They constantly tested God
and provoked the Holy One of Israel.

God was angered and grieved by Israel's disobedience in the wilderness after the Exodus. We also see God express love, hate, compassion, and other emotions in the Scriptures.

Hebrews 13:20–21 is one of the many verses that talk about God's will:

> Now may the God of peace, who brought up from the dead our Lord Jesus—the great Shepherd of the sheep—through the blood of the everlasting covenant, equip you with everything good to do his will, working in us what is pleasing in his sight, through Jesus Christ, to whom be glory forever and ever. Amen.

We also see Jesus demonstrate intellect (Luke 2:52), emotion (John 11:35), and will (Luke 22:15) confirming that he is a Person; and the same is true for the Holy Spirit where we see he has intellect (1 Cor. 2:10–11), emotion (Eph. 4:30), and will (Gal. 5:17).

God is a Person, even though he has no physical body, and that is important for us to understand because this is how we can have a relationship with him. We can't have a relationship with an impersonal force, but we can have a relationship with the Person we know as God.

Psalm 78:40–41; Hebrews 13:20–21

14

Q. What does it mean that God is spirit?

A. *God is spirit* means he does not have a physical body.

In Jesus' encounter with the Samaritan woman at the well, she asked him about the proper place of worship. The temple was in Jerusalem, but the Samaritans were not welcomed there, so they had made their own place of worship in Samaria, which further caused the Jews to criticize them. So when a random kindhearted rabbi showed up at the well in her town, she took advantage of the opportunity to ask this important question.

Jesus answered the woman by telling her that the time had come when it wouldn't matter where a person worshiped because true worshipers worship God in Spirit and truth. Jesus was talking about how he was the true temple that had come to provide direct access to the Father through his death and resurrection. Then Jesus said it again.

> "God is spirit, and those who worship him must worship in
> Spirit and in truth." (John 4:24)

When Jesus said that God is spirit, he was telling us that God has no physical body—he exists as a spirit. And that makes sense when we think about it. God created everything physical, so he could not have a physical body because he existed before anything physical did. This also helps us understand how God can be omnipresent—existing everywhere at once—because he is not confined to a physical body.

But what about verses that talk about the finger of God (Ps. 8:3), the hand of God (Isa. 66:2), or the face of God (Num. 6:25–26)? If God is spirit, how are we to understand these verses? How does a bodiless spirit have a finger?

We have to remember that God is beyond our understanding. There are some aspects of God that we just cannot quite grasp. But we also have to remember that God wants us to know him and to know him well. In light of this tension, there are times when God uses language that we can understand to express truths about him that we cannot understand. This is called *anthropomorphic language*—God being described in the form (*morphe*) of a human (*anthropos*) so we can comprehend him. Because we have trouble understanding that God is spirit, he will use images of a human body to help us know him better. We understand what it means to turn your back, or face, away from someone. It is a sign of rejection. So when we read, "may the LORD make his face shine on you" (Num. 6:25), we understand that to mean God accepting us and giving us his favor. The image of God's face shining on us makes God more understandable.

Jesus said something else about God being spirit that is incredibly important for us today. Because God is spirit, we are to worship him in Spirit and truth. Just as Jesus was trying to move the woman away from thinking in physical terms when it came to worship, so should we. Worship is prompted by the Holy Spirit stirring our hearts and affections for God, which results in genuine, honest worship of him. That is what he is after—the Holy Spirit stirring our spirit to worship God, who is spirit.

John 4:24; Colossians 1:15

15

Q. What does it mean that God is holy?

A. *God is holy* means he is pure and set apart from his creation.

God's holiness means that he is set apart, or distinct, in two main ways. First, he is set apart from sin, which means he is completely sinless and pure. When Adam and Eve sinned in Eden, they, all future people, and all of creation fell under the curse of sin. Every single thing that God created was marred by sin. But God was not. Sin did not stain him. It didn't even touch him. God is still completely holy and pure. Second, God's holiness means that he is set apart from his creation. He is above his creation and not part of it.

One of the most riveting pictures of God's holiness in Scripture takes place in Isaiah 6, where the prophet Isaiah had a vision of God seated on his royal throne with glory all around him. Two seraphim—a type of angel—flew near God calling out to each other, "Holy, holy, holy is the Lord of Armies; his glory fills the whole earth" (Isa. 6:3). The triple use of "holy" is a way of expressing complete and total holiness. The language seems to indicate that the seraphim continued to call this out to each other, over and over.

"Holy, holy, holy. Holy, holy, holy." Again and again. Can you imagine? What an amazing glimpse of the overwhelming holiness of God!

Much later in the book of Revelation, we see a similar scene that is just as powerful. This time four creatures were flying near God, and day and night—never stopping—they cried out, "Holy, holy, holy, Lord God, the Almighty, who was, who is, and who is to come" (Rev. 4:8).

There is one more picture of God's holiness in Scripture that deserves our attention—a curtain. But not just any curtain, the curtain that divided the Holy of Holies from the Holy Place in the temple. God established the temple to be the place for his presence to dwell with his people, and his presence was found in the innermost part of the temple called the Holy of Holies. This is where the ark of the covenant rested, and only the high priest could enter into this area one day a year, on the Day of Atonement. The curtain was a barrier—a physical reminder that access to God was limited because of sin. God is holy. He is set apart and separate from his people because of our sin.

But the high priest entering on the Day of Atonement pictured the hope of reconciliation. There was a way we could approach God again through a mediator. That picture was fulfilled in Christ, our Mediator who came to earth, shed his blood, and opened access to God for all who believe. In Christ, we now have unlimited access to God (Heb. 10:19–22). That is the message God sent when Jesus breathed his last on the cross and that same curtain in the temple was torn from top to bottom. God had reached down and made a way for his people to enter his presence because we had been made holy with Christ's righteousness. God is holy and set apart from sin, and he has made a way for us to be with him, namely, by making us holy and set apart from sin in his Son, Jesus Christ.

Isaiah 6:3; Leviticus 19:2

Q. What does it mean that God is love?

A. *God is love* means he expresses faithful love in all he does and he is the standard of love.

We can throw the word *love* around quite a bit in our culture. One minute we might say we love ice cream, and the next minute we are telling our son or daughter, "I love you." Surely we don't feel about ice cream the same way we do about our children, but we use the same word to describe both. We also live in a culture where love can be short-lived and conditional. Just look at some of the Hollywood marriages that end before the ink on the marriage licenses even dries.

So when we think about God's love, we must be careful that our kids don't come to understand his love based on our understanding and use of love. Instead, we need to provide God's definition of love—true love based on who he is (1 John 4:8)—and allow that to carry over to how we love others. How then should we define God's love?

Perhaps the best way to think about God's love is that it is faithful. God's love doesn't waver. It doesn't falter. It doesn't end. It is not conditional. It is faithful, lasting, and secure.

Another way to think about God's love that really sets it apart from human love is that it is self-giving. God's love looks outward. It looks to give. Man's love is often the opposite. It is inward and looks to receive. Our love is driven by how we feel and what we can get from someone or something. And once that feeling goes away or we stop getting what we want, the love stops. But that is only true of man's love, not God's. God's love faithfully and selflessly continues even when we fail to love him back.

That is the message God sent to us through the Old Testament prophet Hosea. At the beginning of the book of Hosea, God instructed him to marry a woman of promiscuity—a prostitute. Hosea marries a woman named Gomer and they have three children, but then Gomer leaves Hosea for her adulterous lifestyle. At this point God tells Hosea to show love to Gomer and go purchase her back, even if she doesn't love him and has been unfaithful.

> Then the LORD said to me, "Go again; show love to a woman who is loved by another man and is an adulteress, just as the LORD loves the Israelites though they turn to other gods and love raisin cakes." (Hos. 3:1)

If you're wondering about the raisin cakes, God was not worried about Israel's dessert choices—although chocolate is always a better choice. Raisin cakes were most likely used as aphrodisiacs and as part of licentious pagan worship. With that said, why would God put Hosea through this? *Because he wanted to use Hosea as a powerful word picture of his love for his people.* God's faithful love continues for his people even when they are adulterous against him and worship other gods. Even when they don't love him back. And God's self-giving love prompted him to provide his Son, Jesus, to buy us back at the price of his life.

One of the greatest gifts we can give our kids is a proper understanding of God's fixed, unconditional, unfailing love for them. Our kids need to know that even when they fail God—and they will, just as we have—God's love is steadfast and immovable. There is nothing they can ever do to make God love them less and there is nothing they can do to make him love them more. That's because his love is fixed on them based on who he is and not on who they are or what they do or do not do. This is the amazing love of God. And this is why we love him—because he first loved us (1 John 4:19).

1 John 4:8–10; 1 John 4:19

Q. What does it mean that God is just?

A. *God is just* means he always acts in ways that are right and he is the standard of justice.

We live in a time when the concept of *right* and *wrong* is widely debated. What is right and what is wrong are often seen as relative—something may be right for one person but wrong for the next person, or something may be right one day and wrong the next day. The concept of justice is fluid, and it is sometimes rejected altogether.

This poses a problem when we speak of God being just, or doing what is right. Right is relative, so what is his standard of doing what is right? The answer is that *he* is the standard. What is right is what conforms to God's character. If something is done according to his character, it is right. If something is done that goes against his character, it is wrong. As creator, God has the right to determine what is right.

Because God is consistent in always acting according to his character, everything he does is right. This is how Moses put it in Deuteronomy 32:4:

> The Rock—his work is perfect;
> all his ways are just.
> A faithful God, without bias,
> he is righteous and true.

It's one thing to know that all of God's ways are just, but it's another thing to feel that truth. The reason why the world around us tries to redefine what is right and why it doesn't seem to us that God acts justly at times is because we are trying to determine right and justice from our perspective. We want to force our standard of what is right—what is fair—on God, instead of allowing his standard of justice to reshape our perspective of life.

And this is where we need to be careful. Our standard of justice is deeply flawed. Take fairness for example. Fairness is often defined as sameness. To be fair is to treat others the same way. That's how our kids see it, right? Just try giving one of your kids one more cookie than your others and see how that goes over! While there are certainly times when fairness does require sameness, there are many more times when it does not. People are different. To treat everyone the exact same way and call it fairness is to dishonor everyone's personhood. It wouldn't be fair to give a second grade student and a mathematics professor the same exam, would it? Of course not! That wouldn't be fair. But there are times when we may think that God is being unfair because he is not treating us the same way as someone else. Someone else may have been blessed in a way we wanted, and that feels unfair—unjust. But it is not. It's just different.

We see God acting differently, yet fairly, with people in the Bible all the time. God chose Jacob, not Esau. Jesus spent more time with his inner three disciples—Peter, James, and John—than the others. God rejected Saul and accepted David. Because God is perfectly just, we know that he always does what is right, even if it is not the same for everyone.

But there is one area where God does treat us the same—judgment for our sinful rebellion. Because everyone is a sinner, we all have earned death and separation from him. And God will not just turn and look the other way when it comes to our sin. That would be unjust. Instead, he is righteous to judge us for our sin and condemn us to die as our punishment. We wronged an infinitely holy, perfect God, and that rebellion deserves nothing short of eternal separation from him.

But God—one of the greatest word pairings you will find in the Bible—"but God proves his own love for us in that while we were still sinners, Christ died for us" (Rom. 5:8). God is just. And God is love. In his loving justice, he provided his Son Jesus to pay the penalty that we owed for our sin, so that we can be forgiven and have relationship with him.

God is just. Jesus paid the penalty for sin.

God is love. Through Jesus we are adopted into God's family to live with him forever.

Deuteronomy 32:4; Romans 3:26

Q. What does it mean that God is good?

A. *God is good* means all he speaks and does is good and he is the standard of goodness.

Psalm 119:68 declares this of God:

> You are good, and you do what is good; teach me your statutes.

God is good, but how do we define "good"? This is the same issue posed by God's justice, and the answer is the same as well. In the same way that God is the standard of "right," he is also the standard of "good." Everything God does is good because it is done in a way he approves.

In the creation account in Genesis 1, we read repeatedly that God saw that what he had created was good. Then when God had finished creation, he saw all that he had made and declared that it was *very good* (Gen. 1:31). Everything God made was agreeable with his standard of goodness—in this case, everything was made perfectly.

Everything God does and everything he says is good and worthy of his approval. But that is not all that it means for God to be good. It also means that he himself is, in his nature, good and worthy of approval. God is not good just for what he does, but also for who he is.

James 1:17 tells us that "every good and perfect gift is from above, coming down from the Father of lights, who does not change like shifting shadows." We often take God's good gifts for granted, don't we? We either start to believe that we deserve good things, so we don't see them as gifts but what is owed to us, or we fail to connect all the good we experience back to God's faithful provision. We take his good gifts for granted.

That breath you just took—that's a good gift from God. The new day. Family. Food. Every single possession. All of these are good gifts. Your talents, abilities, knowledge, and health. Gifts. When we stop and consider all that God has given us, we become overwhelmed by his goodness and grace to us. Remembering that all that we have is a good gift from God helps us to live generously and with gratitude, contentment, and joy.

But there is one more good gift to mention. It is the greatest gift that came down from above—Jesus. God provided his Son as a gift—a completely undeserved gift—that was given to us so that we may know and experience how good God truly is. Jesus lived among us in perfect obedience to the Father, then he laid down his life as the perfect sacrifice, and finally he exited the tomb in perfect victory over sin and death. That is the gospel—the good news—that God has provided to us as the greatest gift imaginable.

Psalm 119:68; Matthew 19:17

19

Q. What does it mean that God is true?

A. *God is true* means all he speaks and does is true and
he is the standard of truth.

When we speak of God being true, in the broadest terms, we mean that
God exists and he is the one true God (Jer. 10:10–11; John 17:3). But when it
comes to his attribute of being true, we mean far more than that. That God
is true means that all he says and does is true. Everything is said and done
according to his character. There is no deception in his conduct. God will
never mislead or act in any way that is not consistent with who he is. God will
never fail to love or be just, for example. In the same way, there is no dishon-
esty in God's speech. God cannot lie (Titus 1:2).

God being true is incredibly important when it comes to how and why
we can trust the Bible. The Bible is the Word of God, written by men. Those
men were overshadowed by the Holy Spirit in the process to ensure that what
is in the Bible is completely true and free from error. This process is known as
inspiration—God the Spirit moving the writers to record truth. If God is true,
and the Bible is a product of his, then the Bible must be true too.

If it were not for inspiration, then the Bible would be no different from
any other book written by a person. It could have truth in it, as well as lies
or errors; it would be no more authoritative than anything else. We would
never know with confidence who God is, how to know him, and how to live a
life that pleases him. Thankfully, our true God did inspire the writing of the
Bible, and we can place our complete confidence in it and rely on it to know
God and know how to have a relationship with him through Jesus.

As Jesus prayed to the Father the night of his arrest, he asked God to
sanctify (or set apart) his disciples by the truth, and then he declared that

God's Word is truth (John 17:17). We can find encouragement from what Jesus said as we study, apply, and teach our kids what we read in the Bible. The more we study the Bible, the more we will see that it is one big story of Jesus—who is the very Word of God (Luke 24:27). Our true God has given us truth in God's Word to teach us about the one true Word of God.

Jeremiah 10:10–11; Titus 1:2

20

Q. What does it mean that God is wise?

A. *God is wise* means he always wants and does what is best and he is the standard of wisdom.

When we think of God being good, we mean that everything that he does is agreeable with his character. We could look at every single one of God's actions and consider each good. God being wise is a little different than that. When we say that God is wise, we mean that he will bring about the best outcome in everything he does and will also use the best path to reach each of those outcomes. God's wisdom, therefore, concerns more of *why* and *how* God does what he does, while his goodness concerns more of *what* he does.

In Romans 8:28 we read that "all things work together for the good of those who love God, who are called according to his purpose." Paul is not singling out a specific action of God here, but instead he is looking more broadly at how God works to bring about what he desires—in this case, salvation. In the verses that follow this, Paul walks through what can be thought of as a chain of salvation. One action of God leads to the next that leads to the next, and so on—all working together to bring about a person's salvation and ultimately resulting in his or her glorification, when sin will be no more. Paul's point is that God is wise in this process, and the end goal—the *why*—as well as each action along the way—the *how*—is the best, even if those steps may be painful and difficult in the moment.

For example, feeling sorrow over sin is a necessary step toward repentance that leads into salvation. Sorrow isn't pleasant, and some of the ways God may lead us to feel that sorrow are painful. Pain and sorrow don't feel good in the moment, but they are certainly for our best when we think of what they lead to—salvation. We know this as parents because we discipline our children in the same way. We can know, then, that God is indeed wise for bringing pain and sorrow into our lives, because that is the best way to move us to repentance. Repentance then leads to the best possible outcome—our salvation from the eternal sorrow that those separated from God will experience. This is what Paul had in mind when he wrote 1 Corinthians 1:26–31.

> Brothers and sisters, consider your calling: Not many were wise from a human perspective, not many powerful, not many of noble birth. Instead, God has chosen what is foolish in the world to shame the wise, and God has chosen what is weak in the world to shame the strong. God has chosen what is insignificant and despised in the world—what is viewed as nothing—to bring to nothing what is viewed as something, so that no one may boast in his presence. It is from him that you are in Christ Jesus, who became wisdom from God for us—our righteousness, sanctification, and redemption, in order that, as it is written: Let the one who boasts, boast in the Lord.

The gospel seems foolish to the world. God being born as a human and suffering and dying is absurd according to the world's way of thinking. How many of us would have chosen this plan of redemption for the world? How many of us would have begun the church with a rather unimpressive group of men and women in hiding? But God's wisdom is proven by what Jesus did to bring about salvation, and by the early church's flourishing under those unimpressive but Spirit-filled men. God's planned outcome is wise, and the path taken to get there is wise. Gratefully, we are the beneficiaries of that wise plan.

James 3:17; Proverbs 2:6

Q. What does it mean that God is faithful?

A. *God is faithful* means he keeps his promises even when we are not faithful to him.

God being faithful is pretty much like him being true. In fact, many consider God's faithfulness part of his truthfulness, and would see these as two different words for the same attribute. There is nothing wrong with that, of course, but it can be helpful to see God's faithfulness and truthfulness as separate but closely related attributes, because they each lead us in slightly different, but equally important, directions.

As we have seen, God's truthfulness gives us the reason we need to trust in the Bible. Because God is true, we can look back at what he has revealed to us and know that we can believe it. God's faithfulness, on the other hand, pushes us to look forward into the future. Because God is faithful, we can trust that everything he has promised will come to pass one day. We live in a world where promises are broken all the time, but God's promises will never fail. If God has promised it, it will happen. No matter what. Even our disobedience cannot make God quit on what he has promised:

> If we are faithless, he remains faithful, for he cannot deny himself. (2 Tim. 2:13)

And that's important because God's promises are where we find our hope. God has promised that one day he will put an end to sin and death for good. We can trust that promise with hope even when the world seems to be falling apart around us, because God is faithful.

God has promised that, if we have trusted in Jesus, he has forgiven all of our sin. We can trust that promise with hope and experience grace in our lives each day because God is faithful.

God has promised that he will provide for all our needs. We can trust in that promise with hope even when our financial, work, relationship, church, or health situation seems dire, because God is faithful.

At the end of the Great Commission, Jesus told his followers that he would be with them always, even to the end of the age (Matt. 28:20). If God were not faithful, this promise would be meaningless. However, because God is faithful, we know that we can trust in this promise with hope and find great encouragement and strength from it. We are never alone! No matter what, Jesus, our faithful Savior, is with us. He is there with us in the midst of joy as well as sorrow and suffering. Even when it doesn't feel like he is there with us, we can know he is. Because God is faithful.

That is what our kids need to take to heart. We will let them down. Others they look up to will let them down. They will even let themselves down. But God will never let them down. Ever. They can always trust in God and find hope and peace in his promises to them—promises that will help them get through the difficulties they will face in life.

2 Timothy 2:13; Lamentations 3:22–23

22

Q. What does it mean that God is omnipresent?

A. *God is omnipresent* means he is not confined to a body and is everywhere at once.

This is the first of three attributes of God that begin with the prefix *omni*, which means "all." Omnipresence, then, can be thought of as God being "all-present."

David provides a clear view of God's omnipresence in Psalm 139:7–12.

> Where can I go to escape your Spirit?
> Where can I flee from your presence?
> If I go up to heaven, you are there;
> if I make my bed in Sheol, you are there.
> If I live at the eastern horizon
> or settle at the western limits,
> even there your hand will lead me;
> your right hand will hold on to me.
> If I say, "Surely the darkness will hide me,
> and the light around me will be night"—
> even the darkness is not dark to you.
> The night shines like the day;
> darkness and light are alike to you.

David asks where someone can go to get away from God's presence; the answer is an emphatic "nowhere." There is nowhere where God isn't there. Anywhere we go, God is there.

But that doesn't mean that God is just too large to fit in one place, even the universe. It's not like God is partly here and partly over there and partly over there because he is so big. Remember that God is Spirit, so he has no "size" in that way. God is fully everywhere. He is fully here and fully over there and fully over there too.

This doesn't mean that he is fully everywhere in the same way. God is present with a believer differently than he is present with an unbeliever. And even in our lives, sometimes God is present to bless us, and other times he is with us to discipline us.

And that takes us to what our kids need to understand about God's omnipresence. Sure it's kind of interesting and neat to think about, but it matters. It matters because God being with our kids all the time will help them in two very different ways.

First, there will be times when remembering God is with our kids will help them turn from sin. So many sins are committed when people are alone—many of them within our own minds and hearts. It is easier to sin when no one is watching! But when our kids remember they are never truly alone, because God is right there with them, it can make a world of difference in that moment of temptation.

Second, God being everywhere can be a great encouragement to our kids. God is with them and provides his strength, his wisdom, his peace, his love—whatever they need in that moment! This is especially important in the preteen and teen years when our kids are coming to terms with who they are. There will be so many times when they feel that no one understands them or likes them. Preteens and teens can feel so lonely at times, but remembering that God is with them and that he loves them and is molding them into his image can be just the comfort they need. Nothing they face will be too difficult, not because of how great they may be, but because of how great God with them truly is!

Psalm 139:7–12; Matthew 28:20

Q. What does it mean that God is omniscient?

A. *God is omniscient* means he knows all that is, was, will be, and could be.

The second of God's *omni* attributes is his omniscience—God is all-knowing. The apostle John was pretty blunt about this when he wrote that God knows all things (1 John 3:20). David, on the other hand, took a more personal and poetic approach when he wrote that God had searched him and knew him. God knew when he sat and stood; God knew his every thought (Ps. 139:1–2).

Let's drill down on this for a few minutes to try to appreciate this attribute as fully as we can. We can place everything that God knows into three main categories—everything that has happened, everything that will happen, and everything that could have happened.

Knowing everything that happened is actually the easiest of the three categories to understand, but it is still really challenging for us to wrap our minds around. God knows every single thing that has ever happened in human history—and even farther back in eternity before he created.

Right now there are about seven billion people alive on earth. God knows every single thing each of those people has done every single second of their lives. He knows the number of hairs on each of their heads. He knows every cell in their bodies. He knows every thought they have ever had. Every word they have ever spoken. He knows what they like, what they love, what they hate, and what they fear. And that is just for the people alive today! There may have been an additional 100 billion people who have lived previously on the earth, and God knows everything about them too!

But that's not all God knows about what has happened. It actually just begins to scratch the surface! He also knows everything about what every animal and every insect has ever done. He knows every blade of grass, flower, and tree that has ever grown. Every wave that has broken on every beach. Every drop of rain that has ever hit the ground and which particles of dirt they each struck. He knows the size, shape, and weight of every snowflake that has ever fallen. And this is only considering our own planet, one of trillions and trillions! *He knows it all.*

Struggling to grasp the greatness of God's knowledge? Well, we're just getting started! That just covers God's knowledge of what *has* happened. He also knows everything that *will* happen in the future, and perhaps most staggering, he knows everything that *could* have happened:

> "Woe to you, Chorazin! Woe to you, Bethsaida! For if the miracles that were done in you had been done in Tyre and Sidon, they would have repented in sackcloth and ashes long ago." (Matt. 11:21)

Think about all the choices you make every day. God knows what would have happened had you chosen to do something differently for each and every one. Then think about how each choice changes the future decisions you make, and you start seeing how amazing this is.

Just for simplicity, let's suppose that every decision you make only has two options. The first decision you make then gives you a choice of two options more. Those two options would then present two more options, giving you a total of four options. Then those four options would lead to eight and so forth.

After ten choices, you would have had a total of 512 options. So God would know your ten choices and the 502 you did not choose. After twenty choices, you would have had 524,288 options. After thirty choices, you would have had 536,870,912 options. After forty choices, 549,755,813,888 options. After just fifty choices, you would have had 563 trillion different options you could have chosen. After just fifty choices you made, and if each choice only had two options! And God knows every single one of them for you and every other person who has ever lived on the planet.

God is amazing, isn't he?

So what difference does this make for us? We can find comfort in knowing that God knows us that deeply. God knows what we are going through.

He knows what worries us. He knows when we are sad, happy, frustrated, or confused. He knows it all. That is why we should encourage our kids to be real with God when they pray. If they are happy, they should be happy with God. If they are angry, they should let him know. If they are struggling to trust him, they should tell him. We cannot hide anything from a God who knows everything, so why should we even try? God invites us to be genuine before him, because when we are, he is able to meet us where we are, to take us where we need to be.

1 John 3:20; Psalm 139:1–2

Q. What does it mean that God is omnipotent?

A. *God is omnipotent* means he can do anything that is
according to his character.

The third and final of God's *omni* attributes is his omnipotence—God
is all-powerful, which we see in his name "God Almighty" (Gen. 17:1).
Sometimes people will say that God is omnipotent, which means he can do
anything, but that isn't quite right. God actually cannot do *anything* because
his actions are always consistent with his character and with the promises of
his providential activity in the world.

First, God's actions are aligned with his character. For example, because
God is true, he cannot lie. It is impossible for him. God cannot tell a single lie.
Likewise, he cannot stop existing, or stop loving, or commit even a single sin.
So can God do *all* things? Clearly he cannot. But can God do all things that
are *according to his character*? Now that, he certainly can do!

This also means that, because God chooses and promises to act in certain
ways, he cannot do things he has promised not to do, and he cannot *not* do
things he has promised to do. There are things he *could* do, but he has chosen
not to do them. For example, God did not choose to spare his Son from dying
on the cross. He could have—it would even have been within his just character—but he did not. Further, God promised never to flood the entire world
again (Gen. 9:11). While he has the power to flood the entire world again,
he cannot now because he has promised not to. If he were to flood the entire
world again, he would be violating his character and be a liar.

One day a wealthy young man approached Jesus and asked what good
he could do to have eternal life. It's a revealing question when you stop and
think about it. The man assumed there was something he could do to earn

salvation—he didn't understand that salvation is by grace through faith. Of course, Jesus saw through this question and told the man that if he wanted to have eternal life, he would have to sell all he had and follow him. And with that, the man turned and walked away.

The disciples had witnessed this encounter unfold, so Jesus took the opportunity to tell them how difficult it is for a wealthy person to be saved. The astonished disciples asked him who could be saved, then. Here is Jesus' response:

> Jesus looked at them and said, "With man this is impossible, but with God all things are possible." (Matt. 19:26)

It's not just impossible for wealthy people to enter into heaven—it's impossible for *everyone*. That is, apart from God's omnipotence at work. When we think of God's omnipotence, we often think of his power to perform miracles or how he has the power to deliver us from illness and difficulties. There is nothing wrong with that of course, but the greatest way that God has demonstrated his power is by saving us from sin and death through Christ Jesus. Our salvation is the greatest act of power we have ever experienced, and we pray that our children will be able to experience it one day too.

Matthew 19:26; Job 42:2

25

Q. What does it mean that God is infinite?

A. *God is infinite* means he is limitless in all his attributes.

When we say that God is infinite, we mean that he is not limited in any of his attributes as they are properly understood.

> Our Lord is great, vast in power;
> his understanding is infinite. (Ps. 147:5)

For example, God's love has no limit. He has an infinite amount of love, and it never decreases, runs low, or runs out. The same is true of his knowledge. God is not nearing the capacity of all he knows, nor does he need to trade out old information for new information because he is running out of storage space in his mind. There is no limit to what he knows. The concept of infinity is naturally woven into some of God's attributes, such as his omnipotence—his infinite power—but it informs all of his attributes either directly or indirectly.

It's probably easiest for us to understand and appreciate God's infinite nature when we contrast it with our finite nature. Even when we have the best of intentions of being faithful to a promise, we may end up breaking it because of circumstances out of our control. We might promise to meet someone at a certain time, but a traffic jam prevents us from being there when we said we would be. We planned to be faithful, we wanted to be faithful, and we tried to be faithful, but in the end we were unfaithful.

But God is perfectly faithful, in part, because he is infinite. He has infinite power and authority over everything, so circumstances cannot hinder his faithfulness. He has infinite knowledge and wisdom, so nothing catches him by surprise and he never chooses a way that is not best. All of these attributes work with his infinite nature so that he is faithful in all he does.

Teaching our kids what God being infinite means can be helpful in two ways. First, it gives them a bigger picture of God—a picture of who he truly is—which helps them be in greater awe of him. It's amazing to think about God being limitless in all of his attributes! But at the same time, when we think about God being infinite, we are forced to come to terms with our finiteness. Our love is limited. Our knowledge is limited. Our strength is limited. And that's something our kids really need to think about—especially as they move into their teen years when they think they are indeed infinite—that they will live forever and can do anything they want. God's infinity is so great because it humbles us; once it has humbled us, it quickly takes us to a deeper appreciation of what God has done for us, especially what he has done for us in Christ.

Psalm 147:5; 1 Kings 8:27

26

Q. What does it mean that God is immutable?

A. *God is immutable* means he does not change in who he is, his purposes, or his promises.

We live in a world that is rapidly changing all around us. From technology, to governments, to worldviews and cultures, it seems that the only thing that is unchanging is change itself. Many of these changes are beneficial, although some are not, which is why many people don't like or even fear change. Change can be difficult. It forces us into the realm of the unknown.

When it comes to God, however, there is no need to worry or fear change. God is by nature unchanging, or immutable:

> They will perish, but you will endure;
> all of them will wear out like clothing.
> You will change them like a garment,
> and they will pass away.
> But you are the same,
> and your years will never end. (Ps. 102:26–27)

God does not change in who he is—his attributes—in his purposes or plans, or in his promises. However, this does not mean that God is stoic—that he doesn't feel emotion. God expresses different genuine emotions that might "change" at times. Nor does this mean that God is static and uninvolved in his creation. At a single moment in time roughly 2,000 years ago, God sent Jesus, which was a "change" from the prior moment. So to say that God's immutability means he never changes in any way is not precisely true.

It's probably easiest to appreciate God's immutability by thinking about what it would be like for him *not* to be immutable. What would God be like if he could change?

Well, first of all, we would never have a God who is perfect. All change requires either improving or diminishing in some quality. If God were to change in regard to his wisdom for example, that would mean either he wasn't fully wise before and now he is (maybe, because he may change again), or he was perfectly wise and now he isn't.

Second, we would never be sure of our salvation. If God could change, he could change the requirements of salvation—say, from grace through faith to works. Or he might change his mind on securing our salvation. After a billion years in heaven, God could simply change his mind about salvation lasting for eternity and cast us from his presence.

And that takes us to the third ramification of God changing if he could. We would never be sure that God will continue to be our loving, gracious, merciful Father. God could immediately, or gradually, change and become an evil, oppressive, sinister, all-powerful tyrant.

When we think about what could happen if God were not immutable, we see how wonderful an attribute this is. God is God and will remain God forevermore.

Psalm 102:26–27; Malachi 3:6

27

Q. Is God perfect?

A. Yes, God is perfect in all of his attributes, and he lacks nothing.

Just as God is infinite in all of his attributes, he is perfect in each as well:

"Be perfect, therefore, as your heavenly Father is perfect." (Matt. 5:48)

God is not just limitless in his goodness, for example, but he is perfect in his goodness as well. In a sense then, we can think of God's infinity in terms of quantity or capacity and his perfection in terms of quality. God is fully good in both quantity and quality. Because God is perfect in all his attributes, some prefer calling his attributes his "perfections" instead.

God's perfection also means he lacks nothing. There is no additional attribute which he lacks that would make him greater or more complete.

God's love provides a helpful example of why God's perfection in all of his attributes matters. In English, we have just one word for love, but there are multiple words for love in the Greek language of the New Testament. The Bible primarily uses three.

The first word for love is *eros*. This is the erotic or passionate love that is often based on what a person desires from another. This is a love that is more directed inward.

The second word for love is *phileo*. This is a brotherly love and affection that is often based on a mutual benefit in a relationship. This is a love that is directed inward and outward.

The third word for love is *agape*. This is a selfless love that is based on desiring to bring about good for the other person no matter what. This is a love that is directed outward.

It shouldn't be a surprise that is the love God lavishes upon us. God doesn't direct an infinite amount of *phileo* love on us—that would not be good enough. It would be wonderful and undeserved, but it would not be perfect. Instead, God directs his perfect *agape* love on us in unlimited quantities.

Understanding God's perfect love for us really changes the love we have for him and others. In 1 John 4:9, we see that we are to love because God first loved us. Our love is a response to God's love. As we understand God's perfect *agape* love for us more deeply, we will be compelled to strive to love others the same way. We won't be content to extend *phileo* love toward others, as good as that may be. We will want to love them the same way God loves us and loves them as well. And that is so helpful for our kids to know as we want them to grow to love God deeply, and through that love, to love others. We want their love to move from an *eros*-type love that the selfishness of kids often produces, through a *phileo*-type love that shows maturing, to become an *agape*-type love given to them from God.

Matthew 5:48; Deuteronomy 32:4

28

Q. Is there anything or anyone greater than God?

A. No, God is greater than everything and everyone.

If there is one truth that has the power to change us drastically, it is this: God is our greatest treasure. There are many things in life that are truly enjoyable and satisfying. Spending time with family. Enjoying creation. Resting in a hammock. Playing or watching sports. Reading a good book. Eating a wonderful meal. Laughing with friends. These are all great—they are wonderful, even, and there is nothing inherently wrong with enjoying any of them. God designed these things for us to enjoy them, and he delights when we do. However, none of these are ultimately what satisfies us. That is God and God alone:

> There is no one holy like the LORD.
> There is no one besides you!
> And there is no rock like our God. (1 Sam. 2:2)

Our problem is that we often allow other enjoyments—even good ones— to anesthetize us so that we wrongly think we can find contentment in them. But we cannot. Our hearts ache for more, so much more, because our hearts ache deep down for God himself. Knowing God and loving and worshiping him is the greatest joy we can experience. All of our other enjoyments are designed to point us back to that greater reality. The joy of spending time with family should cause us to consider how much greater God—the One who gave us the family—is.

This is why it is not wrong of God to demand that we worship him. Some people push back when they encounter that because it feels wrong. It feels self-serving and egotistical. And it would be if it were anyone else but God demanding it. But when God demands to be worshiped, it is right and proper, because he is the greatest good there is. Not only does he have the right to demand to be worshiped, but worshiping God is for our good because God is drawing us to enjoy our greatest treasure—himself.

We give our kids a great gift if we help them understand this as early as possible. Our kids are like us—they are wired to find contentment and fill that aching in their hearts. But they are also like us in that they will try to fill it with a world of other things besides God, especially if we don't point them to how God is so much greater than anything else they will turn to. The sooner we can help our kids find true contentment in Christ, the more satisfied in him they will become.

Psalm 96:4; 1 Samuel 2:2

29

Q. How much authority does God have?

A. God is a sovereign ruler and has total authority over everything.

As creator of everything, God is the sovereign King, and has complete authority over his creation. This can be thought of as God's positional sovereignty—his right to rule over his creation. But God isn't a powerless or weak King. He is an all-powerful King who demonstrates complete sovereignty over his creation. God is an omnipotent King who always brings his will to pass (Ps. 135:6).

The subject of God's sovereignty can be sensitive for many people. Some people are uncomfortable with the idea of God being in complete control of everything for two reasons. First, it's hard for some people to trust their lives into the hands of another—even if that other person is God. It's easy to believe that no one knows who we are and what we need better than we do, so the more we control our own lives, the better off we will be. But that isn't true. God knows us better than we know ourselves, and God knows what we need much better than we do. We need to remember that God is our good, loving, wise, holy, all-knowing, all-powerful Father whom we can trust to do what is best for us.

The second reason why some people struggle with God's sovereignty is because it seems to take away, or at least erode, free will. If God is sovereign over all and he does whatever he pleases, doesn't that mean that we don't have free will? It makes perfect, logical sense. However, the Bible teaches both, fully. God is completely sovereign. Nothing happens outside of his authority and control. But at the same time, humans have free will. We are responsible for the choices we make and are held accountable for them. Both are true at the same time without either being diminished. God's sovereignty and our free will work together in harmony in a way we cannot fully understand.

But while we cannot understand how they work together, we have to trust that they both do. If we elevate our free will at the expense of God's sovereignty, we attempt to steal his glory, and that is something the Bible will not allow us to do. On the other hand, if we elevate God's sovereignty at the expense of our free will, we are forced to diminish man's responsibility, and that is something the Bible won't allow us to do either. That is why we need to hold fully to both God's sovereignty and our free will in balance with joy.

On the day of Pentecost shortly after Jesus ascended to return to the Father, Peter stood before a crowd of Jews in Jerusalem and preached Jesus. Remember, this was the same Peter who just over a month before had cowered in fear in this city when a little girl accused him of following Jesus. But now, full of the Holy Spirit, Peter preached Jesus boldly.

Peter's thesis was basically that the Jews should have known better. They should have recognized and accepted Jesus as the Messiah. Listen to what he said:

> Fellow Israelites, listen to these words: This Jesus of Nazareth was a man attested to you by God with miracles, wonders, and signs that God did among you through him, just as you yourselves know. Though he was delivered up according to God's determined plan and foreknowledge, you used lawless people to nail him to a cross and kill him. God raised him up, ending the pains of death, because it was not possible for him to be held by death. (Acts 2:22–24)

Do you see what Peter said was the cause of Jesus' crucifixion? It was done according to God's determined plan and foreknowledge—his sovereignty. Case closed, right? God is completely sovereign, even if that comes at the expense of our free will. But wait. Look what he said next: *You nailed him to the cross.* There it is. They were responsible for their actions. Man has free will even if it restricts God's sovereignty, right? Not at all! In this verse we see that God's sovereignty and man's freedom work side by side without tension or problem from God's perspective. It may be a mystery to us, but it isn't for God! Aren't you glad we aren't God, and he is?

Genesis 50:19–20; Acts 2:22–24

30

Q. What is God's providence?

A. God's providence is how he works with people and his creation to bring about what he wants.

While God's sovereignty concerns his right to rule over his creation and his power to do so, God's providence describes the method by which he exercises that sovereignty. You can think of providence as the way God brings about his desired will.

God's providence is experienced by everyone in a general way through his preserving and sustaining creation (Col. 1:17; Heb. 1:3). God did not create the universe and then step away from it, leaving it to run itself. God is still directly involved with keeping the created order going. The planets stay in their orbits by God's providence. Gravity doesn't stop because of God's providence. Rain falls from the sky because of God's providence. We may take all of these things for granted as "nature," but in reality, they are all expressions of God's good and loving providence.

We also experience God's providence through human government. Consider what Romans 13:1 says about how God's providence works through governments:

> Let everyone submit to the governing authorities, since there
> is no authority except from God, and the authorities that exist
> are instituted by God.

God restrains evil through government and moves world leaders to bring about his will. It may be hard to see God's providence in government at times because leaders can often be driven by sin and selfish desires; however, we have to remember that God is sovereign even while man has free will. God's providence is at work even when it is hard to see.

God is also at work providentially—in a specific way—in the lives of his people. Look at Philippians 2:12–13:

> Therefore, my dear friends, just as you have always obeyed, so now, not only in my presence but even more in my absence, work out your own salvation with fear and trembling. For it is God who is working in you both to will and to work according to his good purpose.

Once again we notice the coupling of man's responsibility—we are to work out our salvation—and God's sovereignty—he is the one working in us. God's desire is for his children to grow in Christlikeness, and while we are commanded to work at bringing that to pass, ultimately, it is God's providence that is at work in us to make it happen.

And that takes us to the fourth way God works providentially—through his people. While it benefits us to grow in Christlikeness, we are not the end reason for that growth. We are to grow so that we can be used by God to impact others, especially our children. Here is how Paul put it in Ephesians 2:10:

> For we are his workmanship, created in Christ Jesus for good works, which God prepared ahead of time for us to do.

God already has works planned for our lives—works that will bring him glory and draw others to himself—and he is the one providentially working in us and through us to bring those works to fruition. What an encouragement for our kids to hear that God has great works planned for them!

God's providence is at work all around us and within us, even if we fail to notice it much of the time. But we can trust God that he will continue to work to bring about good in us and through us no matter what.

Romans 13:1; Ephesians 2:10

CREATION

Q. Who created everything?

A. God created the world and everything else in the universe.

If you have ever built something from scratch, you know how challenging it can be. It takes careful planning, attention to detail, the right resources and tools, time, and effort. Sometimes plenty of effort. If you have built something, you probably also have a deeper appreciation for professionals and artisans who can build the same thing you have, only with much more skill and beauty. But as impressive as a table built by a fine craftsman might be, it pales in comparison to God's creation of the universe. Everything we know, except God himself, was created by God as a signpost to his beauty, splendor, power, and glory (Ps. 104:24).

When we think of God's creation of the universe, it is helpful to keep two things in mind. First, God created everything out of nothing. This is known as creation *ex nihilo*. The writer of Hebrews talks about this in Hebrews 11:3.

> By faith we understand that the universe was created by the word of God, so that what is seen was made from things that are not visible.

God creating everything out of nothing gives us a glimpse of his amazing power. Our most beautiful creations all require raw materials, but God's masterpiece of creation was created out of nothing. He created it all only by the power of his spoken Word.

The second thing to keep in mind about God's creation of the universe is that all three Persons of God—the Father, the Son, and the Holy Spirit—were

involved in the act of creation. Sometimes we think that only the Father created, but the Bible records that the Spirit and the Son were involved as well.
We see the Holy Spirit was part of creation in Genesis 1:2.

> Now the earth was formless and empty, darkness covered the
> surface of the watery depths, and the Spirit of God was hover-
> ing over the surface of the waters.

In Job 33:4, we read that the Holy Spirit was not just present, but actively
involved in creation. As for the Son, we read of him creating everything in a
few places, such as Colossians 1:16.

> For everything was created by him,
> in heaven and on earth,
> the visible and the invisible,
> whether thrones or dominions
> or rulers or authorities—
> all things have been created through him and for him.

It should not be surprising that all three Persons worked together in
creating everything. Sometimes we forget that the three Persons of God are
united more closely than we can imagine and they always operate together.
Remembering that they worked together in creation reminds us of their close
fellowship, the fellowship that they invited us to join. It also reminds us that
they are working together in a new creation—executing the plan of redemption to bring us back into relationship with them after we rebelled and turned
from God.

Genesis 1:1; Hebrews 11:3

Q. Why did God create everything?

A. God created everything for his glory.

God is infinitely glorious. He is more beautiful, amazing, and good than we can ever hope to grasp. And that's the problem. He is so far greater than we are that it is hard for us even to begin to understand his glory. That is why he created the universe. It exists to reveal God's glory to us. Let's be clear: God is not glorious *because* he created—that would imply that he needed to create to become glorious. Instead, we need to turn that around. Creation exists because God is glorious and he wanted to give us a glimpse of that glory.

There is a scene early in the book of Revelation where twenty-four elders worship God before his throne. We're not sure who these elders are, and it doesn't really matter at this point; we should simply pay attention to why they say God deserves glory in Revelation 4:11.

> Our Lord and God,
> you are worthy to receive
> glory and honor and power,
> because you have created all things,
> and by your will
> they exist and were created.

God is to be glorified because he created everything, and he created everything solely because he willed it all to be. Isaiah 43:7 specifies that God created every person for his glory, so it is clear that we are included in the twenty-four elders' reason for glorifying God. Everything, including you and your kids, exists for that singular purpose—to reveal God's glory.

But how does that happen? How does creation glorify God? Again, we have to be clear that creation doesn't make God glorious or add to his glory.

Instead creation reveals his glory, and it does that through its beauty, design, and size. The beauty of the universe proves to us that the creator is that much more beautiful. The design of the universe proves to us that the creator is orderly and intelligent. The size of the universe proves to us that the creator is so much bigger than we can imagine.

As amazing as that is, it's even more amazing when we remember that creation as we see it is fallen. Can you imagine how much greater creation was before sin corrupted it? But even now, the fallen universe continues to scream, and whisper, the glory of our God.

When we marvel in God's creation, we glorify God. When we enjoy God's creation, we glorify God. And when we emulate God's amazing creativity through arts, music, and other creative endeavors, we glorify God. Pretty amazing, isn't it? God created such an amazing universe, and he wants us to enjoy it to the fullest for his glory. Our pleasure glorifies God! Yet another reason why he is so glorious!

Revelation 4:11; Isaiah 43:7

3

Q. How did God create everything?

A. God created everything by his spoken word.

"Sticks and stones may break my bones, but words will never hurt me." Most likely, we've all heard that old idiom. It's often told to kids to encourage them not to let someone insulting them or calling them names hurt them. But there's a problem with it. A big one. Words *do* hurt. Sometimes more than a physical wound ever could. Words have power. We have to remember and appreciate that, because everything we know came about by the power of the spoken word. Here's how Psalm 33:6 puts it:

> The heavens were made by the word of the LORD,
> and all the stars, by the breath of his mouth.

God spoke, and *everything* came into existence. That's power! Not only does creation itself reveal God's glory; the method by which he created does as well. But there is even more depth and richness to God's creating by his spoken word. God's method of creation points us to Jesus.

In John's prologue to his Gospel, he describes the background of why and how Jesus came to earth, the story he would unfold in the rest of the book. He uses an interesting title to introduce Jesus. Not Messiah. Not Lord. Not even Son of God. All of these would have been appropriate, but instead John calls Jesus the Word. Look how he begins in John 1:1.

> In the beginning was the Word, and the Word was with God,
> and the Word was God.

That closely echoes Genesis 1:1, where we read that in the beginning, God created everything. John did that on purpose. He wanted to draw our attention right away to the awesome reality that the same power that created the universe—the Word—had now come to the very earth he had created. Just as the spoken word of God brought everything into existence and gave life, so too would Jesus, the Word of God, bring salvation and eternal life as God had intended in Eden.

God's Word is powerful. We are to be in awe of it. But beyond that, we are to be ever-grateful that the Word of God came so that he might break the power of sin and death and that one day he will return and make everything right again on earth and to the farthest reaches of the universe he created.

Psalm 33:6; John 1:1

4

Q. In what condition was everything God created?

A. God created everything perfectly good.

Have you ever wondered why flowers are different colors? Why didn't God make them all one color—say yellow. Wouldn't they still be beautiful? Wouldn't they still be functional? Or why not just create everything in black and white? Why create color at all?

OK, how about taste? Have you ever wondered why God gave us taste buds to taste sweet, sour, bitter, and salty? Why did God give us thousands of taste buds, which are renewed each week, to experience different tastes? Why not give us the ability to taste one thing—say, sweet? Or, why did he give us taste buds at all? He could have designed us to live on a tasteless sludge that would provide all of the nutrients we need. It would be healthier, wouldn't it?

Believe it or not, these questions are not unimportant. They take us right to the heart of what it means that God created the world perfectly good. Everything God created was good because it all perfectly fulfilled its purpose and earned God's full approval. The earth, the waters, the vegetation, all of the animals, people, the stars, the moon, the planets—everything.

And that takes us back to color and taste buds. There was a reason God created both. There is purpose in each, because each was included in God's declaration that everything was very good:

> God saw all that he had made, and it was very good indeed.
> Evening came and then morning: the sixth day. (Gen. 1:31)

Color and taste buds were worthy of God's approval and perfectly fulfilled their purposes.

Let's think about color first. Certainly if all flowers were yellow, they would still declare God's glory to us. But consider how much more flowers full of color shout God's glory. They reinforce even more deeply his creativity and beauty. And they remind us of how much he desires for us to enjoy his creation. If yellow flowers don't excite you, that's fine. How about red ones? Or blue ones? Or orange ones? Or white ones? The list goes on and on. That is why God declared colorful flowers good—because they fulfill the purpose of deeply showing us his artistry in creation.

It's the same idea with taste. God created us with taste buds so that we would enjoy the food he provides. His desire is that we savor a good meal, and in doing so, turn our attention to his goodness and glory in creating the food, giving us our taste buds, and then providing the food to us. Taste was declared good because it fulfills the purpose of deeply showing us God's kindness to us to heap such gifts upon us.

Even now, after the Fall, God's creation is still good—although no longer perfectly good. God still desires for us to enjoy his creation to the fullest as we also steward it well. So go ahead and put an arrangement of fresh-cut flowers on the dining room table and prepare your favorite meal; delight in each. That is what they were created for, and by enjoying them, we fulfill our created purpose of worshiping the creator and provider of it all.

Genesis 1:31; 1 Timothy 4:4

5

Q. How does God rule over his creation?

A. God rules over his creation perfectly and with loving care according to his purposes.

Perhaps many of us struggle to understand how God rules over his creation because we try to understand it through the lens of human government. When we think of ruling, we think of government, so when we think of God ruling, we see him as sort of a government official—like the president. But not many of us know our government officials, especially the president. We probably have never even met them, perhaps never even tried to communicate with them. So to us, they govern from a distance. This is especially true the further removed government is from us. Local government officials feel distant, but then state officials feel even more distant, and national officials still even more distant. We know our government leaders don't know us, and we don't expect them to. Important leaders are too important to know us, or to care specifically about us.

And that's the thinking we carry over to God. Wrongly.

God indeed rules over all, which we read in passages such as Psalm 97:1.

> The LORD reigns! Let the earth rejoice;
> let the many coasts and islands be glad.

But God does not rule from a distance. He has chosen to be with us and rule over his creation through his providence. Jesus being Immanuel—God with us—is all the proof we need of God's desire to rule from near, not far! God sent Jesus to show us who God is and teach about the kingdom of God, and then Jesus sent the Holy Spirit, who resides in those who trust in Christ to lead and guide us in his ways (see Rom. 8:14 and Gal. 5:25).

One of the ways that God rules and brings his purposes to pass in his creation is through his people. God has chosen to position his people as his mediatorial rulers. This is one of the assignments God gave Adam and Eve in Genesis 1:28.

> God blessed them, and God said to them, "Be fruitful, multiply, fill the earth, and subdue it. Rule the fish of the sea, the birds of the sky, and every creature that crawls on the earth."

God appointed man to subdue and rule over the earth, but God did not abdicate his authority. We are still to rule under God's absolute authority, in essence, being his stewards by caring for the creation he still owns but has entrusted to us. Our role, then, is to yield to God's rule in our own lives as we steward his creation well. Living carelessly with creation does not honor its Creator. The world is not unimportant. It is not just where we live and how we survive. The world is designed to reveal God's glory, and our failure to honor it and steward it as such reveals that we do not see and appreciate God's glory ourselves. But when we do care for God's creation as we should, we strengthen the message that it sends out to all who see it—that God is beautiful and amazing and deserving of worship.

Psalm 97:1; 1 Chronicles 29:11–12

Q. What did God create on the first day?

A. On the first day, God created light and formed day and night.

The first day of creation is described in Genesis 1:2–5.

> Now the earth was formless and empty, darkness covered the surface of the watery depths, and the Spirit of God was hovering over the surface of the waters. Then God said, "Let there be light," and there was light. God saw that the light was good, and God separated the light from the darkness. God called the light "day," and the darkness he called "night." There was an evening, and there was a morning: one day.

Notice how creation begins—by God taking a formless, empty, and dark earth and beginning to bring order, structure, and light to it. This is not accidental. God is revealing his character to us right off the bat: he is an orderly God. He also introduces us to the incredibly important concept of "light." All throughout Scripture, God will use light as an image of how people come to know him. Israel was to be a light to the nations (Isa. 49:6). The Bible is a lamp to those who read it (Ps. 119:105). Jesus is the light of the world (John 8:12). And followers of Jesus are to be light on a hill (Matt. 5:16). It is fitting, then, that creation begins with order and light.

We also see God creating by separating—here light from darkness. He will create by the same manner of separating on days two and three as well, forming a parallel structure in the days of creation where days one and four, days two and five, and days three and six relate with each other.

The sun will not be created until day four (day one's parallel day), so the light created here cannot be it. It is most likely that the light created on the first day was the light of God's glory (2 Cor. 4:6). If this is the case, we shouldn't make the mistake of thinking that this was the beginning of God's glory. God's glory is eternal as he is eternal. Instead, this was a way that God's glory might be expressed within his creation through particles and waves he created.

Genesis 1:2–5; John 8:12

Q. What did God create on the second day?

A. On the second day, God created the sky.

The second day of creation is described in Genesis 1:6–8.

> Then God said, "Let there be an expanse between the waters, separating water from water." So God made the expanse and separated the water under the expanse from the water above the expanse. And it was so. God called the expanse "sky." Evening came and then morning: the second day.

As he did on the first day, God again created through the process of separation on the second day. This time, God separated the waters to create an expanse—a space—between them: the sky. The waters that were left below would become the seas on day three, and the waters that were separated above would become moisture in the atmosphere.

The stage is now set for vegetation to grow on the ground with a watering system in place. It won't be surprising to see God create that vegetation on the next day.

Some believe that there was actually more water in the atmosphere from this point of creation moving forward until the flood in Genesis 7. Genesis 7:11 describes the watery depths bursting open as well as the floodgates of the sky opening. The image is of a reversal of the created order of Genesis 1, in an act of "uncreation," judging mankind for their sin. The waters that were separated on day two of creation were joined back together again.

Genesis 1:6–8

8

Q. What did God create on the third day?

A. On the third day, God created land, seas, plants, and trees.

The third day of creation is described in Genesis 1:9–13.

> Then God said, "Let the water under the sky be gathered into one place, and let the dry land appear." And it was so. God called the dry land "earth," and the gathering of the water he called "seas." And God saw that it was good. Then God said, "Let the earth produce vegetation: seed-bearing plants and fruit trees on the earth bearing fruit with seed in it according to their kinds." And it was so. The earth produced vegetation: seed-bearing plants according to their kinds and trees bearing fruit with seed in it according to their kinds. And God saw that it was good. Evening came and then morning: the third day.

The third and final creative act through separation results in the formation of land masses and the seas. Unlike the first two days of creation, the third day includes two different creative acts. God continues creating on this day by creating vegetation, with the capacity to produce fruit with seed to continue to produce more vegetation and fruit.

It may seem odd to include the details of the seeds, especially since it is mentioned more than once. This may have been included to reinforce the intentionality of God's design of creation, but there is another possible reason as well. Seed will be another important image throughout the Old Testament. We will see it again appear two chapters later after Adam and Eve sin and God promises that one of Eve's descendants—her seed—would crush the head of the serpent. This seed is, of course, pointing to Jesus. The rest of the Old Testament centers on the story of that seed coming, and he is traced through several lineages. Through Seth. Through Noah. Through Abraham. And so forth all the way into the New Testament when that Seed is born in a manger in Bethlehem.

Genesis 1:9–13

9

Q. What did God create on the fourth day?

A. On the fourth day, God created the sun, moon, and stars.

The fourth day of creation is described in Genesis 1:14–19.

> Then God said, "Let there be lights in the expanse of the sky to separate the day from the night. They will serve as signs for seasons and for days and years. They will be lights in the expanse of the sky to provide light on the earth." And it was so. God made the two great lights—the greater light to rule over the day and the lesser light to rule over the night—as well as the stars. God placed them in the expanse of the sky to provide light on the earth, to rule the day and the night, and to separate light from darkness. And God saw that it was good. Evening came and then morning: the fourth day.

The first three days of creation work together to form one movement of God creating the earth, the stage of what God would create on the final three days of his active creation. With that stage now complete, God begins to fill the universe he has made.

Day four parallels day one. On day one, God created light. Now on day four, he creates other sources of light in the heavens—the sun, the moon, and stars.

Again, we see God's design at work as he uses these celestial bodies not only to produce light but also to separate day and night and to form the seasons. God gave us a way to tell the passing of time.

Genesis 1:14–19

10

Q. What did God create on the fifth day?

A. On the fifth day, God created birds and sea creatures.

The fifth day of creation is described in Genesis 1:20–23.

> Then God said, "Let the water swarm with living creatures,
> and let birds fly above the earth across the expanse of the sky."
> So God created the large sea-creatures and every living creature
> that moves and swarms in the water, according to their kinds.
> He also created every winged creature according to its kind.
> And God saw that it was good. God blessed them: "Be fruitful,
> multiply, and fill the waters of the seas, and let the birds multi-
> ply on the earth." Evening came and then morning: the fifth day.

The fifth day of creation parallels the second day when the waters were separated and the sky was formed. Now God fills the waters and the skies with sea creatures and birds. Here we notice a progression in terms of life that God created that will culminate on the following day. First, God created vegetation, which is alive, but not in the same way as birds and fish. The next day God will create animals, and then, finally, the pinnacle of creation—man.

We see another first from God on this day as he blesses the birds and creatures of the waters and commands them to be fruitful and multiply. This blessing reveals that animals are in a favored position in creation, although they will be surpassed by mankind.

We also see God's intention for his creation not to be static. The animals were to multiply and spread out—as were humans. There is purpose in God's creation, and he has a will for what was to happen within his creation.

Genesis 1:20–23

Q. What did God create on the sixth day?

A. On the sixth day, God created animals and people.

The sixth day of creation is described in Genesis 1:24–31.

> Then God said, "Let the earth produce living creatures according to their kinds: livestock, creatures that crawl, and the wildlife of the earth according to their kinds." And it was so. So God made the wildlife of the earth according to their kinds, the livestock according to their kinds, and all the creatures that crawl on the ground according to their kinds. And God saw that it was good.
>
> Then God said, "Let us make man in our image, according to our likeness. They will rule the fish of the sea, the birds of the sky, the livestock, the whole earth, and the creatures that crawl on the earth."
>
> > So God created man in his own image;
> > he created him in the image of God;
> > he created them male and female.
>
> God blessed them, and God said to them, "Be fruitful, multiply, fill the earth, and subdue it. Rule the fish of the sea, the birds of the sky, and every creature that crawls on the earth." God also said, "Look, I have given you every seed-bearing plant on the surface of the entire earth and every tree whose fruit contains seed. This will be food for you, for all the wildlife of the earth, for every bird of the sky, and for every creature that crawls on the earth—everything having the breath of life in

it—I have given every green plant for food." And it was so. God saw all that he had made, and it was very good indeed. Evening came and then morning: the sixth day.

The sixth day of creation parallels the third day when God created the land and vegetation. Now, God begins by creating animals to roam on that land. Again, as on the third day, God created in two acts on this day. The second act is the peak of creation—the creation of man—which is why there is much more detail recorded about this day.

We will note for now that man was created uniquely from the rest of creation in that man was created in the image of God. This places man in a special relationship with God and sets man apart from the rest of creation in importance. Man is then blessed and commanded to be fruitful and multiply and fill the earth, as were the birds and sea creatures—but added to man's blessing and instruction is subduing and ruling over the earth.

We also see God's plan for providing food for man, and the other creatures, from what he had created on the third day—vegetation. Most likely, all creatures were originally vegetarian (which is not surprising because eating meat would have required death, a consequence of the Fall). God would change what man could eat after the flood (see Gen. 9). With the creation of man, God is finished with his creation, which we will see on the seventh day.

Genesis 1:24–31

Q. What did God create on the seventh day?

A. On the seventh day, God rested.

The seventh day of creation is described in Genesis 2:1–3.

> So the heavens and the earth and everything in them were completed. On the seventh day God had completed his work that he had done, and he rested on the seventh day from all his work that he had done. God blessed the seventh day and declared it holy, for on it he rested from all his work of creation.

We will quickly notice that the seventh day is somewhat different from the first six. It is not surprising that there is no mention of God speaking because his created work was completed. We also do not see the familiar closing refrain of "there was evening and there was morning" along with the day number. This may have been left off to reveal that God's design was for his creation to stay in a constant state of rest, a rest ruined two chapters later by Adam and Eve's rebellion.

But why did God rest? Surely not because he was weary. Why, then, include this day of God resting in the creation account?

On one hand, this day is important to confirm that God's creation was indeed finished and that it did fully measure up to his standards. The seventh day serves as a period, or perhaps even an exclamation point, on creation with God emphatically declaring that it is over. Everything was truly very good, as he had said.

But at the same time, God is also teaching us two important things. First, God's creation was built on a rhythm of work and rest that we were to emulate. Later, God would command that his people do such through the institution of the Sabbath. While there is debate about if and how Christians are to honor the Sabbath in the New Covenant (more on that later), the principle of our need to rest is traced back to the created order, which tells us that rest is an ongoing need. God designed us to need and enjoy rest—something we are reminded of every day with our need to sleep. God's point may be that we need to remember that *he* is ultimately our provider and sustainer, not us.

The second thing God teaches us through his resting on the seventh day is that he is the provider of our ultimate rest. Hebrews 4 describes salvation as entering our rest—in this case, our rest in Christ. Rest, then, would become an important concept when it comes to describing salvation—not only the end result, but also the way we are saved in the first place by stopping our efforts to be good enough and resting in Christ's sacrifice and receiving his righteousness so that we can be saved and find true rest indeed.

Genesis 2:1–3; Exodus 20:8–10

13

Q. Who were the first people God created?

A. God created Adam and Eve as the first man and woman.

The first man that God created was Adam, a name that comes from the Hebrew word that means "man." Adam, like the rest of creation, was declared good by God. But then, in Genesis 2:18, we read of God declaring part of his creation *not* good:

> Then the LORD God said, "It is not good for the man to be alone. I will make a helper corresponding to him."

Why was it not good for the man to be alone? After all, Adam was in a beautiful garden in the middle of God's perfect creation. Adam ruled over creation, under only God's authority, and Adam had a perfect relationship with God. What was missing from that? What could Adam possibly lack? Companionship.

God created man to be a social being, like he is. God the Father, God the Son, and God the Holy Spirit have enjoyed a perfect relationship for all eternity, and God's desire was for the man he created to enjoy a similar relationship, as well as a relationship with him. One does not take away from the other in God's economy; each adds to the other.

So God brought all of the animals before Adam so that he could name them as part of his mediated rule over creation. While Adam naming the animals reinforces his authority over them, it served another, perhaps more important purpose, as well. As Adam studied each animal to give it its name, he was surely able to make one critical observation—none of the animals was like him. None was a suitable helper and companion for him.

So God caused Adam to fall asleep and created a woman from part of him. The woman would be the companion Adam needed, and her compatibility was immediately proven by her literally being part of him. Adam would later name the woman Eve, which means "living" or "mother of all living," playing off of her role in being the one who would begin the process of producing new life on earth.

Genesis 2:18–23; Ecclesiastes 4:9–12

Q. How did God create Adam and Eve?

A. God formed Adam from the dust of the ground and breathed life into him, and God created Eve from Adam's rib.

God had created the world, but he had not yet sent rain on the land and there was no one to work the ground. So God created Adam to fulfill that role which was first hinted at in the process God chose to create him as described in Genesis 2:7.

> Then the LORD God formed the man out of the dust from the ground and breathed the breath of life into his nostrils, and the man became a living being.

It is likely that God created Adam out of the dust from the ground to emphasize his primary task in creation, and perhaps also because in God's omniscience he knew that Adam would sin and return to that very dust one day (Gen. 3:19). While forming Adam out of the dust doesn't seem to elevate him over the rest of creation, breathing the breath of life into him surely does. This act of God sets mankind apart from the rest of creation.

When it came time to create Eve, God took a different approach. Eve was created from one of Adam's ribs (Gen. 2:21). Nothing God does is unintentional, so we have to ask why God chose that method for creating the first woman. We find the answer a few verses later when God presents the woman to the man in Genesis 2:23.

> And the man said:
> This one, at last, is bone of my bone

and flesh of my flesh;
this one will be called "woman,"
for she was taken from man.

After seeing no suitable companion among all of the animals, Adam at last finds his perfect helper and declares that she is bone of his bone and flesh of his flesh—literally. Adam felt an immediate connection to Eve because she was part of him. God's wisdom in creating Eve the way he did is immediately evident in Adam's declaration and we see it again two verses later when we read that they were naked and felt no shame (Gen. 2:25). The first husband and wife enjoyed a deeply intimate marriage relationship from the start.

Genesis 2:7; Genesis 2:21

Q. In what way did God create Adam and Eve?

A. God created Adam and Eve as male and female, each in his own image.

More important than *how* God created Adam and Eve was the *way* he created them. *How* focuses more on the method or process, while the *way* focuses more on their composition. Adam and Eve were different from the rest of creation—critically so.

Our first clue that Adam and Eve would not be just another part of creation but that they would be the pinnacle of creation is found in what God says as he prepares to create man. Up until this point, we heard the common refrain of "let there be" echo through the days of creation. But now, God says something different, which is recorded in Genesis 1:26.

> Then God said, "Let us make man in our image, according to our likeness. They will rule the fish of the sea, the birds of the sky, the livestock, the whole earth, and the creatures that crawl on the earth."

"Let us make" immediately conveys a more intimate act of creation. God lovingly created everything, and he rules over all with providential care, but his relationship with man and his love and care for him are on a higher level. While this change in what God says hints at the uniqueness of man's creation, what follows clearly conveys that man is indeed special.

Man was made in God's image and likeness. That cannot be said of the rest of creation. Only men and women enjoy this distinction. But what does it mean?

First of all, we should clarify what it does not mean. It does not mean that we are exactly like God. This is clear based on our physical bodies; God is Spirit and has no body (John 4:24). The Hebrew words that are translated as "image" and "likeness" both denote similarity, but they do not mean we are identical to God, in nature. So to be created in God's image and likeness doesn't mean we are exactly like him but that we are similar to him in some way. There is a way, or perhaps several ways, we represent God to the rest of creation.

Some believe that we are made in the image of God in that we alone are like God in demonstrating rational thought and morality. Others believe that we are in the image of God because we have a spiritual dimension that allows us to know him and have a personal relationship with him that is different from the animals' ability to know God. Still others say that we are like God in the authority he gave us as stewards over his creation. The way we rule over creation images his absolute dominion over it. All of these are ways that we are like God and represent him to the world, and there is no reason to pick and choose between them, but we do need to talk about two important notes about being made in the image of God.

First, both males and females are created in God's image. The term "man" in Genesis 1:26 is best understood as humanity, not just males. This is veri-fied elsewhere in Scripture, such as James 3:9, and in our understanding of the heart of God.

Second, because every person is created in the image of God, all peo-ple—no matter their ethnicity, language, socio-economic status, or anything else—have intrinsic worth. As the people of God, we are to love and treat all others with the respect they deserve. And this is critical for our kids to understand, not only so they treat others the way they deserve, but also so they see themselves properly—as God does—with intrinsic worth. Our kids need to understand that their self-worth is not based on what they look like, how smart they are, how athletic they are, or anything else except that they bear the image of God. That is the worth we want our kids to find—the worth they need to find.

Genesis 1:26–27; Colossians 3:10

16

Q. What did God give Adam and Eve besides a body?

A. God gave Adam and Eve a spirit so they could know him.

What makes a person who they are is not only a body. Our true identity—who God made us as individuals—is more than that. Our true and whole identity is found in the union of our body with our soul, or spirit, which God has given us. We read of this spirit in several passages such as Zechariah 12:1.

A pronouncement:

> The word of the LORD concerning Israel.
> A declaration of the LORD,
> who stretched out the heavens,
> laid the foundation of the earth,
> and formed the spirit of man within him.

God has given us a spirit within our body that is the seat of our true identity and the way we can know God and may be in relationship with him. This is one of the ways we are set apart from the rest of creation.

Death, then, is understood as the separation of the spirit from the body. The body goes to the ground, but the spirit lives on, until it is reunited with the body at the resurrection. The only question for a person is where he or she will live for eternity—with God enjoying all the good he designed for us, or apart from God in the absence of anything good. Thankfully, because of Jesus, we may look forward to an eternity with God in resurrected, glorified bodies.

Zechariah 12:1; James 2:26

17

Q. In what condition did God create Adam and Eve?

A. Adam and Eve were created perfect, innocent, and content.

Adam and Eve were perfect people living in a perfect garden in the middle of a perfect world as part of a perfect universe—all bringing glory to a perfect God. We need to understand, though, how Adam and Eve's perfection differed from God's.

Adam and Eve were perfect in that they were everything God created them to be. They were perfectly good—they measured up to God's standard. That does not mean they were perfect like God is perfect in all of his ways. Part of God's perfection is his omniscience, but Adam and Eve were never all-knowing. Nor were they omnipresent or omnipotent.

We also need to appreciate that perfection allows for differences. The three Persons of God are perfect, yet they are different in their roles and they are three different Persons. This is obvious when we consider that Adam and Eve were perfect yet were of different genders and were given different roles by God. As perfect people, Adam and Eve had the capacity to fully glorify God, honor him, worship him, serve him, and know him.

In addition to being perfect, Adam and Eve were innocent. They were entirely without sin. Not only had they not committed any sins, but they did not have a sin nature or natural tendency to desire to sin.

Finally, Adam and Eve were content. God had provided all they needed and they enjoyed perfect relationship with him and one another. They were perfectly satisfied in their service to God, and they enjoyed God's creation all around them. They lacked nothing and needed nothing. God had supplied all of their needs.

Genesis 3:7; Genesis 1:31   .

18

Q. Why did God create Adam and Eve?

A. God created Adam and Eve and all people to love him, worship him, and give him glory.

We were created to be in relationship with God—a relationship that is deep, meaningful, and fully satisfying. That is important to remember, because we are commanded to love, worship, and glorify God—all actions that are directed toward God and seem to benefit him, not us. But in reality, these actions *do* benefit us because they foster our relationship with God.

When Jesus was asked which of the 613 commands in the Old Testament Law was the greatest, he pointed to the commandment to love God fully (Matt. 22:37–38). Our love for God is at the center of our relationship with him and should be what drives everything else—worship, obedience, and service. But God's command to love him is not one directional. Our love for God actually is anchored in his greater love for us as we read in 1 John 4:19.

We love because he first loved us.

God's pure, limitless, outward-focused love for us was best demonstrated on the cross, where he gave us his Son to die in our place for our sin. Such love as this is what compels us to love God in return. God's command to love him isn't a chore, but an invitation to know him, to know what he has done for us, and to love him in response.

When love is the foundation of our relationship with God, the natural result will be that we will worship God in Spirit and truth (John 4:24). Our worship will not be forced or hollow. It will be genuine and deep—being generated from the core of who we are and showing itself through how we live each day. The God who is so amazing and who loves us as he does deserves worship! We see this in Psalm 100:

> Let the whole earth shout triumphantly to God!
> Serve the LORD with gladness;
> come before him with joyful songs.
> Acknowledge that the LORD is God.
> He made us, and we are his—
> his people, the sheep of his pasture.
> Enter his gates with thanksgiving
> and his courts with praise.
> Give thanks to him and bless his name.
> For the LORD is good, and his faithful love endures forever;
> his faithfulness, through all generations.

This psalm does not depict stagnant, rote worship. It pictures vibrant worship that gives us joy and pleasure. We are all worshipers at our core. That is how God designed Adam and Eve and us to be. We are never *not* worshiping. Our problem is that we often worship the wrong things—things other than God, such as sports, family, money, popularity, and influence. Worshiping anything else other than God is idolatry, but we can learn something about the nature of worship from this sin. Why do we worship these other things? Because we want to! We find enjoyment in doing so, or else we wouldn't do it. How much greater, then, should our worship of the one true God be? If we find enjoyment in worshiping broken things in the world—false gods that give us momentary pleasure—how much more enjoyment will we find in worshiping God, who satisfies our greatest needs in himself?

That takes us to the third purpose God gave to Adam and Eve and us. We are to glorify God in all we do, as we read in 1 Corinthians 10:31.

> So, whether you eat or drink, or whatever you do, do everything for the glory of God.

Paul wrote this instruction at the end of a discussion of whether the early Christians were allowed to eat meat from an animal that had been sacrificed to an idol. Some in the early church believed that was wrong, while others believed it was fine; this disagreement caused an argument. Paul addressed that issue and concluded with this overarching principle: Everything we do—even something that seems trivial such as eating a meal—should be done for

God's glory. The key is to always remember that God is the source of all that is good (James 1:17), and when we do that, we will constantly live seeing God's kindness to us and finding purpose in all we do.

Adam and Eve were to love, worship, and glorify God in Eden, and in doing so, they were to enjoy a beautiful relationship with him. We are invited to do the same.

Matthew 22:37–38; Psalm 100:1–5; 1 Corinthians 10:31

19

Q. What were Adam and Eve to do?

A. Adam and Eve were to rule over creation and start a family.

God's instructions to Adam and Eve can be boiled down to ruling over creation and populating the earth, as captured in Genesis 1:28.

> God blessed them, and God said to them, "Be fruitful, multiply, fill the earth, and subdue it. Rule the fish of the sea, the birds of the sky, and every creature that crawls on the earth."

Later we would see God command Adam to work the ground, which was part of how he was to subdue and rule. It's important to note that Adam's obedience to God and one of the ways he worshiped him was by tending a garden. This shows us that God's definitions of worship and service are much broader than ours.

It is also helpful to note that marriage and family are critical parts of God's design for creation. The family is God's building block for creating society and culture. Just as family was important in Eden, it is still important today. Marriage is a gift from God, and all children are a blessing from God.

One of the best ways we can glorify God is by striving to have marriages that reflect faithful love and commitment and by honoring and celebrating marriage, especially when our culture's value of marriage is eroding rapidly. At the same time, we can glorify God by raising children who love Christ and honor him. No matter who you are, your family is your primary ministry and the greatest opportunity you have to reflect the love of God to the world.

Genesis 1:28

20

Q. What command did God give Adam and Eve?

A. God commanded Adam and Eve not to eat from the tree of the knowledge of good and evil.

What do you first think of when you see God's command to Adam in Genesis 2:16–17?

> And the LORD God commanded the man, "You are free to eat from any tree of the garden, but you must not eat from the tree of the knowledge of good and evil, for on the day you eat from it, you will certainly die."

Perhaps you zero in on God's instruction not to eat of the tree of the knowledge of good and evil—and if so, it is easy to see why, with such a strong warning of death attached to it. But we cannot miss the beginning of what God shared—Adam was invited to eat from *any* other tree! God had created the entire universe for man to enjoy and had given him a garden full of trees with lush, perfect fruit. Restricting him from eating the fruit of one tree doesn't seem too harsh when you think of it that way, does it?

Even here, in God's first command, we see an important principle—all of God's commands are for our good. God's heart is not to restrict our joy and withhold good things from us. He desires to give us joy and protect us from that which will harm us.

That might prompt the question of why God placed the tree of the knowledge of good and evil in the garden in the first place. If God wants to protect us, why place that tree in Eden at all? It's a great question—one we can ponder endlessly. But ultimately, it is one we cannot answer. We cannot be certain about God's intention in placing the tree in the garden, because he has not revealed it to us. However, we do know that God knew Adam and Eve would rebel. Further, he knew that he would provide his Son, Jesus, to suffer the punishment of death because of what Adam and Eve, and all humanity, would do. And yet knowing this, God still placed the tree in Eden. Knowing what it would cost (Titus 1:2). That is how much God desires for us to have a meaningful relationship with him. That is how much God loves us.

Genesis 2:16–17; Titus 1:2

SIN

Q. Did Adam and Eve remain perfect, innocent, and content?

A. No, Adam and Eve disobeyed God's command not to eat from the tree of the knowledge of good and evil.

We don't know how much time elapsed between Genesis 2 and Genesis 3. It could have been years, decades, or more. Or it could have been weeks, days, or perhaps even hours. We have no way of telling. But what we do know is that Adam and Eve failed to obey God's single command. This is how Solomon put it in Ecclesiastes 7:29.

> Only see this: I have discovered that God made people upright,
> but they pursued many schemes.

It all began when the serpent asked Eve a question: "Did God really say, 'You can't eat from any tree in the garden'?" (Gen. 3:1). Moments later, Eve would be mulling over in her heart whether God was truly good or whether he was withholding something from her. She ended up believing a snake rather than the living God—a created thing rather than the Creator.

Eve chose to bite into a piece of fruit from the tree of the knowledge of good and evil, and Adam, who was with her, ate as well. While eating of the tree was clearly a sinful act, Adam and Eve lost the battle before that—in the seconds or minutes prior when they chose to disobey God. That is when sin truly entered the world. Eating the fruit was just the external evidence of what had already been decided in the heart. "We don't trust God! He is holding something from us and we want more! What he has given us just isn't enough. We won't listen to his command and we *will* eat of that tree!"

Adam and Eve had everything going for them. And in that one moment of weakness, confusion, and rebellion it all fell down around them.

It's easy for us to shake our heads in disbelief and disappointment in Adam and Eve. We like to think that had *we* been there, things would have been different. *We* would have been smarter. *We* would have been holier. *We* would have been faithful and obedient. At least we like to think that.

But in reality, we would have done the same. Every single one of us. We all would have rebelled against God. We would have done it that day, because we do it every day. We are no better than Adam and Eve. Thank God he gave us a Savior in Christ.

Genesis 3:6; Ecclesiastes 7:29

Q. Why did Adam and Eve eat the fruit from the tree of the knowledge of good and evil?

A. The devil tricked Eve. She wanted to be like God, so she ate the fruit, and so did Adam.

Adam and Eve were free to eat from dozens of trees, hundreds of trees, perhaps thousands of trees in Eden. And every single one of those trees produced gorgeous, sweet-tasting perfect fruit. There was only one tree they could not eat from, and the wily serpent turned God's generous provision of all those trees on its head to trick Eve.

Satan's initial question in Genesis 3:1 hints at his plan. "Did God really say, 'You can't eat from any tree in the garden'?" Read it closely and you can discover his angle. "Look at all of these trees! You can eat from that one? And that one? And those over there? And these over here? And even those few way over there? You can eat of *any* of these trees except for one single tree? That just doesn't make sense. Why not just allow you to eat from every single tree? It's so close to that, isn't it? Why hold just that one tree back from you?"

Eve responded that they could indeed eat from any tree in the garden except for the one in the middle. God said they could not eat of it or touch it, or they would die.

Looking back at God's instructions in Genesis 2, we don't see any limitation on Adam and Eve touching the tree. We have three options then:

1. God told Adam and Eve they couldn't touch the tree, but it isn't recorded in Scripture. The Bible doesn't give us a complete account of all that happened, but it does give us a correct account.

2. God had originally told Adam the prohibition of eating from the tree before Eve was created. Adam may have added the instruction of not touching the tree as an extra layer of protection.

3. Eve added the prohibition of touching the tree herself.

Thinking through these options reveals that two of them have problems, making the third seem most likely. As you read through the first five chapters of Genesis, you will see many different places where something will appear in one place and be referenced again soon after showing a tight cohesiveness of the five chapters. The days of creation parallel each other. The image of Adam being created from the ground, then working the ground, and then returning to the ground. Being naked and unashamed, then being naked and ashamed, then being clothed and ashamed. Death being promised, death occurring, then death being stated over and over again. With this in mind, it seems unlikely that the Holy Spirit would have failed to include the prohibition of touching the tree just a handful of verses before this, had God actually given it to Adam and Eve. Option 1 is possible, but it doesn't seem like the best option.

If option 2 is correct, then Adam would have lied to Eve about what God had said, which would have been the first sin. Moreover, Eve didn't say that they shouldn't touch the tree, as if Adam and Eve had decided that on their own, just to be extra safe. She said that God had told them they could not touch it. Adam would have had to lie about that. Option 2 doesn't seem possible.

That leaves option 3. So why would Eve have added this prohibition? What was going on in her mind and heart?

The serpent's initial question implies that God was unfairly holding something back from her—the tree of knowledge of good and evil. It seems that Eve picked up on this and her response added fuel to that notion. "You know, you might have a point. Come to think of it, we can't even touch that tree!"

This is when the serpent sprung his trap. "No! You will not die" (Gen. 3:4) was the direct lie that came out of its hissing mouth. Then he followed that up with a partial truth. "God knows that you will be wise like God, knowing good and evil." What the serpent didn't say is that Adam and Eve would know good and evil, but they would know it differently from God. God knows the difference between the two, of course, but he is without evil. When Adam and Eve sinned, they came to know good and evil by experiencing evil itself.

At this point, Eve entered a literal death spiral. She saw that the tree was good for food (which of the others were not?), that it looked delightful (again, which of the others were not?), and that it was desirable for obtaining wisdom (the real deciding factor), so she ate and gave some to Adam who was with her.

The serpent's strategy had worked: suggest that God was holding something back unfairly and then weave in partial truths and lies. It worked that day with Eve and it still works with us. We are just like Eve—our kids are as well. We will rationalize disobedience in our minds and hearts and, like Satan, even distort the truth to satisfy ourselves and please our desires. The more we help our kids see this in themselves, and confess, the more we will help them see their sinfulness and their need of a Savior. And the more they see that, the more prone they may be to turning to God in faith. If we love our kids, we will show them their sin, for their own good.

Genesis 3:1–7; 2 Corinthians 11:3

3

Q. Who is the devil?

A. The devil, also called Satan, is a fallen angel who wants to take glory from God.

At some point during creation, which the Bible doesn't specify, God created angels. Angels are heavenly beings, different from people, that serve God. The word *angel* literally means "messenger," and we see them living up to this name by delivering messages from God often throughout Scripture.

At some point after creation, which the Bible also doesn't specify, one of these angels named Lucifer became prideful, rebelled against God, and fell from his place in heaven. A group of angels, perhaps one third of the total, fell along with Lucifer. These fallen angels are now known as demons, and Lucifer, also called Satan or the devil, is their leader. Ezekiel 28, Isaiah 14, and Revelation 12 are passages that seem to piece this account together.

The devil is also called the accuser, for making accusations against believers (Rev. 12:10), and the tempter (Matt. 4:3). The devil's goal is to take glory away from God, which he has been trying to do from Eden and will continue to do until he is finally thrown into the lake of fire (Rev. 20).

Although he is already a defeated foe of God's, the devil is powerful and should not be taken lightly. While God's people have nothing to fear because God is greater than the devil and the demons, Satan and his fallen angels are not to be taken too lightly either. The devil and the demons continue to do all they can to thwart God's plans and rob him of his glory.

Luke 10:18; Revelation 12

4

Q. How does the devil try to take glory from God?

A. The devil tries to take glory from God by lying, stealing, killing, and destroying.

From the very beginning in Eden, the devil has used the same plan to rob glory from God. He lied and tricked Eve. He stole purity and innocence from Adam and Eve. He brought death to Adam and Eve. And he destroyed the good creation that God had created, Adam and Eve's relationship with each other, and Adam and Eve's relationship with God.

Lie. Steal. Kill. Destroy. It was the devil's strategy then, and it is his strategy now.

In one of Jesus' most heated debates with the Jewish leaders, he had this to say about the lies of the devil:

> "You are of your father the devil, and you want to carry out your father's desires. He was a murderer from the beginning and does not stand in the truth, because there is no truth in him. When he tells a lie, he speaks from his own nature, because he is a liar and the father of lies." (John 8:44)

The devil is a liar and the father of all lies because he is the one who indirectly caused the Fall. Satan's desire is to mislead the entire world:

> So the great dragon was thrown out—the ancient serpent, who is called the devil and Satan, the one who deceives the whole world. (Rev. 12:9)

All of the lies we experience, such as false religions and attacks on God, are rooted in the devil. The devil's lies aid him in his desire to steal as well, and one of the main things he tries to steal is life from people:

> "A thief comes only to steal and kill and destroy. I have come so that they may have life and have it in abundance." (John 10:10)

While killing, both physically and spiritually, as we saw in John 8:44 is part of how the devil tries to steal life, it is not the only way. He also steals life by robbing people of joy, meaning, and purpose found in Christ.

All of these activities—lying, stealing, and killing—all lead into the devil's desire to destroy. We see this in Eden when he sought to destroy Adam and Eve's relationship with God and creation itself. We see this in his attempt to destroy Jesus as the worthy Savior in his temptations in the wilderness. And we see this every day all around us if we pay attention:

> Be sober-minded, be alert. Your adversary the devil is prowling around like a roaring lion, looking for anyone he can devour. (1 Pet. 5:8)

The devil is defeated. He knows that. But he isn't going down without a fight.

1 Peter 5:8; John 8:44

5

Q. Will the devil win against God?

A. No, the devil has already lost and will be judged by God one day.

———————————

Sometimes you will hear about a loss or setback that was used to turn things around. Maybe it was a sports team that experienced a crushing loss, which motivated them and ended up turning their season around. Maybe it was a failed business deal that caused a company to rethink its strategies and ended up making wiser choices going in a different direction. Maybe it was a painful event in someone's life that caused him or her to get serious about what they were doing in life. When you hear stories like this, you will often hear the team, company, or person talk about the setback as if it were good—they may even share that they are glad and thankful it happened.

The greatest setback that was actually a victory didn't occur on a sports field or in a company's board room—it happened two thousand years ago on a hill called Calvary. The crucifixion of Jesus was the most evil event in all of history, but it was also the greatest victory ever. Nothing worse has ever happened or ever will happen than the blameless Son of God being nailed to the cross, mocked, and scorned, as he suffered and died. But it was through his suffering and death that sin and death were defeated once and for all. And so was the devil.

The devil will not win against God. We know this because he has already lost. His plan to rob God's glory has failed. It's just a matter of time until he experiences the fullness of his failure.

Here's one thing that is important to remember about the devil. He is not God's opposite or equal, as some see him. The devil is a created being, and that alone confirms that he is under the one true God's authority and power. It was never really a fair fight when you think about it.

We see the devil's weakness before God in the account of Job. Job was a righteous man whom God had blessed with a family and wealth. One day, Satan tells God that Job only worships him because he has given him those blessings. And this is where we see God's sovereignty over the devil. God grants the devil permission to take away Job's possessions, but the devil is not allowed to harm Job (Job 1:12). Then when that fails to turn Job away from God, God allows the devil to harm Job, but he could not kill him (Job 2:6). Both times God places limits on the devil—limits that are not questioned by the devil and that are followed by him.

The devil is powerless before our mighty God. He may be fooling himself for now, but one day he will find out how wrong he has been.

Job 1:12; Revelation 20:10

6

Q. Who was responsible for Adam and Eve eating the fruit?

A. Both Adam and Eve freely chose to disobey God and were responsible for their sin.

It didn't take Adam and Eve long after their first sin to learn the blame game. When God asked Adam what had happened, Adam was quick to blame someone else.

> The man replied, "The woman you gave to be with me—she gave me some fruit from the tree, and I ate." (Gen. 3:12)

It was all true, of course. God had given Eve to Adam. And Eve had indeed given him the fruit to eat. But Adam was not simply stating facts. He was blaming Eve—and God as well! Shortly before this, Adam was overcome with joyful gratitude by God's provision of Eve. But now, because Adam failed in his role to protect her from the lies of the serpent, Adam was placing blame on her.

God turned his attention toward Eve and asked what she had done. She was also quite adept at blaming someone else. This time it was the serpent. "He deceived me and I ate!" Again, true, but hardly an accurate telling of what had happened. Eve had listened, entertained the thought of disobeying God, and then stretched out her hand to take a piece of fruit on her own. No one *made* her do it.

Adam and Eve both failed to confess their own desire to sin. It was certainly true that the serpent was responsible in part, and neither of them helped each other, but in the end, they each gave in to their own desires. James, the half-brother of Jesus, put it this way:

No one undergoing a trial should say, "I am being tempted by God," since God is not tempted by evil, and he himself doesn't tempt anyone. But each person is tempted when he is drawn away and enticed by his own evil desire. Then after desire has conceived, it gives birth to sin, and when sin is fully grown, it gives birth to death. (James 1:13–15)

Adam and Eve were tempted and drawn away from trusting and obeying God by their own desires. Eve wanted to be wise like God. Once that desire anchored in her heart, she made the choice to rebel against God and sinned. While we aren't sure what motivated Adam, we know that he experienced the same journey in his mind and heart and he sinned as well. And in that moment, they both died spiritually; later, they would die physically.

God saw through Adam and Eve's attempts to shift blame—and he sees through ours and our kids' attempts to do the same. We are just as quick to blame someone else—anyone else—for our sins instead of owning up to them and taking responsibility. But God will have none of it. He holds us accountable for our sin (Rom. 14:12). Just after this, God would judge Adam and Eve, as well as the serpent, for their sins. But their judgment would not be without hope. God's plan of redemption that was formed before creation was set into motion.

James 1:13–15; Romans 14:12

Q. What happened to Adam and Eve when they disobeyed God?

A. Adam and Eve became sinful and separated from God when they disobeyed him.

Genesis 2 ends by stating that Adam and Eve were naked and unashamed (Gen. 2:25). It is a curious statement that really doesn't make much sense until after the Fall. Here's the first observable consequence of the first sin:

> Then the eyes of both of them were opened, and they knew they were naked; so they sewed fig leaves together and made coverings for themselves. (Gen. 3:7)

Immediately after sinning, Adam and Eve's intimacy with each other was shattered. While once they were unashamed with each other, shame had now entered their relationship. The result was that they put barriers between themselves—sin had driven them apart. What happened next was even more tragic.

Adam and Eve heard the sound of God coming. The language in the Genesis account suggests that God did this regularly before the Fall. God would come down to earth to fellowship with Adam and Eve in the middle of his creation. But Adam and Eve didn't run toward God this time; instead they hid from him (Gen. 3:9–10). The perfect relationship they had enjoyed with God was lost as well. The man and woman put barriers between themselves and God. From that moment forward, Adam, Eve, and the rest of humanity would continue to experience sin and would continue to put more barriers between themselves and God.

Just a few minutes later, God would tell Adam that he would return to the ground—he would die. It didn't happen that day, but a day would come when he would breathe his last. And so would Eve, as would all of their offspring. We see God proven true in the next chapter, when one of Adam and Eve's sons, Cain, would kill his brother, Abel, in the first death recorded in the Bible. From perfection to a brother killing a brother in one single generation. Then we would read of a man named Lamech bragging about killing someone (Gen. 4:23–24). Then in Genesis 5, in the first lineage of the Bible, we would read a tragic refrain over and over again—"then he died." Death had come and it had come with a vengeance.

But physical death was not the worst part of Adam and Eve's sin. Spiritual death was. Just as physical death is a person's spirit separating from the body, spiritual death is our separation from God. An infinite chasm was created between God and mankind because of the sin committed against a perfectly holy God.

God had warned them, but they chose to listen to the lies of the serpent rather than the truth of God. And nothing would ever be the same.

Genesis 3:9–10; Romans 6:23

8

Q. What did God say would happen to the serpent for its part in the first sin?

A. God said the serpent would be cursed more than any other animal.

God had confronted the man first about what had happened in Eden, and Adam had blamed the woman. God then addressed Eve, and she blamed the serpent. God would then pronounce judgment for each of their parts in the first sin in reverse order. He would start with the serpent, move on to Eve, and finish with Adam. Here is the judgment God declared upon the serpent:

So the Lord God said to the serpent:

> Because you have done this,
> you are cursed more than any livestock
> and more than any wild animal.
> You will move on your belly
> and eat dust all the days of your life. (Gen. 3:14)

The serpent would be more cursed than the other animals and would move on its belly eating dust all the days of its life. While some suggest that the serpent may have had legs before this pronouncement, that isn't necessary. It might be better to see God's judgment speaking of humiliation in general using the characteristics the serpent already possessed. It doesn't get any lower and more humiliating than moving on the ground.

The eating the dust all the days of its life may be God's way of using the serpent's lie to Eve against it. The serpent had told Eve that she would not die, but now, just as Adam would return to the dust in death, so would the serpent—hinted at by the last phrase "all the days of your life." That ending implies that the days are limited and the serpent would die as well. His lie had brought about his own death.

But there may be even more to this judgment. God may have also been judging the devil who was behind the actions of the serpent. The devil would be humiliated. He had sealed his own fate. Seeing this judgment in this two-fold way makes more sense when you read the next verse:

> I will put hostility between you and the woman
> And between your offspring and her offspring.
> He will strike your head,
> And you will strike his heel.

The hostility between the serpent and the woman and their offspring seems to fit better to be speaking about the devil, rather than a serpent. While there are many people who do not like snakes, there seems to be more at stake here. Also, the last part of that verse, as we will see soon, is certainly about Jesus and the devil. The devil would strike at Jesus and wound him, but Jesus would crush his head in return. Even while judging our sin, God is gracious and extends hope to us.

Genesis 3:14–15

9

Q. What did God say would happen to Eve for her part in the first sin?

A. God said Eve would have increased pain giving birth and her relationship with Adam would become difficult.

The judgment of the serpent led right into the judgment of Eve:

He said to the woman:

> I will intensify your labor pains;
> you will bear children with painful effort.
> Your desire will be for your husband,
> yet he will rule over you. (Gen. 3:16)

Eve's judgment centered on her role as Adam's helper and, by extension, as God's servant. First, Eve would experience intense pain in giving birth to children. This was a primary way she could partner with Adam and was also one of the ways she could help fulfill God's command for Adam and her to be fruitful and multiply. Childbearing was an act of worship and service to God, but now Eve would offer that worship and service with great difficulty. Joyful worship was now painful.

Second, Eve's relationship with her husband would be negatively affected in some way. This last sentence is hotly debated and explained in different ways. Some see this as Eve desiring Adam sexually, because the same word for "desire" is also used of sexual intimacy in Song of Songs 7:10–11, but that doesn't seem to fit the context of judgment. Others believe that this points to Eve depending on her husband from this point forward, and he would rule

over her. Still others point to the same use of "desire" in the next chapter
(Gen. 4:7) where it speaks of sin's desire to control Cain to suggest that this
represents a power struggle in the marriage. The woman would desire the
place of authority in the marriage relationship while the husband would seek
to authoritatively rule over her.

While this sentence is not clear, what is plain is that in some way, the
marriage relationship was hindered because of sin. We already saw this happening when Adam and Eve hid from each other and then again moments
later when Adam passed blame on to his wife. And we continue to see sin
plague marriages today. But even in this judgment impacting marriage and
family, we see hope. Adam and Eve would not die right away; they would live
long enough to have children and continue life on earth. And one of those
future descendants who would one day be born in a manger in Bethlehem
would be the answer for all of the pain, suffering, and sorrow sin had brought
upon humanity.

Genesis 3:16

10

Q. What did God say would happen to Adam for his part in the first sin?

A. God said Adam would have to work hard to produce food to eat.

The final and longest judgment was directed toward Adam.

> And he said to the man, "Because you listened to your wife and ate from the tree about which I commanded you, 'Do not eat from it':
>
>> The ground is cursed because of you.
>> You will eat from it by means of painful labor
>> all the days of your life.
>> It will produce thorns and thistles for you,
>> and you will eat the plants of the field.
>> You will eat bread by the sweat of your brow
>> until you return to the ground,
>> since you were taken from it.
>> For you are dust,
>> and you will return to dust." (Gen. 3:17–19)

Just as he did in the judgment of the serpent, God gave a reason for Adam's judgment. Adam is judged because he listened to his wife and ate of the tree. This is not God devaluing the woman as if to say Adam's mistake was merely listening to her; instead it is God pointing out to Adam that he was more culpable. Eve was tricked; he ate willingly. Furthermore, Adam should have stepped in to protect his wife from the lies of the serpent, but he failed to do so. In many ways, he is more accountable than anyone else in the Fall, and his judgment bears that out.

Like Eve's, Adam's judgment centers on his worship and service to God. As Eve's service and worship would be made difficult, so would Adam's. The ground that Adam was supposed to work in joyful service to God would now rebel against him—much like how he had rebelled against God. Adam would experience great difficulty in growing food and providing for his family.

This is also where God restated the overarching judgment of death. While God told Adam that he would return to the ground in death, this judgment was not only for him. All humanity, and creation as well, would experience this consequence of sin. But one day, one of Adam's descendants would wear on his brow a crown made out of the thorns the ground produced because of the Fall, and be buried in death, but death would not be able to contain him.

Genesis 3:17–19; Romans 5:12

Q. What did God promise Adam and Eve would happen one day?

A. God promised Adam and Eve that one of their offspring would strike the head of the serpent one day.

Genesis 3:15 is known as the *protoevangelium*. *Proto* means "first" and *evangelium* is where we get the word "evangelism," or good news. So this verse is the "first good news"—the first mention of God's plan to rescue mankind through Jesus.

> I will put hostility between you and the woman
> And between your offspring and her offspring.
> He will strike your head,
> And you will strike his heel. (Gen. 3:15)

While these words of God were directed toward the serpent, he had someone else in mind for this pronouncement, especially the final sentence, which is where we see a beautiful glimpse of the gospel. A child would be born in Adam and Eve's family, and this offspring would defeat the serpent. The offspring would be Jesus, and he would defeat Satan once and for all, as we read in Hebrews 2:14.

> Now since the children have flesh and blood in common, Jesus also shared in these, so that through his death he might destroy the one holding the power of death—that is, the devil.

The apostle John echoed this in 1 John 3:8.

> The one who commits sin is of the devil, for the devil has
> sinned from the beginning. The Son of God was revealed for
> this purpose: to destroy the devil's works.

But how would Jesus destroy the devil? What would the striking of the head and heel be? The answer would be revealed thousands of years later when a crowd cried out, "Crucify him!" As a beaten and battered Man, Jesus was marched outside the city of Jerusalem, nailed to a cross, and left to die. He gave up his life on the cross, experiencing death and bearing the full weight of the world's sin, and was buried in a tomb. But then, on the third day, he left the tomb, having risen from the dead.

That event—the cross and resurrection of Jesus—would be the fulfillment of God's promise in the *protoevangelium*. Satan would strike Jesus' heel—a powerful blow—on the cross, but that very blow would prove to be fatal to Satan. God would use the cross to overcome sin and death, turning the most evil action ever into the greatest gift the world would ever see.

Genesis 3:15; 1 John 3:8

Q. What happened to Adam and Eve after God judged them?

A. After God judged Adam and Eve, they had to leave the Garden of Eden.

Immediately after God judged Adam for his role in the Fall, the focus shifts from judgment to three signs of hope. First, Adam named his wife Eve—which means "living" because she is the mother of all the living (Gen. 3:20). Death would come, but life would continue. And the Deliverer would come from that life. Hope remained.

After that, God made clothing for Adam and Eve out of skins to replace the leaves they had sown together. God provided covering for Adam and Eve's shame through the death of an animal. This looked forward to when God would instruct his people to offer animal sacrifices to cover their sins symbolically, which in turn anticipated when God would provide Jesus to be the perfect sacrifice, whose blood would cover his people's ultimate shame. Hope of rescue is found in God's gracious provision of coverings for Adam and Eve.

After this, God removed the pair from Eden.

> The LORD God said, "Since the man has become like one of us, knowing good and evil, he must not reach out, take from the tree of life, eat, and live forever." So the LORD God sent him away from the garden of Eden to work the ground from which he was taken. He drove the man out and stationed the cherubim and the flaming, whirling sword east of the garden of Eden to guard the way to the tree of life. (Gen. 3:22–24)

This expulsion, while difficult, was not part of the judgment. The judgment had clearly ended with the naming of Eve and provision of clothing sandwiched between it and this. This wasn't judgment, because it was grace. Notice the reason for the expulsion—so that Adam and Eve would not eat of the Tree of Life and live forever. Had Adam and Eve remained in Eden, they may have eaten from that tree and lived forever—which sounds great, until you consider they would have lived forever in a fallen state, out of the relationship with God he had designed and which they had once enjoyed. God had a better way—a much better way—to provide better—much better—life to mankind. God would provide eternal life and restore his people as completely forgiven, completely righteous children through his Son dying on a different tree on a hill called Calvary. Banishment from Eden kept this hope alive.

Genesis 3:20–24

Q. What effect did Adam's and Eve's sin have on all people?

A. Because of Adam's and Eve's sin, all people since have been born with a sin nature.

Because of Adam's and Eve's sin, or more precisely, because of Adam's sin, every single person since has been born in sin. Everyone, that is, except for Jesus. But why? How does Adam's sin make us sinners today? First, it is important to see this taught in Scripture:

> Therefore, just as sin entered the world through one man, and death through sin, in this way death spread to all people, because all sinned. (Rom. 5:12)

Through Adam, sin and death entered into the entire world and spread to all people. Adam and Eve passed along the sin nature to their children, who passed it along to their children, and on and on. This is known as "inherited sin" from Adam and is mentioned by David in Psalm 51:5.

> Indeed, I was guilty when I was born;
> I was sinful when my mother conceived me.

David was not innocent when he was born, he was guilty and sinful, as we all are because of the sin nature we have each inherited as descendants of Adam.

But there is another, more direct way Adam's sin impacted us. Sin was imputed directly upon us from Adam. To impute something is to give something of yours to someone else. In this case, the "something" is sin, and Adam gave it to us. Some people struggle with this because it doesn't seem quite fair, but none of us can say that we would have succeeded where Adam failed. We also all sin, proving we are far from innocent and deserving of God's judgment in our own right.

But there is a more compelling reason for us to work through our struggles and reach the point where we embrace the idea of our imputed sin from Adam. Because that is not the only thing imputed.

We received Adam's imputed sin.

But Jesus took our imputed sin on himself.

We then received Christ's imputed righteousness in its place.

You see, if we reject the idea that Adam can impute his sin to us because that doesn't seem fair, then we have to reject Christ taking our sin and imputing his righteousness in its place for the same reasons. And that is not something we want to do.

When we humbly see ourselves as we truly are—sinners from birth because of inherited and imputed sin, who rebel against holy God every day because of our own choices to do so—we are forced to recognize our need of a Savior and cry out to him. The beauty of the gospel—God providing Jesus to provide forgiveness—is most clearly seen through the lens of our sinfulness. We weren't good people who needed a little help to be better. We were wretched sinners in desperate need of salvation.

Romans 5:12; Psalm 51:5

Q. What effect did Adam's and Eve's sin have on all of creation?

A. Because of Adam's and Eve's sin, all of creation has been cursed and is no longer as it should be.

The world is full of beauty and splendor. From powerful waterfalls to magnificent creatures to majestic mountains, we are surrounded by the grandeur of creation, which at times can leave us in breathless awe. It's hard to believe that nothing we see is as it should be.

When Adam and Eve rebelled against God, their sin didn't just impact them and all future generations of people; it also affected all of creation.

> For the creation was subjected to futility—not willingly, but because of him who subjected it—in the hope that the creation itself will also be set free from the bondage to decay into the glorious freedom of God's children. (Rom. 8:20–21)

All of creation is under the curse of sin and undergoing decay. Animals die. Vegetation dies. Beaches erode. Rocks wear down. Rivers dry out. Beauty surrounds us, but so do death and decay.

The first sign of creation being under the curse was the thorns and thistles and rebellious ground that God told Adam would be the result of his sin (Gen. 3:17–18). We see it again when Noah exited the ark and God warned him that the animals would be in fear and terror of man, and they may even strike out to kill (Gen. 9:1–5). God had created people to live in harmony with creation, but after the Fall, that harmony vanished.

This is why creation hopes for liberation from bondage. Jesus came so that people might be rescued from sin and death, but he also came for creation to experience the same freedom through him (Matt. 19:28; Acts 3:21). One day, when Jesus returns, creation will be made new, the curse will be removed from all of God's creation, and we will live forever in a new universe that is once again as God intended it to be.

Romans 8:20–21; Revelation 21:1

15

Q. What is sin?

A. Sin is disobeying God by doing what he forbids, not doing what he commands, or not having the right attitude toward him or others.

Imagine you are watching an Olympic archery event. One of the world-class archers steps up to his spot, pulls the bow string back, steadies his aim, and releases the arrow. The arrow springs from the bow and flies through the air 150 miles per hour toward the round target two hundred feet away. But then the arrow begins to dip, and it imbeds itself in the earth's soil several feet short of the target. The archer's shoulders and head sag. He has missed the mark. He has sinned.

That is a helpful word picture based on one use of the word *sin*—to miss the mark in archery. However, this is just a starting point for helping us to understand sin. It is deeper and stronger than that. While there are times when we will try to "hit the mark" and obey God but fall short, there are many more times when we don't try to obey—we sometimes go out of our way to sin. That word picture would show us facing away from the target and releasing our arrow in the wrong direction altogether.

The Bible defines sin as lawlessness in 1 John 3:4.

> Everyone who commits sin practices lawlessness; and sin is lawlessness.

This idea of lawlessness helps us see the seriousness of sin more than the archery definition, but it still needs to be understood more fully. Lawlessness certainly makes us think of doing what we should not be doing, but we also need to understand that sin is also not doing what God has told us to do, as we read in James 4:17.

So it is sin to know the good and yet not do it.

We sin in our actions and also our lack of actions at times. But we still aren't all the way there yet in properly understanding sin. Galatians 5:19–21 gives us a sobering list of sins:

> Now the works of the flesh are obvious: sexual immorality, moral impurity, promiscuity, idolatry, sorcery, hatreds, strife, jealousy, outbursts of anger, selfish ambitions, dissensions, factions, envy, drunkenness, carousing, and anything similar. I am warning you about these things—as I warned you before— that those who practice such things will not inherit the kingdom of God.

Many of those sins we will look at and easily see how they fall under wrongful actions. But what about hatred, jealousy, selfish ambitions, and envy? Those aren't necessarily actions. Those are postures of our hearts and minds. So we need to add that sin is not confined to our actions but can be a wrongful attitude of the heart.

So we may sin in our actions, lack of actions, and attitude. There is one other note we need to mention about sin. While sin may involve other people (such as an outburst of anger at someone else), ultimately, all of our sin is against God. God is the One who has given us the law, so any violation of the law is a direct act of rebellion against him. This is why only God can forgive sin. We should definitely seek forgiveness from others when we wrong them, but we need to remember our need to repent of our sin and confess it to God, the One whom we wronged the most.

1 John 3:4; James 4:17

16

Q. Where does sin begin?

A. Sin begins in the heart, where we choose not to fulfill our created purpose to love, worship, and glorify God as he deserves.

We will often hear someone say they "fell into sin." There are surely times when sin creeps up on us and we stumble into it, just as there are times when it comes at us too fast to process and resist or run. But that is not what normally happens to us when we sin. Usually, we consciously choose to. Sin is an act of the will, rooted in our hearts.

This is what Jesus wanted the crowds around him to understand in Matthew 15. Jesus was trying to break down the legalism that was rampant among the people, taught to them by the religious leaders. The leaders were more concerned about the proper, ceremonial way to wash their hands before eating than about loving God. For them, hollow obedience had replaced loving relationship.

So Jesus combatted this by teaching that it isn't what goes into the mouth that makes a person unclean, but what comes out of the mouth. What comes out of the mouth—what a person says—is rooted in the heart. But the heart doesn't just guide what we say; it also drives what we do.

> "For from the heart come evil thoughts, murders, adulteries, sexual immoralities, thefts, false testimonies, slander." (Matt. 15:19)

Murder, adultery, immorality, stealing, and lying are all sinful actions that are rooted in a sinful heart. When we sin, we yield to our hearts that want to turn away from loving, worshiping, and glorifying God. The heart is where the battle is won or lost.

This is one of the main themes of the Sermon on the Mount (Matt. 5–7). Jesus set out to describe and define who a true disciple of his was, and he shared that one of the major ways a disciple is identified is by the heart. True disciples let God go to work on their hearts, because they know that if God changes their hearts, their actions will follow. What we do isn't the best way to evaluate ourselves; the posture of our hearts is. Helping our kids understand this is critical. We want our kids to focus on heart-change, driven by the gospel and fueled by the Holy Spirit, rather than behavior change. Changed behavior can mask a corrupt heart, but a changed heart will purge corrupt behavior.

Matthew 15:19; Genesis 6:5

17

Q. Is there anyone who does not sin?

A. No, everyone sins.

We are good at finding ways to divide people, whether it be by nation, gender, ethnicity, language, age, political ideology, or even favorite sports team. Yes, as people, we have many differences among us. But we also have some things in common, and one of the most important is that we are all sinners. Every single one of us. Romans 3:23 puts it this way:

> For all have sinned and fall short of the glory of God.

Sin is the great equalizer among people. All the ways we divide ourselves don't matter. It doesn't matter how much money you have, where you were born, your ethnicity, or anything else. You are a sinner in need of a Savior, just like everyone else in the world.

We all sin because we are sinners by nature (Rom. 5:12). Our sin then is the natural outworking of who we really are. This is why we enjoy sinning so much. We are pleasing our most basic nature. This is what is in mind in Isaiah 53:6.

> We all went astray like sheep;
> we all have turned to our own way;
> and the LORD has punished him
> for the iniquity of us all.

Notice that we didn't wander off by accident. We didn't lose sight of the shepherd and try to find him. We didn't fall into a ditch. We turned to our own way and went where we wanted to go, forsaking the shepherd. This is why God punishes sin—because it is an intentional act of rebellion against him. We are not innocent victims—we are intentional perpetrators.

But while God is just to punish sin, he is also gracious to provide someone to pay for our sins in our place—Jesus. We willingly sinned against God. He willingly sent his Son to die for our sins. Jesus willingly gave up his life for us. That is the gospel that has been made known to all of us, and the gospel we all desperately need.

Isaiah 53:6; Romans 3:23

Q. What does every sin deserve?

A. Every sin deserves death and separation from a holy God.

The Bible clearly teaches that every sin deserves death. In Romans 6:23 we read:

> For the wages of sin is death, but the gift of God is eternal life in Christ Jesus our Lord.

Wages are what you earn. You do not hope your employer pays you every two weeks out of the kindness of her heart; you expect a paycheck because you earned it. It is your wage for the work you completed the prior two weeks. So every sin has earned us death, separation from God, and his wrath. Right after talking about several sins, Paul wrote the following in Ephesians 5:6:

> Let no one deceive you with empty arguments, for God's wrath is coming on the disobedient because of these things.

Death, separation, and wrath. That is what every sin deserves. But what about jaywalking? If a person only committed that one sin, would he really deserve to die, be separated from God forever, and be under his wrath?

Yes. Yes, he would.

The problem is that sins are not measured by the badness of the action, but by the greatness of the One who was wronged. All sins are against a perfectly holy and just God, so any sin, no matter how small it seems to be, is an act of open, hostile rebellion against our perfect God. This is why James wrote that if someone keeps the whole law but fails in one point, he has become guilty of breaking all of it (James 2:10). Every sin has the same legal effect.

But that doesn't mean that all sins are the same in other ways. First, sins will have different earthly consequences, some being more severe than others. Jaywalking and murder have much different consequences. Second, some sins will impact our relationship with God more than others. Some sins might enslave us and leave us feeling defeated and demoralized, driving us away from God and his grace toward shame and isolation, while others are much easier for us to confess and rest in God's absolute forgiveness through Christ.

We need to take every sin seriously. knowing that every single sin dishonors God. That is also why we need to fight against sin in our lives, all the while resting in God's never-ending grace.

Romans 6:23; Ephesians 5:6

19

Q. How does sin impact a person's relationship with God?

A. Because God is perfect, no one can be sinful and have a relationship with God.

———————

Imagine that you are thirsty and someone hands you a glass of pure, cold water. Just as the glass is about to touch your lips, the person stops you and explains that he had just placed an ever-so-small drop of poison in that glass of water moments before and thought you might want to know. Would you still drink the water?

Of course not! It doesn't matter how little poison was put in the glass—it is still contaminated and dangerous to drink. That is a word picture of why we cannot have a relationship with a holy God. He is pure and perfect and must separate all sin from himself. Holy God cannot be in relationship with sinful people while sin remains.

This is what we see demonstrated in the call of Isaiah. Isaiah was an Old Testament prophet called by God to preach some of the most compelling messages of the coming Messiah to God's people. We read of Isaiah's call in Isaiah 6 where he has a vision of God sitting on his throne. Here is how he responded:

> Then I said:
>
>> Woe is me for I am ruined
>> because I am a man of unclean lips
>> and live among a people of unclean lips,
>> and because my eyes have seen the King,
>> the Lord of Armies. (Isa. 6:5)

Notice that Isaiah's natural response to being in God's presence is woe—because he knows that he is a sinner in the presence of a holy God. We see a similar response from Peter when he realized who Jesus was (Luke 5:8).

God's holiness barring sinful people from having a relationship with him is perhaps most clearly pictured in the Holy of Holies in the tabernacle, and later the temple. This was the innermost portion of the temple complex where God's presence dwelled. It was blocked off from the outer room—the Holy Place—by a thick curtain or veil. The message is clear—access to a holy God is blocked because of the sin of people. However, one day a year, the high priest could enter the Holy of Holies, after making careful sacrifice for his sin. He would enter the Holy of Holies to make atonement for the sins of the people. God's message was also that access is available to him through a mediator.

When Jesus died on the cross, that veil was torn in two from top to bottom, symbolizing that access to God had opened up from God through Jesus, the Mediator. Now, in Christ, we have full access to holy God because all of our sin has been cleansed and we have been given Jesus' righteousness. Once access to God's presence was blocked, but now it is wide open, and we are invited to enter with confidence and joy.

Isaiah 6:5; Hebrews 9:3–10

20

Q. Do people have to die and stay separated from God because of sin?

A. No, God has provided a way to be forgiven of sin, to be saved from death, and to enjoy a relationship with him.

It is easy to get discouraged when you read through the Old Testament. There is so much rebellion and sin by God's people and discipline by God in response. Page after page of waiting for things to take a turn for the better only to find they were in fact getting worse.

Mankind was hopelessly stuck in sin, unable to do anything about it. Nothing had worked. Not relying on national identity. Not being religious enough. Not finding better leaders. Nothing. And that is exactly what we are supposed to feel when we read the Old Testament—the full weight of the effects of sin on all of us. We are supposed to feel dread. We need to feel it.

But in the midst of the despair, we also find hope. Peppered all throughout the Old Testament is God's recurring message to his people—I will provide a Deliverer! Sin and death will be conquered! I will make a way! One of the most powerful of these messages of hope is found in Isaiah 53:3–5 where we read about the coming Messiah—Jesus.

> He was despised and rejected by men,
> a man of suffering who knew what sickness was.
> He was like someone people turned away from;
> he was despised, and we didn't value him.
> Yet he himself bore our sicknesses,
> and he carried our pains;

but we in turn regarded him stricken,
struck down by God, and afflicted.
But he was pierced because of our rebellion,
crushed because of our iniquities;
punishment for our peace was on him,
and we are healed by his wounds.

Jesus would be rejected by his people, suffer, and die. But through his suffering and death, Jesus would bear our sin so that we might find peace and healing at last. There was a way! It would be Jesus.

We did nothing to deserve rescue. We deserve the just punishment for our sins. But God chose to provide Jesus by his grace. This is the beauty of the gospel—it was driven solely by the amazing love of God, as we read in John 3:16:

"For God loved the world in this way: He gave his one and only Son, so that everyone who believes in him will not perish but have eternal life."

As much as we deserved death and separation from God, his love provided a way. That way is Jesus.

Isaiah 53:3–5; John 3:16

JESUS

Q. How can a person be saved from sin and have eternal life with God?

A. Only through faith in the God the Son can a person be saved from sin and receive eternal life with God.

It was the darkest day creation had experienced to that point. Adam and Eve had rebelled against God, and sin entered the world. From that day forward, nothing was as it should have been. Mankind's relationship with God was severed, and relationships with one another were plagued by sin and strife. The perfect world God had created for mankind to enjoy was also stained by sin, and life on it became exceedingly difficult.

But even in the midst of God's pronouncing judgment on Adam and Eve for their sin against him, we see his mercy, love, and grace shine through. A descendant was promised, and when he came, he would crush the enemy and put an end to sin and death. For the next several thousand years, generation after generation waited expectantly for that deliverer to come. While the picture of who this rescuer would be came into sharper focus, one giant mystery remained: how exactly would this deliverer provide the answer for mankind's sin?

Then the answer arrived, surprisingly, in a manger in the little town of Bethlehem. The Son of God, Jesus, had taken on flesh and had come to be the Deliverer at last. Jesus lived a sinless life of perfect obedience to the Father, laid down his life to pay the penalty of sin, and then rose from the dead to show that sin and death had been defeated once and for all.

The Bible says that everyone who places their faith in Jesus—who he is and what he has done—will be saved.

> If you confess with your mouth, "Jesus is Lord," and believe
> in your heart that God raised him from the dead, you will be
> saved. (Rom. 10:9)

Such a profound problem solved by such a simple solution. Anyone who trusts in Jesus will be saved and have eternal life with God. So easy from our perspective—but so costly from God's.

But is there another way? No there is not. Jesus is the only way. He said so himself:

> Jesus told him, "I am the way, the truth, and the life. No one
> comes to the Father except through me." (John 14:6)

Only faith in Jesus will save us, but thankfully, it is not blind faith. There is plenty of evidence for our faith. It is rational to trust in Jesus for salvation.

Some people struggle with Jesus being the only way we can be saved. It seems unfair that God would provide such exclusive access to him. But turn that around—what if God had made another way to be saved besides the death of Jesus? What would that say about God? Jesus' death wouldn't be necessary, making God cruel and unloving for willing for his Son to suffer and die needlessly.

But Jesus is the only way to God. Jesus is God's one and only loving provision so that whoever believes in him will have eternal life.

Romans 10:9; John 14:6

Q. Has God the Son always existed?

A. Yes, God the Son has always existed, just as the Father and the Holy Spirit have.

When we hear "son" we tend to think of a male who was born to parents. Thus, some people think the Son of God was born—or at least created—at some point. But God the Son has always existed because he is fully God, and one of God's attributes is eternality. The apostle John opened his Gospel with this foundational truth:

> In the beginning was the Word, and the Word was with God, and the word was God. He was with God in the beginning. (John 1:1–2)

Jesus is the Word, the Son of God, and he has always existed. If there were still any doubt, John followed these verses with the statement that the Word created everything, requiring him to be eternal. If the Word were created, then he would have had to create himself, which is impossible.

Later on in John 17:24, Jesus mentioned his eternality in his prayer to the Father just before his arrest in the garden:

> "Father, I want those you have given me to be with me where I am, so that they will see my glory, which you have given me because you loved me before the world's foundation."

Not only do we see that the Son of God is eternal, but that the Father has loved him eternally as well. God the Father, God the Son, and God the Holy Spirit have enjoyed an eternal relationship of love within God's triune nature.

So does this really matter? Does it make a difference to us that the Son of God is eternal? Without a doubt. If the Son of God were not eternal, then he would not be fully God, and therefore not God at all. If we were to remove any single attribute of God, he would no longer remain God. God is either fully and completely God or he is not God at all. It's that simple. And if the Son of God were not eternal, and therefore not God, then he would not have been the sufficient sinless sacrifice needed to provide salvation to the world.

The eternality of the Son of God may not seem that critical, but if salvation is, then it is too.

John 1:12; Colossians 1:16–17

3

Q. By what other name do we know God the Son?

A. We also know God the Son as Jesus.

———————————

Leave it to Mark, author of the shortest Gospel, to cut to the chase and spoil the ending. Here is how he opened his Gospel:

> The beginning of the gospel of Jesus Christ, the Son of God. (Mark 1:1)

You cannot be much clearer than that. The Son of God is Jesus. Matthew provided a little more context of why God chose the name *Jesus* for the Son of God in his Gospel:

> "She will give birth to a son, and you are to name him Jesus, because he will save his people from their sins." (Matt. 1:21)

The Son of God was named Jesus when he took on flesh because he would save his people from their sins. It may be hard to see the connection until we understand that the name *Jesus* is the same name as *Joshua* in the Old Testament. OK, still not there? What if we were told that the name means "The Lord Saves" or "The Lord Is Salvation"? So the angel told Joseph that Mary would have a baby and they should name him "The Lord Saves" because he would save his people from their sins. There we go.

There are a couple other interesting parallels between Jesus and Joshua besides their name. Both delivered God's people by defeating their enemies— Joshua by defeating those who were in the Promised Land and Jesus by defeating sin and death. Both led God's people into a land of rest—Joshua bringing the people literally into the Promised Land and giving them rest from war there, and Jesus bringing the people spiritually into salvation and giving them rest from sin (see Heb. 4).

God used the ministry of Joshua to paint a compelling picture of what he would do through Jesus. Joshua was the shadow of who would come and what he would do, a shadow of the Son of God we know as Jesus.

Matthew 1:21; Mark 1:1

Q. Is Jesus God or man?

A. Jesus is both fully God and fully man.

Sometimes doctrines don't quite add up. Take Jesus being fully God and fully man, for example. Jesus is 100 percent God, and he took on the flesh and became 100 percent man. And in this case, 100 percent plus 100 percent equals 100 percent. That math will get you a bad grade in a school classroom, but it is exactly right when it comes to the doctrine of who Jesus is.

But before we can really see why that math works for Jesus being God and man, let's first see where we find this proven in Scripture. Let's start with Jesus being fully God. To see this, we can turn to Colossians 2:9.

> For the entire fullness of God's nature dwells bodily in Christ.

The fullness of God's nature is in Jesus. That's 100 percent. Jesus is not 50 percent God. He is not 75 percent God. He isn't even 99 percent God. He is 100 percent God. Let's consider some of the evidence of Jesus demonstrating the attributes of God, which proves his divinity.

Jesus claimed to be eternal (John 8:58; 17:5). Only God is eternal. Jesus also claimed that he would be with all of his disciples always—which is a mark of omnipresence (Matt. 28:20). At various times Jesus demonstrated omniscience (Matt. 16:21; Mark 2:8; Luke 6:8; 11:17; John 4:29). Jesus also claimed to be omnipotent and demonstrated divine power on earth (Matt. 28:18; Mark 5:11–15; John 9:30–33). Jesus claimed to be able to forgive sins (Mark 2:1–12) and to give life (John 5:21), which are also two things only God can do. Finally, Jesus was called "the Son of God" and "Lord" by others, claimed to be one with God (John 10:30–33), and accepted worship on several occasions (Matt. 28:9).

But while Jesus is 100 percent God, he is also 100 percent man. Second John 7 is just as clear about this as Colossians 2:9 was about his deity:

> Many deceivers have gone out into the world; they do not confess the coming of Jesus Christ in the flesh. This is the deceiver and the antichrist.

To deny that Jesus is fully human is to be a deceiver and to be against Christ. But the humanity of Jesus is not something we have to confess without evidence. Jesus was born and grew (Luke 2:52). He hungered and thirsted (Matt. 4:2; John 19:28), and he grew weary (John 4:6). Jesus bled and died and even after the resurrection had a body that could be touched (John 20:17).

So Jesus is 100 percent human. And 100 percent God. Which added together is 100 percent. But how does that work and why does it matter? Let's work backward. There is only one Jesus, so the total of who he is must be 100 percent, or in other words, he is fully who he is. But we cannot say that Jesus is less than 100 percent of either his humanity or deity. To do so would leave him as either subhuman (less than fully man) or sub-God (less than fully God). Neither can we say that Jesus' deity and humanity are mixed. That would result in a hybrid being who is neither God nor man. Instead, we are left stating that Jesus is fully God and fully man without mixture or compromise of either essence. The math may not work in a school classroom, but the doctrine of the Son of God being a man—Immanuel—works perfectly.

Colossians 2:9; 2 John 7

Q. Why did God the Son become human?

A. God the Son became human to please the Father and provide forgiveness of sin.

Sometimes we might think that everything Jesus did was for us. And while that is true in one sense, it is not quite complete. Everything Jesus did, he ultimately did for the Father. Listen to what Jesus said of the Father in John 4:34.

> "My food is to do the will of him who sent me and to finish his work," Jesus told them.

And again in John 17:4 in his prayer with the Father.

> "I have glorified you on the earth by completing the work you gave me to do."

Clearly, Jesus' priority was to please the Father and bring him glory. But that doesn't mean that he also didn't do what he did for us out of his love. This is not an either-or proposition. Jesus didn't have to either desire to please the Father or show his love for us. Both are true. Jesus pleased the Father *through* his loving act of living perfectly and sacrificing himself for us to provide forgiveness of sin:

> What the law could not do since it was weakened by the flesh,
> God did. He condemned sin in the flesh by sending his own
> Son in the likeness of sinful flesh as a sin offering. (Rom. 8:3)

God provided Jesus to do what nothing else could do—provide the solution for sin and death through his sacrifice in our place. The penalty of sin was death—human death—which is why Jesus had to become a man. Jesus came to earth and took our sin on himself and became sin so that we might become his righteousness (2 Cor. 5:21). What an amazing act of love and humility! To think of the Creator wrapping himself in his creation just to be rejected, scorned, and put to death. This is what Paul marveled at in Philippians 2:5–8.

Adopt the same attitude as that of Christ Jesus,

> who, existing in the form of God,
> did not consider equality with God
> as something to be exploited.
> Instead he emptied himself
> by assuming the form of a servant,
> taking on the likeness of humanity.
> And when he had come as a man,
> he humbled himself by becoming obedient
> to the point of death—
> even to death on a cross.

This is the amazing love of Christ Jesus for us. This is the unwavering obedience of Christ Jesus to the Father. This is the beauty of the gospel.

John 17:4; Philippians 2:5–8

6

Q. How was Jesus born?

A. Jesus was born of the virgin Mary.

All the way back in the Old Testament book of Isaiah, God made an amazing promise about Jesus through his prophet:

> Therefore, the Lord himself will give you a sign: See, the virgin will conceive, have a son, and name him Immanuel. (Isa. 7:14)

Several hundred years later, the angel Gabriel appeared to a young girl named Mary with a perplexing message. Mary, a virgin engaged to be married to a man named Joseph, would conceive and give birth to a son, whom she would name Jesus. Mary would fulfill God's prophecy through Isaiah and give birth to the Son of God—truly Immanuel, which means "God with us."

Some argue that the word *virgin* in the Bible can simply mean a young woman and may not necessarily mean a person who was sexually pure. The argument is that this is what is in mind here, because a virgin birth is impossible. However, notice how the conversation between Mary and Gabriel continues:

> Mary asked the angel, "How can this be, since I have not had sexual relations with a man?"
>
> The angel replied to her: "The Holy Spirit will come upon you, and the power of the Most High will overshadow you. Therefore, the holy one to be born will be called the Son of God." (Luke 1:34–35)

Notice that Mary directly references her sexual purity and asks how it would be possible for her to have a baby. Her response doesn't make sense if she had been just a young woman, and not a virgin. Then you see Gabriel respond that the Holy Spirit would bring this about. This would not be a normal conception. In Matthew's Gospel, we read of the angel sharing this news with Joseph, Mary's fiancé, and we read there that he married her but kept her a virgin until after she had given birth to Jesus (Matt. 1:24–25). It seems clear that the Bible is not merely talking about a young woman fulfilling Isaiah's prophecy, but an actual virgin.

The same God who created everything by his spoken word, parted the Red Sea for his people to cross on dry ground, made the walls of Jericho fall, and rained fire from heaven to consume a drenched altar, conceived Jesus in a virgin's womb. The message was clear—this was going to be a special child indeed.

Isaiah 7:14; Luke 1:34–35

7

Q. Why was Jesus born of a virgin?

A. Jesus was born of a virgin to reveal he is the Son of God and to protect him from inheriting a sinful nature.

The more obvious reason for the virgin birth was to fulfill prophecy (Isa. 7:14) and to reveal that Jesus was not a normal baby and person—he is the Son of God. Right from the start of his life, it was apparent that Jesus was special—he was unique. His birth was something only God could do which foreshadows how the salvation that Jesus would provide is also something only God can do.

That's important, of course, but there is another reason as well. We would see many other signs that Jesus is God, but the virgin birth accomplished something only it could do. And to understand this, we have to think about how Adam's sin has been inherited by and imputed to all people.

In Romans 5:12 we read that sin entered the world through one man, Adam, and it spread to everyone:

> Therefore, just as sin entered the world through one man, and death through sin, in this way death spread to all people, because all sinned.

This sin was inherited through the natural process of childbirth. Sinful, fallen parents give birth to sinful, fallen children, who grow up to be sinful, fallen parents who give birth to sinful, fallen children and so on. There is no way around this. Sinful people cannot give birth to sinless children. But at the same time, Adam's sin was also directly imputed to each of us because Adam was our representative in Eden.

And this is why the virgin birth was necessary. Had Jesus been conceived like any other baby, he would have been born in sin. He would have inherited sin through Joseph and Mary, and Adam's sin would have been imputed to him as well. But because the Holy Spirit overshadowed the conception of Jesus, he was protected from being born with a sin nature like the rest of us (Luke 1:35). The virgin birth preserved Jesus' sinless nature and life, as John explained:

> You know that he was revealed so that he might take away sins, and there is no sin in him. (1 John 3:5)

And just to be clear that Jesus' sinlessness extended into his nature, and not just his actions, the writer of Hebrews says this about him:

> For this is the kind of high priest we need: holy, innocent, undefiled, separated from sinners, and exalted above the heavens. (Heb. 7:26)

Jesus was separate from sinners through his lack of a sin nature thanks to the virgin birth. Just as the Holy Spirit overshadowed the writers of Scripture to write the Bible without errors but allowed for their voices to come through, he also overshadowed the conception of Mary so that Jesus would be fully God, fully man, but without sin so he would be the sinless sacrifice we need.

1 John 3:5; Hebrews 7:26

8

Q. What title is given to Jesus?

A. Jesus is given the title of Christ, or the Messiah.

From the moment God judged the sin of Adam and Eve in the garden, God promised that a rescuer—the Messiah—would come to make all things right again. The story of the Old Testament is the story of this Messiah coming. Every book and every story points toward the Messiah through direct prophecies that gave more details of who he would be and what he would do, as well as by tracing his family tree from generation to generation as his arrival drew nearer. This coming Messiah would be the One through whom all the families of the world would be blessed (Gen. 12:3), and God's people ached for his arrival, especially when their continued sins brought about God's discipline through foreign nations taking them into captivity.

Then at last, in God's perfect timing (Gal. 4:4), Jesus the Messiah was born. Some argue that Jesus was not the Messiah, but just a good teacher who was misunderstood, or that his followers claimed he was the Messiah on their own. But the Bible provides ample evidence showing that Jesus claimed to be the Messiah and acted like the Messiah because he is indeed the Messiah.

In Jesus' encounter with the Samaritan woman at the well, the idea of proper worship was discussed, which led to this interchange between the two:

> The woman said to him, "I know that the Messiah is coming" (who is called Christ). "When he comes, he will explain everything to us."
>
> Jesus told her, "I, the one speaking to you, am he." (John 4:25–26)

That is a pretty clear claim by Jesus that he is the Messiah. He made a similarly bold statement in the synagogue of his hometown (Luke 4:21), and he entered Jerusalem on a donkey expressly to fulfill the messianic prophecy of Zechariah 9:9 (Matt. 21:1–7).

His followers recognized Jesus was the Messiah, as we see in Peter's sermon at Pentecost just weeks after the crucifixion and resurrection:

> "Therefore let all the house of Israel know with certainty that God has made this Jesus, whom you crucified, both Lord and Messiah." (Acts 2:36)

Many of the people of Israel also were willing to believe Jesus was the Messiah, which is why they greeted him with shouts of acclaim as he entered Jerusalem (Matt. 21:9). But many of those same people were probably in the same crowd that shouted "Crucify him" just days later. The reason was that they had the wrong understanding of who the Messiah would be and what the Messiah would do. They were expecting a military or political leader who would rescue them from Rome. But when it became clear that Jesus would not do that, they turned on him. They simply could not grasp that he was a greater Deliverer—he was there to rescue them from the greater enemy of sin and death.

There are hundreds of prophecies about the Messiah in the Old Testament, including that he would be a descendant of David (2 Sam. 7:12–16), be born of a virgin (Isa. 7:14), be born in Bethlehem (Micah 5:2), be a prophet (Deut. 18:15–19), be a kinsman redeemer (Ruth 4:4–9), perform signs of healings (Isa. 35:5–6), enter Jerusalem on a donkey (Zech. 9:9), be the rejected cornerstone (Ps. 118:22–24), be lifted up (Num. 21:6–9), be the suffering servant (Isa. 52–53), be the Passover Lamb (Exod. 12:1–51), and be resurrected (Ps. 16:8–11). Jesus fulfilled all of these prophecies, offering overwhelming proof that he is truly the Messiah.

John 4:25–26; Acts 2:36

9

Q. What did Jesus do while he was on earth?

A. While Jesus was on earth, he traveled through Galilee, Samaria, and Judea teaching and performing miracles.

───────────

After Jesus was born around 4 BC, we don't read anything about him in the Gospels until he began his earthly ministry when he was around thirty years old except for the one episode when he was left behind in the temple as a twelve-year-old. Jesus began his ministry with a three-to-five-month period of preparation including his interactions with John, his baptism and temptation, and his first miracle of turning water into wine.

After that, Jesus spent about eight months traveling through Judea teaching, performing miracles, and gathering his disciples. When John was arrested, Jesus moved his ministry to Galilee for about eighteen months where he continued publicly revealing that he was the Messiah.

Near the end of that time, the Jewish leaders, who had been open to considering who Jesus was, rejected him and began to plot a way to get rid of him. Jesus then shifted to more of a private ministry to equip his disciples for around six months. This is also a time when Jesus would avoid the Jewish leaders, especially by not spending as much time in Judea. The region of Judea, which included Jerusalem and the temple, was home to most of the Jewish leaders and because of this was a more dangerous place for Jesus to be as time went on. Galilee was a safer area because the Galileans tended to be more of a working class people and not as strict about the Jewish customs and traditions.

At this point, after roughly three years of ministry, Jesus turned his attention to go to Jerusalem, where he knew he would be crucified, and spent the next six months presenting himself to the people more publicly again, as he also continued to prepare the disciples. Jesus' final week leading up to the crucifixion and resurrection was packed with activities and takes up large portions of the Gospels.

The four Gospels—Matthew, Mark, Luke, and John—give us great pictures of what Jesus did during his earthly ministry; but even as detailed as they are, they don't give us all of what Jesus did. As John ended his Gospel, it almost seems he was frustrated that he could only scratch the surface of all of what he saw Jesus do. There was surely so much more he wanted to share. Here's how he ended his writing:

> And there are also many other things that Jesus did, which, if every one of them were written down, I suppose not even the world itself could contain the books that would be written. (John 21:25)

John 21:25; Mark 1:38–39

10

Q. What did Jesus teach when he was on earth?

A. Jesus taught about who God is, God's kingdom, and how to live in a way that brings God glory.

Jesus was an amazing teacher. Even people who don't believe that Jesus is the Son of God acknowledge that he was an extraordinarily powerful teacher. He was a master storyteller who used relatable object lessons and analogies, asked probing questions, and said memorable things, whether he was teaching a multitude in the middle of the day or one person in the darkness of night.

But more important than *how* Jesus taught is *what* he taught. All of what Jesus taught ultimately revealed who God is, his kingdom, and how people can know him and live for him through Jesus.

Three of Jesus' larger public teachings stand out and deserve to be mentioned: the Sermon on the Mount, the Olivet Discourse, and the Upper Room Discourse. In the Sermon on the Mount (Matt. 5:1–7:29), Jesus taught extensively what it looks like to be his disciples and what true righteousness is—not what we do on the outside, but a heart changed by the gospel on the inside that carries over to changed living on the outside. In the Olivet Discourse (Matt. 24:1–25:46), Jesus shared about his future return and the signs that would accompany it. In the Upper Room Discourse (John 14:1–17:26), Jesus prepared his disciples for his departure and told them about the Holy Spirit whom he would send.

In addition to these longer teachings, the Gospels also contain dozens of short parables, many of which focused on the kingdom of God (see Matt. 13). Jesus used these kingdom parables to teach about how the kingdom would grow, who would be part of the kingdom, and the great value of the kingdom.

While many of Jesus' teachings were to groups, some of his teachings were shared with just one person in private settings. Two of the more well-known were Jesus' conversations with Nicodemus (John 3:1–21) and the Samaritan woman (John 4:5–26). Nicodemus was a Jewish leader who came to Jesus at night, most likely to avoid being seen with him. Jesus taught Nicodemus about the need for new birth and faith. Jesus encountered the Samaritan woman at a well when she came to draw water. Jesus taught her about the living water that he can provide and what true worship looks like.

While Jesus' teachings were very different in terms of the size of the audience, the location, and the method used to teach, they all were united in theme. Jesus traveled throughout Judea, Israel, and even Samaria teaching that he is the Son of God—the one way to know the Father and be part of God's kingdom.

Matthew 5:3–10; Matthew 7:13–23; John 15:9–17

Q. Why did Jesus perform miracles?

A. Jesus performed miracles to glorify God, to prove he is the Son of God, and because he loves people.

When John the Baptist was arrested and in prison, he heard news of what Jesus was doing, so he sent word to Jesus asking if he was indeed the expected One. Here is how Jesus replied in Matthew 11:4–6.

> Jesus replied to them, "Go and report to John what you hear and see: The blind receive their sight, the lame walk, those with leprosy are cleansed, the deaf hear, the dead are raised, and the poor are told the good news, and blessed is the one who isn't offended by me."

The evidence Jesus gave to encourage John that he had been right to point people to him as the Lamb of God who takes away the sin of the world (John 1:29) was his miracles. Every miracle Jesus performed was to help people see that there was something unique about him and to confirm that he truly is the Son of God. When Jesus healed, he was showing his unique ability to miraculously overcome disease and infirmity. When Jesus fed people miraculously, he was showing he has the ability to provide supernaturally. When Jesus demonstrated power over nature, he was showing his authority as Creator. When Jesus cast out demons, he was showing his authority as sovereign King.

We can see this especially in the seven miracles John chose to highlight in his Gospel. John even refers to the miracles as *signs* to highlight that they point to something, namely that Jesus is the Messiah, the Son of God.

- Sign 1: Turning Water to Wine (John 2:1–11): Demonstrates that Jesus has the power to create that which is good and is reminiscent of creation.
- Sign 2: Healing Official's Son (John 4:43–54): Demonstrates that Jesus has the power to act from a distance and also affirms the power of faith in him.
- Sign 3: Healing at Pool of Bethesda (John 5:1–9): Demonstrates that Jesus has the power to heal and act independently of a person's faith, and that he can bring comfort to the needy.
- Sign 4: Feeding of 5,000+ (John 6:1–5): Demonstrates that Jesus has the power to provide food in overabundance and hints at Jesus being the bread of life.
- Sign 5: Walking on Water (John 6:16–25): Demonstrates that Jesus has the power to control nature and that he can empower his disciples to do what is normally impossible.
- Sign 6: Healing the Man Born Blind (John 9:1–41): Demonstrates that Jesus has the power to give vision to the blind and alludes to the greater gift of spiritual sight.
- Sign 7: Raising Lazarus (John 11:1–44): Demonstrates that Jesus has power over life and death and prepares his followers for his own resurrection.

While the primary motive of Jesus' miracles was to reveal his identity as the Son of God and thereby draw people to faith in him, there was another reason for his miracles. We see it in several places including Matthew 14:14.

> When he went ashore, he saw a large crowd, had compassion on them, and healed their sick.

The word *compassion* means an extremely deep stirring of the soul or heart. We can find comfort in knowing Jesus also performed miracles out of his deep love for people, and that same love is directed toward us.

Matthew 11:2–5; Matthew 14:14

12

Q. What three offices does Jesus fulfill?

A. Jesus is the perfect fulfillment of the offices of Prophet, Priest, and King.

God's people were given three offices in the Old Testament—prophet, priest, and king. The prophet was a person who spoke God's Word with accuracy and power. The priest represented the people before God, offered sacrifices on their behalf, and prayed and interceded for them. Priests mediated between God and God's people. The king ruled over the people and guided them to obey God.

Each of these three offices looked forward to someone who would come and hold all three perfectly. A future prophet was promised in Deuteronomy 18:15.

> The LORD your God will raise up for you a prophet like me
> from among your own brothers.

A few verses later, we read that God would put his words in this prophet's mouth and that he would tell the people everything God commanded. Hebrews 1:1–2 tells us that God spoke to his people in many different ways in the past, but he had spoken in that time through his Son, Jesus. Jesus is the perfect prophet who fully revealed God because he is the Word of God himself.

As God gave instructions for how the first high priest, Aaron, was to conduct the rituals on the Day of Atonement, we read of a step that revealed the inability of any human priest to be the true intercessor God's people needed:

> "Aaron will present the bull for his sin offering and make
> atonement for himself and his household." (Lev. 16:6)

Neither Aaron nor any other human high priest could ever be the perfect intercessor because none of them were perfect. They needed an intercessor as well. But in Hebrews 9:11–12 we read that there was indeed one perfect intercessor—Jesus.

> But Christ has appeared as a high priest of the good things that have come. In the greater and more perfect tabernacle not made with hands (that is, not of this creation), he entered the most holy place once for all time, not by the blood of goats and calves, but by his own blood, having obtained eternal redemption.

Finally, when King David wanted to build the temple, God would not allow him to, but he did make a covenant with him that promised a future King who would rule forever:

> "When your time comes and you rest with your fathers, I will raise up after you your descendant, who will come from your body, and I will establish his kingdom. He is the one who will build a house for my name, and I will establish the throne of his kingdom forever." (2 Sam. 7:12–13)

Every human king's throne came to an end. But Jesus would be the King who would indeed have an eternal throne. Revelation 19:16 describes the return of Jesus. When he returns, he will be wearing a robe with "King of kings and Lord of lords" written on it.

Jesus is not just the perfect prophet revealing God to his people. He is not just the perfect priest interceding for his people. He is not just the perfect king ruling over his people. He is all three together—prophet, priest, and king—perfectly fulfilling all three offices.

Deuteronomy 18:15; Leviticus 16:6; 2 Samuel 7:12–13

Q. How does Jesus perfectly fulfill the office of Prophet?

A. Jesus perfectly revealed the Father to us and was the fulfillment of what all the other prophets spoke.

If there is a prime example of the change the Holy Spirit can bring in a person, it has to be Peter. During the crucifixion, Peter tried to follow Jesus at a safe distance in Jerusalem, but when he was accused of being one of his followers, he denied Jesus three times. But then, about forty days later, the same Peter stood before a large crowd of Jews in Jerusalem and preached that Jesus is the Messiah, the Son of God. Why the change? *Because Peter wasn't actually the same.* He was filled with the Holy Spirit.

As Peter preached to the crowd, he quoted Deuteronomy 18 where Moses had said a prophet would come from among the people and that they should listen to him or be cut off. He then added that Samuel and the other prophets foretold what would happen as well (Acts 3:22–26). His point was that Jesus was that prophet and the people hadn't listened to him just a few weeks before, but they should now.

While Peter made a compelling case that Jesus was the fulfillment of the perfect prophet, there is a better one. Jesus referred to himself as a prophet in Matthew 13:57.

And they were offended by him.

> Jesus said to them, "A prophet is not without honor except in his hometown and in his household."

But Jesus wasn't just *a* prophet, he was *the* prophet. Jesus was unique in his office as prophet. First, he perfectly revealed God's word as the Word of

God. All of the other prophets could only reveal God in part, but Jesus fully revealed him. Second, Jesus was different from the Old Testament prophets in that he was the One of whom all the other prophets spoke. Jesus didn't speak of someone else, but of himself. Third, Jesus was different from the Old Testament prophets in that he was not just a messenger, but he was the very message itself. The other prophets had pointed others to their messages, while Jesus pointed others to himself.

Because Jesus is the perfect Prophet, we can know God and be known by him. Jesus didn't just tell us *about* God; he laid down his life so that we can know God.

Matthew 13:57; Acts 3:22–24

14

Q. How does Jesus perfectly fulfill the office of Priest?

A. Jesus was the perfect sacrifice made for us and continues to intercede to the Father on our behalf as our great High Priest.

There is a curious encounter between Abraham and a man named Melchizedek recorded in Genesis 14:17–20. Abraham was returning home from a victorious battle when Melchizedek, king of Salem and a priest of God, came out to him and blessed him. Abraham, in turn, gave Melchizedek one tenth of everything—a tithe. And that's it. That's the encounter. After that, Melchizedek is only mentioned in the Old Testament once more in Psalm 110 when the Messiah is said to be a priest coming in the line of Melchizedek.

Melchizedek is then mentioned again by the writer of Hebrews who explained that Jesus was a greater priest than the other priests because he was a priest in the pattern of Melchizedek, not Aaron:

> And this becomes clearer if another priest like Melchizedek appears, who did not become a priest based on a legal regulation about physical descent but based on the power of an indestructible life. For it has been testified:
>
> You are a priest forever
> according to the order of Melchizedek. (Heb. 7:15–17)

The writer explained that Abraham tithed to Melchizedek, which is important. The lesser person always tithes to the greater person, meaning Melchizedek was greater than Abraham. Going a step further, Aaron was a descendant of Abraham and the ancestor is always greater than the descendant. So if Abraham was not greater than Melchizedek, then his ancestor Aaron could not be greater than Melchizedek either. Jesus, a priest in the pattern of Melchizedek, is therefore greater than any priest in the line of Aaron.

Jesus is not only the perfect priest because he is of a better pattern; he is the perfect priest because he became the perfect *sacrifice*. All the other priests sacrificed lambs, goats, and bulls for the people, but Jesus sacrificed himself for the people. This is what the writer of Hebrews says of Jesus later in Hebrews 9:26.

> Otherwise, he would have had to suffer many times since the foundation of the world. But now he has appeared one time, at the end of the ages, for the removal of sin by the sacrifice of himself.

Jesus offered himself one time as the perfect sacrifice—a sacrifice which did what the thousands upon thousands of animal sacrifices could never do—remove sin from God's people. All of those animal sacrifices looked forward to the one sacrifice that would be effective—the sacrifice of Jesus.

There is still another way in which Jesus is the perfect priest—he is able to make ongoing intercession for us to the Father:

> Therefore, he is able to save completely those who come to God through him, since he always lives to intercede for them. (Heb. 7:25)

Jesus is always in the presence of the Father. He is able to make perfect intercession because he knows us and has experienced everything we experience (Heb. 4:14–16) and also because he knows God, being God himself. As God, Jesus can extend one arm toward the Father, and as man, he can extend the other arm toward us, bringing us together with God (1 Tim. 2:5). Jesus is the mediator Job cried out for in Job 9:33! In Jesus we have the perfect priest—the One who was sacrificed on our behalf and who advocates to the Father for us affirming our salvation based on his sacrifice.

Hebrews 9:26; Hebrews 7:25

Q. How does Jesus perfectly fulfill the office of King?

A. Jesus perfectly reigns over his people as King of kings.

God had delivered the children of Israel out of Egypt through amazing miracles. He had provided for them supernaturally as they wandered in the wilderness. He had fought for them in battle to defeat all of their foes in the Promised Land. And he had been so patient with them, providing judge after judge as they continued to wallow in their pattern of sin. But all of this wasn't good enough for them. The people wanted a king—a human king like all of the nations around them. God was their King—their perfect King—and he was going to send them a perfect human King one day, but that wasn't good enough. They wanted a king in their timing and in their way.

God warned his people that human kings would tax them heavily, haul off their sons to fight in wars, burden them with immense, expensive building projects, and more. But that didn't matter. They still wanted a king. So God gave them what they wanted. Which is sometimes the only way people will learn.

The first king was Saul, who certainly looked the part. But he was barely into his reign when he sinned against God out of fear and was rejected by God.

The second king was David, who defeated Goliath and became a mighty warrior, leading his people in many successful battles. But David took another man's wife and then had him murdered to cover his sin.

The third king was Solomon, who, when asked by God to name what he wanted from him, asked for wisdom. God gave Solomon that request and he became the wisest man ever, but he wasn't wise enough. Solomon married many wives and pursued idolatry because of them. Because of Solomon's sin, the kingdom was torn in two when his son, Rehoboam, became king. All the rest of the two nations' kings fell far short of being the king the people needed.

Looking the part wasn't enough. Being a heroic fighter wasn't enough. Being wise wasn't enough. No king was good enough because every single one was a sinner in need of a greater King—King Jesus.

Jesus was born in David's line (Luke 1:32–33), revealing he had a right to the throne. He proved that he is the King his people needed because he rules with perfect authority and wisdom. But Jesus isn't just a perfect King for his people on earth; he is a greater King than that, as he explained during his trial leading up to the crucifixion:

> "My kingdom is not of this world," said Jesus. "If my kingdom were of this world, my servants would fight, so that I wouldn't be handed over to the Jews. But as it is, my kingdom is not from here." (John 18:36)

Jesus is King of kings and Lord of lords over everything. He is King over the universe which is seen, and he is King over the spiritual realm which is unseen.

John 18:36; Matthew 22:42–45

16

Q. What did Jesus do to provide forgiveness of sin?

A. Jesus provided forgiveness of sin by living a perfect life and dying on the cross to pay the punishment for sin.

When we think of what Jesus did to provide forgiveness of sin, we usually think of his death on the cross. And that is understandable because death was the punishment for our sin. Death was owed, and through Jesus, death was paid. This is known as substitutionary atonement. Some people don't quite understand how Jesus dying on the cross pays for anyone else's sins, so perhaps an illustration might help.

Suppose you parked illegally and received an expensive parking ticket. You go to court and the judge asks if you are guilty or innocent. You state that you are innocent and begin to share some reasons why your car was parked where it shouldn't have been parked. The judge listens for a few moments and then stops you and asks one direct question: were you or were you not parked illegally? You confess that you were, and he rightly finds you guilty, and orders you to pay the fine on the ticket.

You explain to the judge that you simply do not have the money to pay the ticket. It is impossible for you to pay it. The judge responds sympathetically, but he says that justice demands that the fine be paid. He would not be just if he allowed you to get away without paying it. But at this point, he stands up, takes off his robe, walks next to you, and removes his wallet. He pulls out enough money to pay the fine, places it on the bench, and says your fine has been paid. You are free to go.

Is the judge just? Without a doubt. Justice was served because the fine was paid. It doesn't matter who paid it, as long as it was paid. And that is what God did for us when Jesus left his place of glory, came to earth, and laid down his life for us.

However, Jesus did more than that—his perfect life mattered too. Look at what Paul wrote of Jesus in 2 Corinthians 5:21.

> He made the one who did not know sin to be sin for us, so that in him we might become the righteousness of God.

Jesus didn't just take our sin and pay our sin penalty, as great as that is. He also gave us something in its place—his righteousness. And that is why Jesus living a perfect life of obedience to the Father mattered. Had Jesus just taken our sin, it would leave us neutral before God. But because we receive credit for his righteousness, we are fully accepted by God. When God sees us, he sees us as completely sinless and fully obedient children.

2 Corinthians 5:21; Romans 3:26

Q. Did Jesus deserve to die on the cross?

A. No, Jesus did not deserve to die on the cross; he was sinless and blameless before God.

After Jesus was baptized, the Holy Spirit led him into the wilderness to be tempted by the devil (Matt. 4:1). Jesus fasted for forty days before the devil tempted him three times, but each time Jesus refused to give in to temptation. Instead, he responded with God's Word. Jesus was served by angels (Matt. 4:11) and then began his earthly ministry.

Being tempted by the devil is a curious way to begin a ministry, but there is an important reason why it happened—to prove that Jesus would succeed where Adam had failed. Jesus is the second Adam; and just as the first Adam represented all humanity, but failed, and brought sin and death into the world, Jesus proved that he would not give in to temptation and sin, revealing that he would live a perfect life, die, rise again, and bring life into the world.

The temptation also reveals that Jesus is the true Israel. While the people of Israel grumbled against God and rebelled against him as they failed to acknowledge his faithful provision, Jesus spent forty days in the wilderness without grumbling or sinning, trusting the Father's provision.

Jesus would continue living a sinless life in full obedience to the Father— even to the point of giving up his life on the cross. The Bible is clear that Jesus was sinless so that he could be the perfect sacrifice:

> For we do not have a high priest who is unable to sympathize with our weaknesses, but one who has been tempted in every way as we are, yet without sin. (Heb. 4:15)

We see this in 1 John 3:5 as well:

> You know that he was revealed so that he might take away sins,
> and there is no sin in him.

And 1 Peter 2:22:

> He did not commit sin, and no deceit was found in his mouth.

The frequency of the Bible talking about Jesus' sinlessness lets us know how important it is. Jesus did not deserve to die on the cross. He was innocent and without sin. God could not find any fault in him, and the only way the leaders could was by lying about him. But even though Jesus was innocent, he willingly laid down his life so that he could pay the sin penalty owed by others.

Hebrews 4:15; 1 John 3:5; 1 Peter 2:22

18

Q. What happened on the third day after Jesus was crucified?

A. On the third day, Jesus rose from the dead and left the grave.

———————

It was still very early on Sunday morning, so early the light was just starting to peak through the darkness. Some of the women—Mary Magdalene, Mary the mother of James, and Salome—were on their way to Jesus' tomb to anoint his body with more spices. Apparently, in the haste to finish preparing the body on Friday before the Sabbath began, the job had not been completed. But when the women arrived, they found something wasn't right—the body was gone.

The four Gospels record what happened next in dizzying speed. An angel speaks with the women and tells them that Jesus had risen. The women run to report what happened to the disciples. Peter and John run to the tomb to investigate, and after going in, realize that Jesus had indeed been raised. They scatter from the empty tomb. Mary Magdalene returns to the tomb by herself and Jesus appears to her. Later that day, Jesus appears to two disciples on the road to Emmaus.

On day one of the resurrection, we already have several witnesses that the tomb was empty, and news is starting to spread that Jesus is no longer dead—he is alive! In the days ahead, it would become apparent that Jesus was physically resurrected from the dead, showing that he had defeated sin and death. But the resurrection of Jesus means even more than that. Because Jesus rose from the dead, we have hope that we will too if we trust in him:

> But as it is, Christ has been raised from the dead, the firstfruits
> of those who have fallen asleep. (1 Cor. 15:20)

Others had been raised from the dead, like Lazarus, but Jesus was the firstfruit of a new kind of resurrection. Everyone else who had been raised ended up dying again. They were raised to the same fallen, broken bodies as before. But Jesus was raised anew. He was the first to be raised like this, but not the last. All of us who belong to him will also be raised into newness one day (1 Cor. 15:23). The resurrection of Jesus gives us confidence in our salvation as we look back, but it also gives us hope of our future as we look ahead.

1 Corinthians 15:20; Mark 16:6

19

Q. Is there any evidence that Jesus rose from the dead?

A. Yes, many witnesses saw Jesus after he rose from the dead.

How confident would you be in believing an extraordinary claim by one other person? Would a second witness verifying it make you feel better about believing it? How about a third? A fourth? A fifth? A five hundredth? The more witnesses there are to verify something, the stronger the case is for believing it.

When Jesus rose from the dead, there were not just a few witnesses who saw him, spoke with him, ate with him, and even touched him. There were hundreds, including more than five hundred at once (1 Cor. 15:4–8).

But hundreds of witnesses and an empty tomb didn't satisfy everyone. Some still presented arguments against Jesus' resurrection. Here are three of the most common ones.

+ *The Wrong Tomb Theory:* This theory suggests that everyone went to the wrong tomb. They found an empty tomb because Jesus' body was still in another tomb—the correct one somewhere else. There are several problems with this theory. First, how many tombs would have had Roman guards and a seal on them? Second, the tomb belonged to Joseph of Arimathea, who would have surely remembered where it was. Third, if the disciples had gone to the wrong tomb and reported that Jesus was alive, the Jewish leaders would have simply gone to the correct tomb and produced the body to stop the reports of the resurrection from the start.

- *The Swoon Theory:* This theory suggests that Jesus did not die on the cross, but merely passed out, or swooned, and later was revived in the coolness of the tomb, snuck out, and then was later reported alive by people because he always had been alive. He never died. Once again, there are several problems with this theory. First, a Roman soldier, an expert in executions, had verified that Jesus was dead. Had the soldier been incorrect, he was at risk of being put to death himself— he would have been sure. Second, even if Jesus did not die, how would he have unwrapped himself in the tomb and then moved the large stone out of the way by himself? He would have been extremely weak from the blood loss and the beatings and scourging he had endured. Third, even if he were able to move the stone, how would he have sneaked past the Roman guards outside the tomb?

- *The Stolen Body Theory:* This theory suggests that the disciples stole the body so they could report that Jesus had risen from the dead. And once again, this theory is riddled with problems. First, how did the group of disciples, who were afraid and in hiding, muster the courage to steal the body and the ability to overpower the guards? Second, if they chose to steal the body and lie about the resurrection, why would they have begun so soon after the resurrection? It would have been wiser and safer to wait a while. Third, according to tradition, all of the disciples were martyred for their claims that Jesus rose from the dead. Why would they all die for a lie? Wouldn't at least one have confessed that it was all a conspiracy?

As you can see, it takes more faith to believe that Jesus did *not* rise from the dead than that he did! The question of the empty tomb is critical. If Jesus did not rise again, our faith is meaningless. However, if he did indeed rise from the dead, then he is the Son of God and our faith is reasonable and secure.

1 Corinthians 15:4–8; John 20:19

Q. Where is Jesus now?

A. Forty days after Jesus rose, he ascended into heaven to return to his place of glory with the Father where he will remain until his return.

After the resurrection, Jesus remained on earth for forty days. During that time, he appeared to his followers to verify his resurrection and build their faith, but he also spent time preparing them to continue the mission after his departure. Then just before Pentecost, he returned to heaven in what is called the ascension:

> After he had said this, he was taken up as they were watching, and a cloud took him out of their sight. While he was going, they were gazing into heaven, and suddenly two men in white clothes stood by them. They said, "Men of Galilee, why do you stand looking up into heaven? This same Jesus, who has been taken from you into heaven, will come in the same way that you have seen him going into heaven." (Acts 1:9–11)

But why did Jesus leave? Why didn't he stay on earth and continue showing himself as the risen Savior? It's a great question. Here are three reasons why he ascended.

First, it verified that his work of salvation was complete. There was nothing left for him to do to provide salvation:

> The Son is the radiance of God's glory and the exact expression of his nature, sustaining all things by his powerful word. After

making purification for sins, he sat down at the right hand of
the Majesty on high. (Heb. 1:3)

Sitting down symbolizes that his work is done. Sitting at the Father's
right hand shows us that Jesus returned to the place of honor and glory he
enjoyed before coming to earth (John 17:5).

Second, Jesus ascended so that he could prepare a place for his followers:

"If I go away and prepare a place for you, I will come again and
take you to myself, so that where I am you may be also." (John
14:3)

Jesus left so that he could complete this place, but he has promised to
return and take us with him there.

Third, Jesus left so that he could send the Holy Spirit to work in us and
through us as his church:

"Nevertheless, I am telling you the truth. It is for your benefit
that I go away, because if I don't go away the Counselor will not
come to you. If I go, I will send him to you." (John 16:7)

It may not be clear how we are better off with the Holy Spirit than Jesus,
but we should believe Jesus and be grateful that he left. But when we look at
how the Holy Spirit benefited the first disciples by contrasting how they followed Jesus in the Gospels with how they served Jesus in Acts and beyond, we
can begin to see what Jesus meant. The Holy Spirit made a huge difference in
their lives and empowered them to boldly proclaim Jesus and grow the early
church rapidly and deeply. The great news is that we have the same Holy
Spirit who wants to do the same in us and through us.

Acts 1:9–11; Hebrews 1:3

SALVATION

Q. What does it mean to be righteous?

A. *To be righteous* is to obey God fully and live in a way that pleases him.

To understand what it means for a person to be righteous, we first have to think about the standard of righteousness—God. God is wholly righteous, meaning everything he does is right, good, and according to his character. But it is more than that. That makes righteousness seem to be outside of God—an activity rather than one of his attributes. So God is wholly righteous also in his character. All of his attributes are good and right. This is what we read in Deuteronomy 32:4.

> The Rock—his work is perfect;
> all his ways are just.
> A faithful God, without bias,
> he is righteous and true.

For a person to be righteous then, he or she would need to be the same. Everything he or she does would have to be right and good according to God's standard. Every single action. Every single word spoken. Every second lived for the fullest display of God's glory. Not a single sin could be committed.

But that would be the easy part! A righteous person would also need to have inner character that is wholly right and good in accordance with God's standard of righteousness. Every thought would need to center on bringing God glory. Complete selflessness and joyful obedience in the heart.

That is what it would mean for a person to be righteous. A good and righteous person on the inside who lives externally in the same way. That is the person who pleases God and who would be accepted by him.

Deuteronomy 32:4

Q. Can anyone be saved by his or her own righteousness?

A. No, no one is righteous enough to be saved.

When you understand what righteousness means—what it requires to be wholly righteous—it is plain to see that no one can be saved by his or her own righteousness. None of us can be good enough to meet God's standard of perfect righteousness. That is what we read in Romans 3:10—there is no one righteous, not even one.

The problem is that we often want to think that we are righteous enough for God. We take advantage of God's love and kindness and believe he will "grade us on a curve." Surely he doesn't expect perfection, right? That is completely unreasonable! So as long as we try to be good and are good enough— mostly good or even more good than bad—we'll be OK. Right?

Wrong. God is loving and gracious and kind. That is absolutely true. But he is also just. He cannot "grade on a curve" because that is not just. But even more than that, we tend to inflate our "good" works and think they are better than they really are. Listen to what Proverbs 21:2 says about this:

> All a person's ways seem right to him,
> but the LORD weighs hearts.

Our ways often *seem* right to us, but they are not. Ever. Because our ways are not God's ways (Isa. 55:8). If they were, they wouldn't be our ways, they would be his ways! You want to know what God thinks of our ways—our attempts to be righteous? Look at Isaiah 64:6.

> All of us have become like something unclean,
> and all our righteous acts are like a polluted garment;

all of us wither like a leaf,

and our iniquities carry us away like the wind.

Our righteous acts are like polluted garments—or filthy rags. Imagine trying to clean yourself with a washcloth that was caked with mud and worse. How clean would you end up getting? That is what happens to us when we try to clean ourselves up with our own righteous acts. We go the wrong way. The reason is simple—our righteous acts take us further away from the truth we need to understand and appreciate—we need another way to be saved that is outside of us. We need a Savior. We need Jesus. Righteous acts do not reveal that. Humble brokenness and desperation before God do.

Proverbs 21:2; Isaiah 64:6

Q. Who will be saved?

A. Anyone who repents of sin and trusts in Jesus will be saved.

If no one can be saved by his or her own righteousness, who will be saved? This is the beauty of the gospel: anyone who repents and trusts in Jesus will be saved. Anyone.

Here is how Paul put it in Romans 10:9–10.

> If you confess with your mouth, "Jesus is Lord," and believe in your heart that God raised him from the dead, you will be saved. One believes with the heart, resulting in righteousness, and one confesses with the mouth, resulting in salvation.

Jesus has done what we cannot do. He has made a way for all of our sin to be forgiven and removed from us, and in its place, he has given us his righteousness—his perfect righteousness that meets God's standard because Jesus is God. All we need to do is repent of our sin and trust in Jesus. That's it.

Salvation, then, is an incredible gift from God. We are given what we could not earn and what we do not deserve. All of the work has been done by God. God sent his Son into the world to die the death we deserve so that our sin penalty could be paid. God raised Jesus from the dead, and he provided the Holy Spirit to work through his people, the church, and convict us of our sin and draw us to trust in Christ. All we need to do is repent and believe in this loving gift that God has given us. As Jesus himself said in John 3:16,

> "For God loved the world in this way: he gave his one and only Son, so that everyone who believes in him will not perish but have eternal life."

That is the good news for everyone. It doesn't matter what ethnicity you are. What your age is. Where you live. What language you speak. How much money you have. How many "good" things you have done, or how much bad you have done. If you trust in Jesus, you will be saved. Period. Full stop. That is the grace of God. And that is the message that we need to share with our kids early and often. We need to help them face their sinfulness, but we also need to quickly take them to salvation through Jesus.

Romans 10:9–10; John 3:16

4

Q. How were people saved before Jesus came to earth?

A. People were saved by faith that God would provide Jesus one day.

So if a person is saved by trusting in Jesus, how were people saved in the Old Testament before he came? Doesn't that mean that no one could have been saved before Jesus? Or were they saved by obeying the Law instead?

Yes, people were saved before Jesus came, but no, they were not saved by obeying the Law. People were saved in the Old Testament the same way people are saved today—through faith. Habakkuk 2:4 says that the righteous will live by faith. Remember, we cannot obey enough, and we are broken and sinful on the inside anyway. The Law was never intended to save; it was intended to show our need for salvation. This is how Paul put it in Romans 3:20.

> For no one will be justified in his sight by the works of the law, because the knowledge of sin comes through the law.

Instead of being saved by obeying the Law, people were saved by their faith in God's unfolding plan to send Jesus one day. People were held accountable for what they knew. So while Abraham, for example, did not know exactly who Jesus would be and what he would do, God had revealed some of his plan to Abraham. Abraham knew that God had promised that all of the people of the world would be blessed through one of his descendants one day. That is what Abraham ended up believing in—after first doubting God's ability to provide an heir—and that is the faith that God rewarded as we read in Genesis 15:6.

Abram believed the LORD, and he credited it to him as righteousness.

This verse is quoted by Paul in Romans and James in his epistle to drive this home. Salvation has always been, and always will be, by faith alone. Faith in God's promise to send the deliverer to crush the serpent's head. The people in the Old Testament knew him just as that—or as one who would be born of a certain family—or as one who would be born of a virgin in Bethlehem. That was what they trusted in. We now know him as Jesus, and we have a record of his life. Jesus is the one we trust for our salvation.

Habakkuk 2:4; Genesis 15:6

5

Q. How did people in the Old Testament show their faith that God would forgive their sin?

A. People in the Old Testament showed their faith in God by offering animal sacrifices to him.

Faith is often misunderstood as something just inside of us. And while it is true that faith largely rests in our minds and hearts, it doesn't just stay there. Faith is active. Faith works. That is what James says in much of his epistle. You cannot say you have faith but have nothing to show from it. Faith should be seen!

People in the Old Testament showed their faith that God would provide a way to forgive their sins through the sacrificial system. Animals were sacrificed, and their blood shed, in an act of faith. This bloodshed was vital as we read in Hebrews 9:22.

> According to the law almost everything is purified with blood,
> and without the shedding of blood there is no forgiveness.

Forgiveness requires the shedding of blood. And if it isn't our blood, it has to be the blood of another. The sacrificial system used the blood of bulls and goats, among other offerings, to picture forgiveness of sin.

There were five primary sacrifices in the Old Testament. We read about them in the first five chapters of the book of Leviticus.

- The Burnt Offering (Leviticus 1): This was a voluntary sacrifice where the animal was completely burned by fire. This offering was a way a person could demonstrate total surrender to God, pictured in the animal sacrifice being totally consumed in flames.

+ The Grain Offering (Leviticus 2): This was another voluntary offering where grain was offered instead of an animal. This offering represented an awareness of, and gratitude toward, God's provision in one's life. Someone giving this offering to God was also expressing a desire to live with generosity toward others.

+ The Fellowship Offering (Leviticus 3): A third voluntary offering, this sacrifice featured the giving of an unblemished animal to God. This offering represented an awareness of being in fellowship, or communion, with God.

+ The Sin Offering (Leviticus 4): The fourth type of sacrifice was not voluntary. The sin offering was necessary to offer to God because of a person's problem of sin—the sins they committed against holy God. This offering was also given for accidental sins a person committed.

+ The Guilt Offering (Leviticus 5): The final sacrifice was not voluntary either, and was offered when a person committed a particular sin and wanted to make restitution.

These five sacrifices were offered by individuals throughout the year, but there was one other sacrifice offered by the high priest once a year on behalf of all the people. This sacrifice was made on the Day of Atonement (Leviticus 16) and symbolized the removal of sin from the people as a whole. All of the sacrifices revealed the people's faith that their sin deserved death and that God was providing a way that it could be forgiven by the shedding of another's blood—ultimately the blood of Jesus.

Hebrews 9:22; Leviticus 16

6

Q. What did the animal sacrifices represent?

A. The animal sacrifices represented Jesus, the perfect sacrifice who was to come.

All of the sacrifices ultimately pointed to Jesus, the perfect sacrifice, who would be offered. This is why John referred to Jesus as the Lamb who came to take away the sins of the world (John 1:29).

The people of the Old Testament performed sacrifice after sacrifice year after year. They had to continue offering sacrifices because their sin was never ultimately dealt with. It always remained. So the sacrifices were not really designed to deal with their sin, but instead were intended to demonstrate their faith that a way—a final way, a real way—was coming, and that way was found in the Person of Jesus (see Heb. 10:19–22).

Perhaps the greatest picture of how the sacrifices pointed to Jesus is found in the two goats that were part of the Day of Atonement. One of the tasks the high priest was to complete on the Day of Atonement was to take two goats and sacrifice one and release the other. First, he was to sacrifice one of the goats, as we read in Leviticus 16:15–16.

> "When he slaughters the male goat for the people's sin offering and brings its blood inside the curtain, he will do the same with its blood as he did with the bull's blood: He is to sprinkle it against the mercy seat and in front of it. He will make atonement for the most holy place in this way for all their sins because of the Israelites' impurities and rebellious acts."

The priest would sacrifice the first goat in front of the people and then take its blood and splatter it on the mercy seat above the ark of the covenant in the Holy of Holies. This bloodshed represented atonement for the sins of the people.

Then the priest would return from within the Holy of Holies and take the second goat—the scapegoat—and lay his hands on its head. This symbolized him placing all the sins of the people on the goat. The people would then release the goat into the wild as we read in Leviticus 16:22.

> "The goat will carry all their iniquities into a desolate land, and the man will release it there."

One goat was slaughtered and its blood paid for sin. The other goat carried the people's sins away from the people. This is a gripping picture of what Jesus would do, once and for all. When Jesus died on the cross, his blood was shed to provide forgiveness of sin and when we trust in him, all of our sin is placed on him, and it is removed from us forevermore (Ps. 103:12). That was what God was picturing in the Day of Atonement, and that is what we have experienced in Christ.

John 1:29; Hebrews 10:19–22

7

Q. How did Jesus being fully human make it possible for people to be saved?

A. Because Jesus is fully human, he was able to die the death sin deserves.

The wages of sin is death (Rom. 6:23). But our sin has not just earned any kind of death; it has earned our death—human death. God is just, so his penalty will always fit the crime. Because humans rebelled against God, human death is the rightful punishment. The Old Testament sacrifices were given as a reminder—foreshadowing—of this truth. Human death was owed and it would be paid one day. The death of animals just wasn't good enough, as we read in Hebrews 10:3–4.

> But in the sacrifices there is a reminder of sins year after year. For it is impossible for the blood of bulls and goats to take away sins.

It was impossible for the blood of bulls and goats to take away sin because their deaths were not human deaths. There had to be another way to pay for human sins. Because every person is born in sin, his or her death should be the only way to pay for his or her sins. Right?

And that is where Jesus stepped in. The Son of God took on the flesh and became fully human so that he could give up his life for others. He had to take on the flesh, or else it wouldn't work. Human sin deserves human death.

But there is more to it than that. There were other reasons Jesus became human. In becoming a man, he was able to reveal God to the world fully. Since we have seen Jesus, we have seen God. We can know God in ways we never could have before.

Jesus also became a man to provide us with an example for living. Jesus obeyed God perfectly and gave us a model to follow. His perfect obedience also proved that he fulfilled all of the Law. Jesus lived in perfect righteousness, which is credited to us when we trust in him (2 Cor. 5:21).

Finally, Jesus became a man so he could become a sympathetic high priest for us (Heb. 4:15). There is nothing we experience that he has not experienced to an even greater degree than we have or ever will. We are tempted to sin; so was he. We feel alone at times; so did he. We are mocked, scorned, and rejected for sharing the gospel; so was he.

Jesus became a man primarily to provide salvation for us through the sacrifice of his life, but, as is the beautiful way of God, he went above and beyond. Jesus' humanity also helps us and comforts as we live each day. When we think no one cares or understands, all we need to remember is that Jesus does. And that should bring us the comfort we need.

Hebrews 10:3–4; Romans 6:23

8

Q. How did Jesus being fully God make it possible for people to be saved?

A. Because Jesus is fully God, he was able to be the perfect sacrifice for the sins of the world.

Because Jesus is a human, he could pay the human death that was owed. But because he is also God, his life was of infinite worth, and therefore, he could pay for the sins of many people. His death wouldn't be restricted to paying the penalty for just one other person. All who trust in him will be saved through his death. This is how Jesus put it in Matthew 20:28.

> "Just as the Son of Man did not come to be served, but to serve, and to give his life as a ransom for many."

The only way Jesus' death could serve many was because he is God. A human could not offer that sacrifice.

But just as there were additional reasons for Jesus taking on the flesh, there are other reasons it is important he is God. For one, Jesus' sacrifice showed that salvation is truly from God alone. Salvation is outside of us—something we could never do on our own.

And second, Jesus being God enables him to be the perfect Mediator who can stretch out one arm to God the Father in his deity and stretch out the other arm to mankind in his humanity, bringing us together. We are like Job, longing for someone who could approach God and speak to him on our behalf but who could also come to us and speak to us on God's behalf (Job 9:33). We need a mediator—a perfect interpreter—who can cross that divide. That mediator is Jesus, the God-man (1 Tim. 2:5).

Our salvation rests on Jesus being fully man and fully God. Take either away and our salvation would fall apart. But put them together and you have the one and only way that a righteous God could bring sinners to salvation.

Matthew 20:28; Job 9:33; 1 Timothy 2:5

Q. What does it mean to repent?

A. *To repent* is to be grieved by sin and turn from it.

John the Baptist's primary role was to be the forerunner of Jesus. His task was to prepare the way for the coming of Jesus and announce his arrival, which he did. In Matthew 3:2 we read what John's message was: "Repent, because the kingdom of heaven has come near." John was urging the people to repent—to be grieved by their sin and turn from it—in preparation to hear Jesus and respond to him. It's not surprising, then, that the message Jesus preached was the same:

> From then on Jesus began to preach, "Repent, because the kingdom of heaven has come near." (Matt. 4:17)

Like John, Jesus was calling on people to repent. Without repentance, they would not be able to experience the kingdom that had come near in and through him.

Repentance is critical for salvation. Without it, we cannot be saved (Luke 24:46–47). We must want to turn from our sin as we read in Romans 6:1–2.

> What should we say then? Should we continue in sin so that grace may multiply? Absolutely not! How can we who died to sin still live in it?

As we can see, repentance is much more than being OK with sin but wishing we didn't do it. It's much more than being sorry we get caught in sin or have to experience the consequences of our sin. It is being *grieved* by our sin—repulsed by it. We need to reach the point where our loathing of sin surpasses the enjoyment we get out of it. That is true repentance.

In this way, repentance is defined narrowly—a grieving of sin and turning from it. However, we can define repentance a little more broadly as not only turning *from* sin but also turning *to* Christ in faith. Repentance, then, can be thought of as two directional. Many times our kids will be sorry they got caught doing something wrong or they will say they are sorry to avoid punishment, but that is not true repentance. We need to help them see that God wants more than that—he demands more than that. We can pray that God will soften our kids' hearts so that they reach the point of being sorry that they sin. That is the repentance that guides them to Christ and the salvation from sin he offers.

Matthew 4:7; Luke 24:46–47

Q. What does it mean to trust in Jesus?

A. *To trust in Jesus* is to believe that Jesus is the Son of God, to have faith that he paid for your sin, and to love and follow him.

The Bible uses many different synonyms for *trust*, including "faith," "believe," and even "obey." While these are all good biblical words, *trust* is probably the best and clearest word to use today. When many people hear the word *faith*, they immediately think of blind faith, but that isn't what biblical faith is. When they hear "believe," they may think of merely accepting facts, but again, biblical belief is more than that. When they hear "obey," they just think of doing what should be done, but once more, biblical obedience is more than that. "Trust," though, seems to capture more of the heart of what the Bible has in mind because it carries with it the idea of acting on what is believed.

Take sitting on a chair for example. Whenever we sit on a chair, we at least subconsciously evaluate the chair and decide whether it will hold us up. If we believe it will, we choose to sit on it. That is the idea conveyed most clearly in the word *trust*. You trust the chair, so you sit on it.

This is why *believe* may not be as effective of a word in our current culture. To us, to believe means intellectual agreement, and that is not the fullness of what the Bible has in mind in trusting in Jesus. The Bible says that even the demons believe in God, but they are far from saved:

> You believe that God is one. Good! Even the demons believe—
> and they shudder. (James 2:19)

Demons agree that God is who he is, but they have not entrusted themselves to him. So trust is more than agreement, and it is also more than approval. We can agree that something is true, and then we can agree that something is true and approve of it. But that is still not enough. There needs to be that element of trusting—of acting on it—such as we read in Romans 10:9.

> If you confess with your mouth, "Jesus is Lord," and believe in your heart that God raised him from the dead, you will be saved.

We can see from this verse that trust is a posture of the heart that involves the mind and results in action, in this case confession. That provides the fuller picture of trust that we need to help our kids see. We are to trust our salvation, and also our very lives, to Jesus. True trust, then, not only eyes what we need for salvation, but also what the rest of our lives will look like as his followers.

Romans 10:9; John 1:12

Q. What is grace?

A. *Grace* is God giving us good things that we do not deserve.

It's hard to understand grace apart from humility, which is perhaps why it is such a foreign concept in our culture today, which feels a greater and deeper sense of entitlement than ever before. We feel that we deserve pretty much everything—everything that is good more precisely. And when you feel you deserve everything, there's no room left for gifts. But that is exactly what grace is—a gift—undeserved good things from God. So for us to appreciate grace, we really need to approach it with deep humility, recognizing that we don't deserve *anything* good from God.

While grace is, by its broadest definition, receiving anything good from God, we often think of it more narrowly in the context of salvation. Salvation itself is given to us by grace. We do nothing at all to deserve God's salvation, yet he gives it to us freely through his Son because of his graciousness. We see this in Ephesians 2:8–9.

> For you are saved by grace through faith, and this is not from yourselves; it is God's gift.

And again in Romans 3:24.

> They are justified freely by his grace through the redemption that is in Christ Jesus.

We are saved by grace from start to finish. Jesus was given out of God's grace. We are saved by God's grace. Each day we wake up is a further gift of

God's grace. All of our possessions are provided out of God's grace. Our family and our friends are given out of God's grace. Every single good thing God provides (James 1:17) is given out of his grace. We deserve none of it. But it is only when we humble ourselves that we can truly see the beauty and the lavishness of God's grace. Through our humility truly comes greater awe of God and joy.

Ephesians 2:8–9; Romans 3:24

12

Q. What is mercy?

A. *Mercy* is God not giving us punishment that we deserve.

Mercy is the counterpart to grace. While grace is God's provision of good things we do not deserve, mercy is God's withholding the punishment we do deserve. God gives us what is good out of his grace, and he doesn't give us what is bad out of his mercy. And when it comes to salvation, what we deserve is really bad indeed. Because of our sin, we deserve not salvation but eternal separation from God, without anything good. That is what God's mercy withholds from us (Titus 3:5). But we also experience God's mercy around us every day—our problem is that we don't quite see it.

Just as humility is necessary for us to really appreciate grace, it is also needed for us to appreciate mercy. We have to understand how serious our sin and rebellion is. We need to accept that reality and come to terms with how our sinfulness collides with God's justice. That is when we will truly begin to understand mercy.

Jesus told a powerful parable in Matthew 18:23–35 to help his followers understand mercy. There was a king who decided it was time to collect the debts his servants owed. One servant owed him ten thousand talents—roughly two hundred thousand years of wages. The servant, of course, did not have money to repay the king, so the king ordered his family and all his possessions to be sold to pay the debt.

The servant heard this and fell down face first and pleaded and begged for the king to give him more time to repay the debt. When the king saw this, he felt compassion and forgave the entire loan. A fortune was forgiven just like that!

That same servant left the king and saw a fellow servant who owed him one hundred denarii—about four months' wages. He grabbed that servant and demanded that he pay him back his debt. The second servant fell down and begged him to be patient and give him more time to repay the debt. But the first servant was unwilling and had him thrown into prison.

Word of what had happened reached the king, and he called the servant in. "You wicked servant!" he told him. "I forgave you all that debt because you begged me. Shouldn't you also have had mercy on your fellow servant, as I had mercy on you?" (Matt. 18:32–33). The king then had the servant thrown into prison until he could pay back his debt.

Now we have to admit that this is an absurd parable. How could a servant who was really forgiven such an outrageous debt fail to forgive such a modest one? And right after his debt was forgiven even! It is outrageous because it was meant to be. Jesus wanted us to remember the debt that we were forgiven—our lives—out of God's mercy. If we truly grasp that level of mercy, we will be compelled to demonstrate mercy to others. No one owes us what we owed God.

Matthew 18:23–35; Titus 3:5

Q. What is atonement?

A. *Atonement* is Jesus living a perfect life and paying our sin penalty to make us right with God.

To *atone* is to repair, satisfy, or make amends. When it comes to salvation, the atonement is God's justice being satisfied by the life and death of Jesus so that we can be made right again with God. Because of what Jesus has done, amends have been made and our relationship with God has been repaired. This is known more fully as "substitutionary atonement," because Jesus satisfied God's justice through his *substitute* death on our behalf.

Romans 3:25–26 is one of the clearer passages describing the atonement:

> God presented him as an atoning sacrifice in his blood, received through faith, to demonstrate his righteousness, because in his restraint God passed over the sins previously committed. God presented him to demonstrate his righteousness at the present time, so that he would be righteous and declare righteous the one who has faith in Jesus.

We can see that God provided Jesus to be an atoning sacrifice on the cross and that we benefit from his atoning work through faith. But we also see that the atonement is more than just Jesus paying our sin penalty in our place. It also includes our being declared righteous by God, which happens when Jesus' righteousness is credited to us. This is why the atonement also includes Jesus living a perfect life of obedience along with his sacrifice on the cross.

Peter describes the atonement, without using the actual word, in 1 Peter 3:18.

> For Christ also suffered for sins once for all, the righteous for the unrighteous, that he might bring you to God.

This definition of the atonement is a little simpler, but it still includes both aspects of Jesus' sacrifice and righteousness, and it also gets more to the purpose of the atonement—to bring us to God. God's justice required the atonement. Payment for sin had to be made. But God's love compelled the atonement. God wanted to restore our relationship with him. That is the beauty of the atonement—it binds God's perfect justice and perfect love together without diminishing either.

Romans 3:25–26; 2 Corinthians 5:19–21

Q. What is regeneration?

A. *Regeneration* is the Holy Spirit causing us to be born again, giving us new hearts that love God.

How we see people apart from the gospel is critical. If we see people as basically good, perhaps needing a little help from God, we won't see the beauty and depth of the gospel. However, if we see people as ruined by sin—dead in sin actually (Eph. 2:1)—then we can begin to see the splendor of the gospel. God didn't just help sick people get well; he gave dead people life!

And that is where regeneration comes in. Regeneration literally means to come alive again, and it describes how the Holy Spirit gives us a new heart—new life—at salvation, so that we can love God. This is how Paul put it in his letter to Titus:

> He saved us—not by works of righteousness that we had done, but according to his mercy—through the washing of regeneration and renewal by the Holy Spirit. He poured out his Spirit on us abundantly through Jesus Christ our Savior. (Titus 3:5–6)

Our salvation is not based on anything we have done. It is an act of God's mercy and grace brought about by the Holy Spirit regenerating and renewing us. Without this act of the Holy Spirit, we could not be saved. This is what Jesus said about our need for this new life in his conversation with Nicodemus:

> Jesus replied, "Truly I tell you, unless someone is born again, he cannot see the kingdom of God." (John 3:3)

Jesus was pretty clear here. Whenever he began something with "truly," that meant that what he was about to say was important—as if everything else he said wasn't important too! But this was Jesus' way of saying, "Lean in and pay close attention because what I am about to tell you really, really matters." And in this case, Jesus wanted us to know that being born again—regenerated—is an absolute requirement for seeing God's kingdom. We must be born again, but thankfully, we are just as passive in this new birth as we were in our physical births. God the Holy Spirit is the One at work in regeneration. We are the recipients of yet another act of God's kindness and grace.

Titus 3:5–6; John 3:3

Q. What is justification?

A. *Justification* is God declaring that we are forgiven of our sins and that we are righteous.

Imagine that you are seated in a courtroom at the end of a trial. The defendant is led in and told to stand as the judge prepares to render her verdict. She recounts the charges against the defendant and then declares that she finds him not guilty. And with the two words "not guilty," the defendant is immediately free to go. There are no longer any grounds to hold him. He is an innocent man.

That is the idea of justification—God's declaration that we are not guilty, we are forgiven and righteous in his eyes. Justification only happens because of what Jesus has done for us, as we read in Romans 3:24.

> They are justified freely by his grace through the redemption
> that is in Christ Jesus.

We are justified—declared not guilty—by God's grace through redemption in Jesus. So the moment we trust in Christ, God declares that we are from that moment forward completely forgiven and in right standing with him. It is important to note that God *declares* that we are good; he doesn't *make* us good. That may seem like a slight difference, but it is important, and here's why: While we are forgiven of our sin, we still continue to sin. Our conduct is far from good. So God does not make us—people who are not good—good. He can declare us good, but he does not make us good in that moment. That will happen one day in the future when we are glorified and we finally put off all sin and act according to what God has declared about us.

This is why being justified is so important for us to remember as we continue to struggle with sin in our lives. In those moments when we sin, we may be tempted to question our salvation. Does God really love us? Has he really forgiven us? It sure may not feel that way in the moment. But when we remember that God has declared us forgiven and that we have been given Jesus' righteousness, we can maintain confidence in our salvation, and the gratitude we feel for God's unwavering love of us should drive us to repent of our sin.

This is what Paul had in mind a little later in Romans.

> Who can bring an accusation against God's elect? God is the one who justifies. Who is the one who condemns? Christ Jesus is the one who died, but even more, has been raised; he also is at the right hand of God and intercedes for us. (Rom. 8:33–34)

Paul takes us back to a courtroom setting, but this time we are the defendants, and it isn't at the end of the case, but the beginning. His first question is, *Who can bring a charge against us?* Without a charge, the case cannot proceed and we would be free to go. His answer is that no one can bring a charge against us because God has justified us already! We are free to go. But Paul asks another question: *Who can condemn us?* Who can find us guilty? Once again, the answer is "no one," because Jesus has already been condemned in our place, and he intercedes before the Judge, telling him that he has paid our sin punishment in our place. Even if someone could make an accusation, there is no one who could find us guilty. Paul asks one more question in the next verse—*Who can separate us from the love of God?* If someone somehow could make a charge and could even find us guilty, who could carry out the sentence? Once again, the answer is that no one can. Paul spends the next few verses emphatically sharing that no one and nothing can separate us from God's love. We are secure! No one can bring a charge. No one can condemn. No one can carry out a sentence. All because we have been justified by God.

Romans 3:24; Romans 8:33–34

Q. What is adoption?

A. *Adoption* is God bringing us into his family as his children.

There isn't much in life more beautiful than adoption. Parents choose a child to bring into their family to become their son or daughter—as if he or she were born into the family from the start. From that day forward, the adopted child has a brand new identity and is fully part of a new family. Adoption is one of the most powerful expressions of love that we can encounter.

The reason why adoption is so beautiful is because it was designed by God and comes straight from his heart. When we trust in Jesus, God adopts us into his family and we become his children and coheirs with Jesus. Here is what we read about our adoption in Romans 8:15.

> You did not receive a spirit of slavery to fall back into fear. Instead, you received the Spirit of adoption, by whom we cry out, "Abba, Father!"

Because we are in Christ and have been adopted as God's children, we are completely secure in our salvation. In Roman adoption, all of the adoptee's former debts and obligations were taken on by his or her new parents and he or she was viewed as a full part of the family as if he or she were born into it. This is what God does for us! He takes our sin debt from us and gives us all of the benefits of being his children. Because of this, there is no reason for us to be afraid of losing our salvation or being punished for our sin. Jesus already paid our punishment in our place and we are now part of God's family for good.

The best part of adoption, though, is the new way we can relate with God as our Father. *Abba* was a term of endearment that a child would call his or her father. *Daddy* or *Papa* would be closest to it for us. When we trust in Christ, God becomes our Daddy. That is simply amazing. We get to call the God of the Universe, the One who created everything, our Daddy from that day forward. Not everyone can do this. While God acts fatherly toward all people, he is only Father to those who have trusted in Jesus and who have been adopted by him. Before we trusted in Jesus we could not call the Father Daddy, but now we can. We can talk with God as our loving Father (Matt. 6:9) and we share in Jesus' glory with him (Rom. 8:17). We were once enemies of God (Rom. 5:10), but now we are his children. All because of Jesus.

Romans 8:15; Ephesians 1:15

17

Q. What is sanctification?

A. *Sanctification* is where we gradually grow to live more like Jesus.

You have most likely heard of a sanctuary—either as part of a church building or perhaps in relation to an animal preserve. A sanctuary is a place that is set apart for a certain purpose. In the church building's case, it is set apart for worship; while in the animal preserve's case, it is set apart as a place where certain animals are protected. That helps us understand what sanctification is—where we gradually grow to live more like Jesus, which sets us apart from the world around us. We are different—in a good way—when we live like Jesus. It shouldn't be surprising, then, to hear that we get the word *sanctification* from the same word that we get *holy*. They both mean about the same thing—to be set apart. So as we are sanctified, we become more holy, like God.

So how does this happen? Does it take place automatically, or is it something we must do on our own? Well, the answer is in the middle somewhere. We are sanctified by God working through us, but we still need to work at it ourselves. It doesn't happen automatically in us. Here is the first part of that—that sanctification is a work of God in us:

> For we are his workmanship, created in Christ Jesus for good works, which God prepared ahead of time for us to do. (Eph. 2:10)

We are God's handiwork, created for good works which God prepared ahead of time—before we were even created, way back in eternity past! That makes it pretty clear that God is the One who works through us to bring about our sanctification. But look at what Paul says about our sanctification in Philippians 2:12–13.

> Therefore, my dear friends, just as you have always obeyed, so now, not only in my presence but even more in my absence, work out your own salvation with fear and trembling. For it is God who is working in you both to will and to work according to his good purpose.

Once again we see that God is the One working in us, but we also see that we are to work out our salvation. Now, we have to be careful not to misread this. Prepositions matter. We don't work *for* our salvation; we work *out* our salvation. We work at growing in the salvation that was given to us by grace and nothing we did.

So which is it, then? Who does the work of sanctification? God or us? Yes and yes. God is the One who is primarily at work—we need him to be. We cannot produce this kind of change on our own. However, we are not passive in the process. We work together with God, out of our love for him and gratitude for what he had done, to grow in our faith. Our salvation is by grace, but that doesn't mean that there isn't work involved. Grace leaves no room for any of our effort in earning our salvation, but leaves plenty of room for our effort in working it out. Work *from* salvation is not opposed to grace; work *for* it is.

This process of growing in sanctification begins at our new birth (1 Cor. 6:11; Titus 3:5; 1 John 3:9), continues to increase gradually during our lifetime when we become more like Christ each day (Phil. 3:13–14; Col. 3:10), and reaches perfection in the future when we are finally rid of our fallen bodies and have been glorified with Christ (Heb. 12:23; Rev. 21:27).

Ephesians 2:10; Philippians 2:12–13

18

Q. What is glorification?

A. *Glorification* is when believers will be made completely right and perfect again in the restored creation.

As amazing as this world and universe is, it is not as it should be. When Adam and Eve rebelled against God, they fell, and all of the rest of creation fell with them. And because of this, creation groans—not a groan from the agony of death, but with the anticipation of new birth one day (Rom. 8:22). This new birth is when God will make all of creation completely right and perfect once again. On that future day, God will remove the curse from creation and sin will no longer plague it. Death and decay will be no more, and all of creation will be as good as Eden—even better.

At the same time, we will also be made new, as we read in Philippians 3:20–21.

> But our citizenship is in heaven, and we eagerly wait for a Savior from there, the Lord Jesus Christ. He will transform the body of our humble condition into the likeness of his glorious body, by the power that enables him to subject everything to himself.

Our current bodies will be changed into new, glorious bodies that will no longer be contaminated by sin and subjected to the curse. Our new bodies will be imperishable, they won't wear out or break down, and they will be perfect. No more disease. No more sickness. No more disabilities. We will all have full use of our bodies and minds. But as amazing as that will be, the best part will be that our sin nature will be done away with. We will no longer sin, struggle with sin, or be tempted to sin. We will finally be able to see God clearly, love him fully, and worship and serve him without hindrance. For the first time we will experience life, a relationship with God, and creation as we should—in fullness.

Our future glorification produces deep longing and hope in us. We long for the day when we will experience perfection to arrive, but at the same time we live with unwavering hope—confident expectation—that it is coming in God's perfect timing.

Philippians 3:20–21; 1 Corinthians 15:38–50

19

Q. What does Jesus take from us and give us when we are saved?

A. When we are saved, Jesus takes our sin and gives us his righteousness.

Any sports fan knows there have been plenty of terrible trades in sports history. Superstars have been traded for next to nothing. Multiple players have been traded for one player who ended up not making much of a difference while the others went on to greatly help the other team. What makes these trades so bad is that they were so lopsided—one team got an amazing deal while the other got robbed. On the contrary, the best trades are usually the ones where both teams ended up winning in the end. They just aren't as memorable.

When it comes to the worst trades ever made, one stands head and shoulders above the rest—the clear winner of this title. Only this trade didn't happen in a sports team's office. It happened when we came to faith in Christ.

The moment we trusted in Christ, the most lopsided trade ever happened. Jesus took our sin from us and traded it for his righteousness. What a terrible trade looking at it from the outside, but can there be any more beautiful trade for those of us who have experienced it? We read about this trade in 2 Corinthians 5:21.

> He made the one who did not know sin to be sin for us, so that
> in him we might become the righteousness of God.

Imagine Jesus holding two jars and we are holding two jars as well. Jesus' jars are labeled "sin" and "righteousness." The first jar is completely empty—not even a molecule of sin is in it. The second jar is completely full—overflowing even—with righteousness. Jesus was sinless and completely righteous. Our jars are labeled the same. But our "sin" jar is completely full while our "righteousness" jar is completely empty.

So here is the trade. Jesus reaches out and pours all of our sin jar's contents into his own sin jar. He then pours from his righteousness jar into our righteousness jar, but both are full in the end. So there we are, with an empty sin jar and a full righteousness jar. And that is exactly how God sees us from that day forward. All of our sin is gone—as far as the east is from the west (Ps. 103:12)—and we have been given Jesus' righteousness. There it is. The worst and greatest trade ever.

2 Corinthians 5:21; Romans 3:22

20

Q. Can someone who has truly trusted in Christ fall away from God?

A. No, all true Christians persevere to the end.

One of our greatest comforts as Christians is that our salvation is secure. When we trust in Christ, we are adopted into God's family as his children and our new identity cannot be taken away from us (Rom. 8:12–17). We also become a new creation; the old is gone and the new has come (2 Cor. 5:17). But the most comforting proof that we are secure in Christ came from what he said about our salvation in John 10:28–29.

> I give them eternal life, and they will never perish. No one will snatch them out of my hand. My Father, who has given them to me, is greater than all. No one is able to snatch them out of the Father's hand.

Let's break down what Jesus said into three main ideas that prove we will persevere until the end and that we cannot lose our salvation.

1. **Jesus gives us eternal life.** Carefully notice what Jesus says he gives us—eternal life. Not life. Not a chance for eternal life. He gives us eternal life itself. That is important because it proves that we are completely secure in our salvation. The moment you trusted in Christ, he gave you eternal life, which means, by definition, it is yours forever. There is nothing you can do to lose it, or else Jesus couldn't give it to you.

2. **Jesus says we will never perish.** We aren't supposed to use double negatives in English because they are grammatically incorrect. However, in biblical Greek, they are fine to use as a way to emphasize the impossibility of something. Jesus used a double negative here, which would be more accurately

translated as "they will not never perish." The idea is that it is completely impossible for us to perish once we are in Christ.

3. **No one can snatch us out of Jesus' hand.** Imagine a baby trying to pry a marble out of the hand of a bodybuilder. It's just not going to happen, right? There is no way a tiny baby can force open the muscular hand of a grown man who has trained his muscles to be incredibly strong. That is the picture Jesus wants us to have in mind when he says no one can snatch us out of his hand. Actually, that picture isn't good enough! We are completely secure in the hands of Jesus. We aren't going anywhere.

Any one of these statements would have been enough on its own. But Jesus gave us all three because he wanted to be crystal clear that we have nothing to fear—our salvation is secure. Knowing that is a great comfort and should motivate us not to live however we want, but to live in a way that pleases Christ out of our gratitude for what he has done for us. We are saved and we are kept safe by him. That is why we seek to put sin to death in us and live in a way that glorifies him. He deserves nothing less from us.

John 10:28–29; Romans 8:35–39

THE BIBLE

Q. What is the Bible?

A. The Bible is God's revelation, or explanation, of himself to us.

The word *Bible* simply means "book," but the Bible is not any book. The Bible is God's special revelation of himself to us; it is the way he has chosen for us to know him. We can learn quite a bit about God from nature through general revelation, but it is only through the words he gave us in the Bible that we can truly know him. The Bible provides what we need to know God, trust in Jesus for salvation, and live a life pleasing to him as a response to what he has done for us.

While the Bible is a fairly long book, it is far from a complete record of who God is and what he has done. This is how John ended his Gospel:

> And there are also many other things that Jesus did, which, if every one of them were written down, I suppose not even the world itself could contain the books that would be written. (John 21:25)

There is just no way to record all there is to know about God and all he has done in a library of books, let alone a single book. So there are many things we don't know about God that we wish we did. For example, the Bible doesn't address what Adam and Eve did after the Fall except that they had children. We don't know if Jonah repented, what happened to Paul when he was under house arrest in Rome, and pretty much anything of Jesus' life between his birth and when he began his ministry at around thirty years old. But while we would like to know these things, and knowing could even be helpful, none of them are essential for us to know. God has given all we *need* to know in the Bible, not everything we *want* to know.

What God has chosen to reveal to us, he wants us to understand. Sure, there are some difficult things to understand in the Bible, even Peter admitted this (2 Pet. 3:16); but overall, the Bible beautifully reveals the greatness of God in ways that we can understand, as we read in Psalm 119:130:

> The revelation of your words brings light
> and gives understanding to the inexperienced.

The Bible is a priceless treasure because it is the very words of God—words of life that he has given to us. It is only through the Bible that we can come to know Jesus, trust in him, and experience salvation and eternal life with God.

John 21:25; Psalm 119:130

Q. Who wrote the Bible?

A. Men who were inspired by the Holy Spirit wrote the Bible.

———————

The Bible is a compilation of sixty-six books written by more than forty different authors. Many of the books mention the author's name in the book itself, such as Paul's letters, but we have to piece together the authors from some books based on evidence we find in the book, in other books of the Bible, or elsewhere. For example, because we know that Luke wrote the Gospel of Luke, we also know he wrote the book of Acts, because it is a continuation of the Gospel, and the introduction of Acts ties the two books together.

The authors of Scripture were a diverse group of men that included shepherds, fishermen, a tax collector, a physician, prophets, kings, and even the half-brother of Jesus. Many of the authors wrote only one book, while several wrote more than one. Moses wrote five—Genesis, Exodus, Leviticus, Numbers, and Deuteronomy—although Deuteronomy 34 was written by someone else, perhaps Joshua, because it records Moses' death. Moses also wrote at least one of the psalms. John also wrote five books—the Gospel of John, 1 John, 2 John, 3 John, and Revelation. Paul wrote thirteen books, nearly half of the books of the New Testament.

The situations from which the authors wrote were just as diverse as the authors themselves. The Bible was written over about a 1,500-year span in history, with the Old Testament being written roughly between 1,500–400 BC and the New Testament being written between about AD 40–95. The Bible was written in three languages—the Old Testament in Hebrew, and the New Testament in Greek, with some Aramaic mixed into both. It was written from three continents—Asia, Africa, and Europe. Men wrote from prisons, palaces, the wilderness, exile, and more.

Yet with all of this variety of authors, languages, times, and locations, the Bible is completely unified in its message of the story of Jesus and how we can be saved through trusting in him. This unity of message without compromise or error reveals that the Bible was not just written by men, but by men guided by the Holy Spirit to record God's Word faithfully.

2 Peter 1:20–21

Q. What does inspiration mean?

A. *Inspiration* is God moving the writers of Scripture to write what he wanted them to write.

If more than forty people attempted to write a book more than 1,500 years in three languages spread across three continents, there is no way that the finished project would be consistent. It would be all over the place! There is no way that the authors would present a consistent central message, and there would be contradictions and mistakes throughout the book. But that is exactly how the Bible was written, only it is absolutely consistent in its message about Jesus and it is without contradiction or error. So how did that happen? The answer is critical—the Bible was produced by God, not the human authors. God gave the Bible to us through guiding the human authors to write what he wanted written, in a process called "inspiration."

When we think of biblical inspiration, we can't think of that word the way we normally do, as when someone is inspired to paint a scene, write a song, cook a meal, or invent something new. What we mean in those cases is that a person got an idea or was moved in his or her creativity. That isn't what is in mind with biblical inspiration though. Biblical inspiration is the process of God moving the writers of Scripture to write his words in the Bible faithfully. We find this term in 2 Timothy 3:16.

> All Scripture is inspired by God and is profitable for teaching,
> for rebuking, for correcting, for training in righteousness.

The Greek word translated as "inspired" is sometimes translated as "breathed out," which adds color to what it means. The source of the Bible is God, and it comes from him, just as his breath does. While this verse is key for clarifying that all Scripture is inspired as well as the value of the Bible, it doesn't really explain *how* God inspired the writers. This is where 2 Peter 1:20–21 helps:

> Above all, you know this: No prophecy of Scripture comes from the prophet's own interpretation, because no prophecy ever came by the will of man; instead, men spoke from God as they were carried along by the Holy Spirit.

First, we see that the books of the Bible, prophecy, did not come from the writers themselves, but from God, echoing 2 Timothy 3:16. But we also see how this happened. The men were "carried along by the Holy Spirit." The Greek word for "carried along" was used one other place in the Bible, in Acts 27:8, which describes a ship being "carried along" by the wind. That picture really helps us understand the process more clearly. Just like the wind comes behind a sail and pushes a ship along, the Holy Spirit came behind the writers and moved them to write what he wanted them to write. But just as a ship has the ability to steer a course even with the wind pushing it, so did the writers of Scripture. We see this in how they wrote with different styles and different vocabularies—the Holy Spirit didn't merely dictate the words to the author. Rather, the Spirit allowed the writers to use their own experiences, vocabularies, rhetorical devices, and perspectives—and yet, every word was still *exactly* what God wanted. Inspiration truly is an amazing thing!

For example, John was a fisherman, so the Greek he used in his books was pretty basic. Luke, on the other hand, was a doctor, and his Greek was more developed. He also used much more medical language than the other authors, which would be expected. *Grace* was a word favored by Paul. It shows up in his writings far more than in the other authors' books. And this is why we have more than one Gospel. God gave each of the writers the freedom to tell the story of Jesus from his own perspective. Matthew told the story of Jesus the Messiah to the Jewish audience. Mark told the story of Jesus the Servant to the Roman audience. Luke told the story of Jesus the Son of Man to the Greek audience. And John told the story of Jesus the Son of God to the world. All tell the story of Jesus from their own perspectives without contradiction.

This is the beauty of inspiration.

2 Timothy 3:16; 2 Peter 1:20–21

4

Q. Is the Bible true?

A. Yes, the Bible is true and has no error.

The truthfulness of the Bible is one of the most important doctrines of the Christian faith. If we reject this one, all of the other doctrines move off of solid ground onto a slippery slope. Everything we know about God, Jesus, the Holy Spirit, sin, salvation, the church, and so much more is rooted in Scripture. So if we cannot be sure that the Bible is true, all of these other doctrines unravel, as does the core of our faith.

So we have to stand on the truthfulness of God's Word, but thankfully, we don't have to take that stand on blind faith. There are many ways we can know the Bible is true from inside the Bible and outside of it as well, such as archaeology, history, and manuscript evidence. But perhaps the most compelling evidence is Jesus' claim that the Bible is true. He said exactly so in his prayer to the Father in John 17:17.

> "Sanctify them by the truth; your word is truth."

There were a number of instances during Jesus' earthly ministry when he used Old Testament passages, and even single words and verb tenses, in debates with the religious leaders to prove an important point. And then there was this part of his Sermon on the Mount in Matthew 5:17–18.

> "Don't think that I came to abolish the Law or the Prophets. I did not come to abolish but to fulfill. For truly I tell you, until heaven and earth pass away, not the smallest letter or one stroke of a letter will pass away from the law until all things are accomplished."

The smallest letter in Hebrew is *yod*, which looks like an apostrophe. The smallest stroke is a small mark similar to what differentiates a capital *Q* from a capital *O*. Jesus was affirming that even these tiny marks in the Scripture matter and that all of Scripture will be fulfilled and be proven true.

But perhaps one of Jesus' strongest affirmations for the truthfulness of Scripture came when some of the religious leaders pressed him to show them a sign to prove he was the Messiah. Now, we have to remember that Jesus had been performing plenty of signs before this, but apparently they weren't good enough for the leaders. Jesus knew that no sign he would give would satisfy them—their hearts were hardened. So this is how he responded in Matthew 12:39–40:

> He answered them, "An evil and adulterous generation demands a sign, but no sign will be given to it except the sign of the prophet Jonah. For as Jonah was in the belly of the huge fish three days and three nights, so the Son of Man will be in the heart of the earth three days and three nights."

Jesus used Jonah in the fish's belly for three days and three nights as a sign pointing toward his burial for three days and three nights. Now, if Jesus didn't affirm that the book of Jonah is true and that Jonah actually was in a fish for three days and three nights, his sign falls apart. It isn't wise to use fiction to point toward reality. This is quite helpful because one of the Old Testament accounts that people have the most trouble with is this one—Jonah in the fish. It is comforting to know that Jesus held to the historicity of Jonah.

And that takes us to an important point of what the truthfulness of Scripture allows, such as figures of speech, idioms, and expressions. Some skeptics point out that Jesus was not in the grave three days and three nights. If you count from Friday afternoon through Sunday morning, you get three days and two nights. But this is not an error. In that day, any part of a day was considered one day and night, so because Jesus was in the grave for part of three days—Friday, Saturday, and Sunday—it was considered as three days and three nights.

The truthfulness of the Bible also allows for the faithful recording of sins, such as Satan's lies, without condoning them, as well as approximations (such as five thousand men being fed), free quotations (where a Bible passage is not quoted exactly), language of appearance (such as *sunrise*), and different accounts of the same event, as long as there is no contradiction between them.

The sign above the cross is a good example of that last one. Matthew records that the sign read *This Is Jesus, the King of the Jews* (Matt. 27:37), Mark recorded that it read *The King of the Jews* (Mark 15:26), Luke that it read *This Is the King of the Jews* (Luke 23:38), and John that it read *Jesus of Nazareth, the King of the Jews* (John 19:19). This may seem like a contradiction at first, but each author wrote from his own perspective, and they actually did not contradict each other. The full sign read, *This Is Jesus of Nazareth the King of the Jews.* For whatever reason, none of the four writers were compelled to record the full statement; instead, each just shared the part that he considered most important. Four accounts of one true event.

God has given us his true Word so that we can have full confidence in what we read in it and in turn so that we can place our trust in Jesus. Following Jesus takes faith, but it is certainly not blind faith.

John 17:17; Matthew 5:17–18

5

Q. How is the Bible true if it was written by men?

A. The Holy Spirit guided the process of men writing the Bible to protect it from error.

We can have full confidence that the Bible is free from error because the Holy Spirit guided the process. Men on their own would not have been able to write the Bible without error, but the Holy Spirit's involvement enabled them to do just that.

The Holy Spirit wasn't done with the Bible with inspiration, though. He also helps us to read the Bible correctly as he reveals truth to us through what is called "illumination" and also to properly understand what the writers meant through what is called "interpretation."

Illumination, or being enlightened, is described in Ephesians 1:18.

> I pray that the eyes of your heart may be enlightened so that you may know what is the hope of his calling, what is the wealth of his glorious inheritance in the saints.

Because God is so far beyond us (Isa. 55:8), we cannot know the mind of God without the Holy Spirit helping us see and understand his truth (see 1 Cor. 2:9–3:2). So the Holy Spirit helped the writers record truth, and then he helps us to read and understand that truth.

But at the same time, the Holy Spirit helps us to interpret what the writers of Scripture meant—what God is communicating to us. There is always one, and only one, proper interpretation of Scripture. There is only one meaning for what we read. For example, when you come to a red octagonal sign with a white border and large white letters that read STOP, you don't have a discussion with the passengers in the car about what it means to them. If you drive through that STOP sign and a police officer pulls you over, you won't get out of a ticket by explaining that you interpreted that as stop talking, so you did. No, we know that sign has one meaning—one interpretation: stop your car. The Holy Spirit guides us to interpret Scripture properly so that God's truth is communicated to us, as we read in Psalm 119:34.

> Help me understand your instruction,
> and I will obey it
> and follow it with all my heart.

Part of how we interpret the Bible properly is by studying the Bible in its context—what surrounds it. For example, if someone were to shout out to you, "Stop, drop, and roll!" you would not stop walking, fall to the ground, and look for a piece of bread. You would know from the context that *roll* means to roll your body. When we read the Bible, we need to keep in mind cultural context—the Bible is a Near Eastern book from 2,000 years ago, not a modern Western book; historical context—what was happening at that time; literary context—what the book's genre is, such as prophetic or Gospel; canonical context—where the book is in the "canon" or collection of Scripture; and then the section, paragraph, and sentence context. Reading the Bible in the proper context is one of the main ways that we can properly interpret the Bible with the Holy Spirit's guidance.

Inspiration, illumination, and interpretation work together to form the backbone of how we are to read and study the Bible properly. And it is when we properly read and study the Bible that we will be able to apply it and live in a way that pleases God and brings him glory.

2 Timothy 3:16; 2 Peter 1:20–21

Q. How is the Bible organized?

A. The Bible contains 66 books—39 in the Old
Testament and 27 in the New Testament.

The Bible is divided into two main parts: the Old Testament, which was written between roughly 1500–400 BC, and the New Testament, which was written between about AD 40–95. These two parts are also sometimes called the Old Covenant and the New Covenant to more closely connect them with the Mosaic Covenant, which provides the context for the Old Testament, and the New Covenant, which provides the context for the New Testament.

There were also a number of extrabiblical books written during these times, such as those contained in the Apocrypha, Pseudepigrapha, and the Gnostic Gospels. These books were not included in the Bible because they failed the fivefold test that the early church used to identify the genuine Scriptures given by God. The five tests were:

- **Divine Inspiration:** Did the book directly claim to be inspired by God (such as including the phrase "thus says the Lord") or show clear signs of inspiration?
- **Prophetic Authorship:** Was the author a prophet or an apostle or a close associate writing under the authority of one?
- **Church Acceptance:** Was the book widely accepted by the church and included as part of their worship gatherings?
- **Absence of Error:** Was the book free of errors in history, theology, and so forth?
- **Agreement with Scripture:** Do the central teachings of the book align with the teachings of the other books of the Bible?

Although the sixty-six books of the Bible were recognized in practice earlier, threats to the core teachings of the church led to two gatherings of the church leaders, called councils, to formally recognize which books were part of the Bible. The thirty-nine Old Testament books were officially recognized in this way at the Council of Jamnia in AD 90, while the twenty-seven New Testament books were officially recognized at the Council of Carthage in AD 397.

While some people are concerned whether or not the early church chose the right books to be in the Bible, when we stop and think about it, we shouldn't be worried. God gave them wisdom in the tests they used, but more importantly the same Holy Spirit who overshadowed the inspiration of the Bible surely also guided the formation of the sixty-six books of the Bible as well.

Q. What are the five divisions of the Old Testament?

A. The Old Testament is made up of the law, history, writings, major prophets, and minor prophets.

The books of the Old Testament are not organized in chronological order, but are instead based on literary style. The first five books we see are the books of the Law, Genesis through Deuteronomy. These five books are also known as the Torah or the Pentateuch and are ordered in somewhat of a chronological order. Within the books of the Law we learn about creation, the Fall, God's forming of a covenant people through Abraham, and the tracing of that people into Egypt and back to the border of the Promised Land, having received the Mosaic Law along the way.

The next twelve books are the books of History from Joshua through Esther. These books pick up where the Law left off and follow the people's conquest of the Promised Land, life under the Judges, and then under the united and the divided monarchies, and finally the falls of both the northern and southern kingdoms, the captivities, and the eventual return into the land.

The next five books are the books of the Writings, or poetry, from Job through Song of Songs. These books describe God, worship, the meaning of life, suffering, and wisdom.

The next five books are the books of the major prophets from Isaiah through Daniel, followed by the twelve books of the minor prophets from Hosea through Malachi. These books describe God's prophetic warnings and encouragements to his people and set the stage for the coming Messiah.

Q. What is the difference between the major and minor prophets?

A. The difference between the major and minor prophets is the length of the books, not their importance.

No, the minor prophets are not less important. Let's just clear that up right off the bat. The only reason the minor prophets are called that is because they are shorter than the five major prophets—Isaiah, Jeremiah, Lamentations, Ezekiel, and Daniel. While the major prophets, especially Isaiah, Jeremiah, and Daniel, tend to get more attention, their shorter counterparts are full of great content too.

In the book of Hosea, we see a beautiful picture of God's faithful covenant love to us through Hosea's marriage to an unfaithful wife named Gomer. In Amos, we are shown the vital importance of sincere worship and social justice. In Jonah we see God's heart for the nations—even the ruthless enemies of his people. And in Habakkuk, we interact with some hard questions of life, such as why the wicked prosper.

The minor prophets also contain some of the most beloved and meaningful prophecies about Jesus in the Bible. Micah 5:2 tells us that the Messiah would be born in the tiny town of Bethlehem. Zechariah 9:9 reveals that the Messiah would enter Jerusalem on a donkey, which Jesus did on Palm Sunday. Zechariah 11:12–13 tells us that the Messiah would be betrayed for thirty pieces of silver and Zechariah 13:7 that the shepherd would be struck down and the sheep would scatter. Finally, Malachi 3:1 tells us that a forerunner, who would be John the Baptist, would prepare the way for the arrival of the Messiah.

Q. What are the five divisions of the New Testament?

A. The New Testament is made up of the Gospels, history, Pauline epistles, general epistles, and prophecy.

Like the Old Testament, the books of the New Testament are not organized in chronological order, but by literary style. First come the four Gospels—Matthew through John. These books tell the story of Jesus' life and ministry on earth from his birth to the point of his ascension. Matthew, Mark, and Luke are known as the Synoptic Gospels because they describe these events from a similar view (*synoptic* means "same view"), while John takes a much different approach. The authors of the four Gospels wrote each of their books to different primary audiences and had different goals in how they portrayed Jesus.

Matthew wrote to the Jews to show that Jesus is the long-awaited Messiah. This is why Matthew used more Old Testament quotes than any other Gospel. Mark wrote to the Romans to show that Jesus is the obedient servant, which is why he showed Jesus in almost constant action. Luke wrote to the Greeks to show that Jesus is Son of Man. He emphasized Jesus' humanity and his teachings. John wrote to the entire world to show that Jesus is Son of God. John didn't care much about chronology and actually only covered a brief period of Jesus' ministry. He was more concerned with structuring his Gospel to clearly show the deity of Jesus, such as through his seven sign miracles and seven "I Am" statements.

After the Gospels comes the one book of history in the New Testament—Acts. Acts was written by Luke as the second half of his Gospel account and picks up with the ascension of Jesus and traces the development of the early church all the way until Paul's imprisonment in Rome.

Next come the thirteen epistles written by Paul—Romans through Philemon. The first nine are Paul's epistles written to churches in order from longest to shortest. The last four are the epistles he wrote to individuals, again arranged by length.

Next come the eight General Epistles—Hebrews through Jude—written by people other than Paul (although some believe Paul wrote Hebrews). These again are structured from longest to shortest.

Finally, we reach the one book of prophecy, Revelation, to conclude the New Testament. This book describes John's vision of Jesus' return that God gave him on the island of Patmos.

Q. What is an epistle?

A. *An epistle* is a letter, usually written to local churches in different cities.

We don't write letters very often any more. It's much easier for us to send an e-mail or a text instead. But in the New Testament period, writing a letter was about the only way you could communicate with someone far away. Letters, or epistles, in that day were structured a little differently from our letters or e-mails, and certainly our texts. The first part of their letters was actually what we tend to put last—who the letter is from. This was followed by the names of the recipient or recipients and a brief greeting. For example, here is how Paul began the epistle to the Philippians:

> Paul and Timothy, servants of Christ Jesus:
> To all the saints in Christ Jesus who are in Philippi, including the overseers and deacons.
> Grace to you and peace from God our Father and the Lord Jesus Christ. (Phil. 1:1–2)

You will notice that Paul used a very similar greeting of grace and peace, always in that order, in most of his letters. After the opening salutation, the writer shared a prayer or blessing such as in Philippians 1:3, where Paul continued with "I give thanks to my God for every remembrance of you" followed by several verses of encouragement.

The body of the letter came next, and once again, Paul followed a specific pattern in his epistles. Paul would always share doctrine first and then follow that up with practical application of what he had just taught. For example, Romans 1–11 is the doctrine of salvation, while Romans 12–16 is application of how we live out our salvation. The closing greeting was the last part of the letter where the author would greet other people besides the recipients, or people the writer wanted to single out. Paul's closing greeting in Romans 16:3–16 was one of his longest.

While the epistles were written to specific recipients, it is clear from several that the writers always intended for them to be shared with churches in the surrounding cities. This was one of the evidences for including the epistles we have in the Bible—because the letters were copied and shared with other churches as part of their worship.

Q. What is the Bible about?

A. The Bible is the story of God providing Jesus to save us from our sin.

It was Easter Sunday—*the* Easter Sunday—and two disciples were walking the six miles back from Jerusalem to the town of Emmaus. As the pair traveled, they were discussing what had happened in the city the week before. They talked excitedly and even argued some as they tried to get their arms around what they had witnessed.

At some point the two noticed a man who had been traveling alone had joined them. "What are you two talking about?" he asked.

The two stopped in their tracks. Their faces fell, part in disbelief, part in sadness.

"Are you the only person who hasn't heard the things that just took place?"

"What things?" the man responded.

The two told the lone traveler what had happened to Jesus the week before—both the highs and the lows. They ended their account with the news that some had reported that Jesus was alive, but when some of the other disciples had gone to the tomb to investigate, they hadn't seen him.

The two disciples on the road had the facts of what had happened right. They just hadn't reached the point of understanding, and believing, that what they had heard about Jesus being alive was true. They had not experienced the joy of the resurrection.

At this point, the man—who was Jesus whom they were prevented from recognizing—replied:

He said to them, "How foolish and slow you are to believe all that the prophets have spoken! Wasn't it necessary for the Messiah to suffer these things and enter into his glory?" Then beginning with Moses and all the Prophets, he interpreted for them the things concerning himself in all the Scriptures. (Luke 24:25–27)

It's a little jarring to see Jesus call someone else foolish, so we want to be sure we understand why he did. The two disciples were foolish because they had all that they needed—the Old Testament—yet did not grasp what it was really about. They knew the Old Testament prophets had written about the Messiah, but they, like essentially all others in their context, probably thought the Messiah would be a military or political leader, rising to power and defeating the enemies of the Jews—the Romans, in that day. Instead, they saw the one they thought was the Messiah, not crushing Rome, but being crushed by Rome on the cross.

That's why Jesus had to explain to them the gospel, the good news. He was the Messiah, but a different kind of Messiah than they expected. He was a suffering Messiah. He came to give his life as a ransom. And he walked them through how all the Bible is one big story about him.

This is a critical passage because it provides the proper lens through which we read all of Scripture. We don't read passages and stories by themselves—we read each one as part of the bigger story of God sending Jesus to provide forgiveness for sin. Everything we read in both the Old Testament and New Testament is designed to help us understand God's holiness, our sin and need of salvation, and the plan to send Jesus to pay our sin penalty in our place and rise from the dead to defeat sin and death. This is what the Emmaus disciples missed, and this is what we need to be sure to see.

It might be helpful to think of the Bible's big story in six main "acts":

- **Act 1: God Creates Everything Good (Genesis 1–2)**
  God created everything good, and Adam and Eve enjoyed a perfect relationship with each other and with God. Their worship and service to God were perfect and completely satisfying.

- **Act 2: Adam and Eve Sin and All of Creation Falls (Genesis 3)**
  Adam and Eve chose to rebel against God by disobeying him. At that very instant, Adam and Eve fell, and they took creation down with them. Their perfect relationship with God was broken, as was their

relationship with each other. Nothing in creation was as it should have been any longer. Worship and service to God became difficult and people began to try to search for fulfillment in ways other than God.

- ### Act 3: Mankind Tries to Make Things Right and Fails (Genesis 4–Malachi 4)

  The rest of the Old Testament records mankind's struggle with sin. At times we see people rebelling against God even more, and at other times we see people trying to make things right with God by trusting in religion, whom their ancestors were, or their higher level of obedience to God than others around them. Of course none of these ways work. But as sad as this part of the story is, it is saturated with hope. God gradually revealed more and more of his plan to provide the one way people could be saved: through Jesus.

- ### Act 4: Jesus Comes to Provide Salvation (Matthew 1–John 21)

  Jesus is born, lives a sinless perfectly righteous life, performs miracles to prove he is the Son of God, and teaches about God's kingdom. Jesus is rejected by his own people, arrested and crucified, and then he dies, is buried, and rises again. When we trust in Jesus, he takes our sin and pays its penalty and gives us his righteousness in its place.

- ### Act 5: The Church Begins the Mission of Sharing the Gospel (Acts 1–Revelation 20)

  Jesus returns to his place of glory with the Father, but just before he does, he gives his followers the task to carry on the mission of sharing the gospel. He also promises to send the Holy Spirit, and when he arrives, he empowers the church to boldly proclaim Jesus. The church grows and continues through today.

- ### Act 6: Jesus Returns and Makes Everything Good Again (Revelation 21–22)

  One day, Jesus will return, and when he does, he will make everything right again. Sin and death will finally be done away with and all who have trusted in him will receive new, glorified bodies and live with God forever in the perfect new creation.

That is the story the Bible tells. That is his story.

Luke 24:16–44; 2 Timothy 3:14–15

Q. What else does the Bible teach us?

A. The Bible teaches us how we can live to please God.

While the big story of the Bible centers on Jesus and how he came to provide salvation for those who trust in him, that isn't all the Bible teaches. It also shows us how we can live in a way that pleases God in response to the salvation he has given us in Christ. That nuance is critical. We live to please God not so that we can earn his love and favor, but because he has *already* given it to us fully in Christ. In other words, we obey *from* God's acceptance, not *for* God's acceptance.

As we think about how God has been so kind and gracious to us and how Jesus laid down his life for us to provide the way our sins have been forgiven, the Holy Spirit goes to work in our hearts and changes our desires from pleasing ourselves to pleasing God. We please him because we want to, not because we have to. Because obeying God gives us joy and pleases us as we please him. It is a matter of heart change, not behavior change. A changed heart will lead to changed behavior, but changed behavior does not necessarily lead to a changed heart. And that is what God wants from us—hearts that are changed to love and please him in all we do as acts of worship.

Thankfully, we don't have to guess how to please God—the Bible tells us:

> All Scripture is inspired by God and is profitable for teaching, for rebuking, for correcting, for training in righteousness, so that the man of God may be complete, equipped for every good work. (2 Tim. 3:16–17)

The Bible is full of instructions for how we can please God. We are to put away the works of the flesh, we are to be part of a local church, we are to show others the love of Christ and tell them the gospel. When we read these imperatives, we should want to live them out as fully as we can. And the amazing thing is, obeying not only pleases God, but it is for our good as well. God's commands are both for his glory and our good.

But there will be times when our sinful flesh drowns out our hearts' desire to please God and we will give in. The Bible also helps us in these times by correcting us and helping us repent of our sin and turn back to God.

One way we can know we are saved is a changed heart that loves God more. Another way is a desire to read the Bible more to learn how to please him. And still another way is joyfully obeying God.

Salvation. Heart change. Life change. That is the gospel.

2 Timothy 3:16; Psalm 19:7–11

Q. What do the Ten Commandments teach us?

A. The Ten Commandments teach us to love God and love people.

We often see our faith as something just between us and God—one to one. We focus so much on being right with God personally, and we don't often think of others. While our faith is indeed a personal faith, it is not *just* a personal faith. God wants our faith to carry over to others as we love them. And that makes sense. God loves others so he would want us to love them as well.

This is at the heart of the Ten Commandments. While the Ten Commandments are no more important than God's other commandments (there are 613 total commandments in the Old Testament), they do provide a snapshot of God's heart behind all of them. And it is critical that we see that—God's commandments are given for a reason. They are not arbitrary; neither are they designed to rob us of our joy and limit what we can do in life. Each of God's commandments reflects his character and leads to loving him more and loving others more.

Most of us probably get the importance of loving God more and why he commands that. But what about loving other people more? Does that really matter to God, and if so, does it matter as much as loving him?

While in one sense it is more important to love God than others because he should be our greatest treasure, it isn't quite that clear-cut. The Ten Commandments weave loving God and loving people together. If we truly love God, we *will* love others. We cannot truly love God without loving others. Neither can we truly love others without loving God, because the love we need to have for them comes from him—unconditional, selfless love that we don't have within ourselves.

So it is more important that we love God, but when we do, we will love others. Our love for others proves our love for God, so in that sense, our love for others is just as important. Here is how Proverbs 14:31 puts it:

> The one who oppresses the poor person insults his Maker,
> but one who is kind to the needy honors him.

If we fail to love the poor and oppress them or even allow them to be oppressed, who are we really offending? That's right—God. And if we are kind to the poor, whom do we really honor? Right again—God. Jesus said something similar in Matthew 25:31–46. When we care for the poor, we do that for him; when we fail to care for them, we do that against him. That is how much God cares about us loving others.

Here is one other passage from the Old Testament that shows God's deep desire that we love others. God gave the following instructions in Leviticus on how to harvest a field:

> "When you reap the harvest of your land, you are not to reap
> all the way to the edge of your field or gather the gleanings of
> your harvest. Leave them for the poor and the resident alien; I
> am the LORD your God." (Lev. 23:22)

God commanded that his people purposefully leave the grain in the corners of their fields for the poor. Can you imagine how challenging that might have been for so many families that were struggling to make ends meet? But that is God's heart. He cares for the poor, and when the farmers obeyed his commands, they surely had enough. After all, God is the One who provides the rain and causes the crops to grow!

Loving God and loving people. That is the heart behind the Ten Commandments.

Proverbs 14:31; Matthew 25:31–46

Q. What are the first four commandments about?

A. The first four commandments are about our relationship with God.

The Ten Commandments are commonly divided into two tables, or parts. The first table consists of four commandments that focus on our relationship with God and address not having any gods other than God, not making or worshiping idols, not misusing the Lord's name, and remembering the Sabbath to keep it holy. We can think of these as vertical commandments, and they can be summarized by Deuteronomy 6:5.

> Love the LORD your God with all your heart, with all your soul, and with all your strength.

If we love God with all of our heart, soul, and strength, we will not have any other gods besides him, make or worship idols, misuse his name, or fail to honor and worship him as part of our normal rhythm of life. Love is the key. This motivation of love is found just before God gave the Ten Commandments in what is considered the preamble of the Ten Commandments:

> Then God spoke all these words: I am the LORD your God, who brought you out of the land of Egypt, out of the place of slavery. (Exod. 20:1–2)

As God prepared to share the commandments that followed with his people, he wanted them to stop and consider who he is and what he had done. He was not just the Lord God to them; he was the Lord *their* God. He had a relationship with them, and he also had a past with them. The children of Israel had seen what God had done on their behalf—how he had delivered them out of slavery in Egypt through miracles. This was God's way of reminding his people of his power and his goodness. That is why they were to obey what he was about to tell them—because he is all-powerful and has the authority to tell them what to do, but also because he cared for them and had proven his love for them. Knowing who God is and what he had done for them should have been the motivation they needed to follow God with a fearful love—a combination of respect for their Creator with love for their Deliverer. And this is what we want to help our kids develop too. We want our kids to respect the authority of God and take him seriously, but at the same time we want them to love God deeply. Respect without love leads toward cold obedience. Love without respect leads to permissive living. But respect and love coupled together lead to joyful obedience.

Exodus 20:1–11; Deuteronomy 5:1–15

Q. What are the last six commandments about?

A. The last six commandments are about our relationships with others.

The second table of the Ten Commandments focuses on our relationships with others—our horizontal relationships. These commandments address honoring our parents, not committing murder or adultery, and not stealing, giving false witness, or coveting things that don't belong to us. These six commandments are summarized by the last part of Leviticus 19:18.

> Do not take revenge or bear a grudge against members of your community, but love your neighbor as yourself; I am the LORD.

The idea of loving our neighbors as ourselves doesn't suggest that we are supposed to have a vain, self-serving love of ourselves. Instead, it means that just as we take care of ourselves—such as eating when we are hungry, resting when we are tired, and protecting ourselves from harm—we should do so for others too. If our neighbor is hungry and has no food, we should care enough to give him or her food. We see this in each of the commandments of the second table. If we break any one of them, we harm someone else by our failure to love them.

So what is our motivation for loving others besides God's commandment that we do so? We find the answer at the very end of Leviticus 19:18 and also in the first table of commandments that precedes this one. Our love for others is based on our love for God. If we love God, we will also love others—people whom he created, who are image-bearers of God, and whom he loves. God loves people, we love God, so we love people too. It's that simple.

Exodus 20:13–17; Deuteronomy 5:17–22

Q. What is the first commandment?

A. The first commandment is to have no gods other than God.

The children of Israel had lived as slaves in Egypt for more than four hundred years. That's a long time to live in a land where the people worshiped a variety of gods. That is going to rub off on you sooner or later. To make matters worse, when God gave the Ten Commandments the children of Israel were heading toward the Promised Land, which was inhabited by people who worshiped a bunch of different gods too. False gods were behind them, ahead of them, and all around them, which explains why God's first command was for his people to not have any other gods besides him:

Do not have other gods besides me. (Exod. 20:3)

In some ways this first commandment is a linchpin for all the rest. If we get this one right, the others will fall into place. It's just as important for us today as it was for the children of Israel then because we too are surrounded by a number of false gods, only they don't come in the form of a stone or wooden idol (which God addresses next) or through some form of organized religion. Our idols look more like homes, wealth, comfort, family, careers, grades, sports, clothes, and even ourselves. We can make a god out of just about anything, and when we do, we set ourselves up to break God's other commandments.

We covet and steal because we have made a god out of wealth and possessions. If only we can have that one item, or that certain amount in our bank account, we will be happy. That is what will truly satisfy us, not God.

We lie because someone else is a threat to our success or our happiness. We take credit for something we didn't do at work to get ahead, or we don't report all of our taxable income because we would rather use the money we'd have to pay in taxes for a vacation.

We commit adultery because we want to feed our desires of the flesh; we want what we believe will make us happy, no matter the cost. No matter who it hurts.

The first commandment calls for us to put all of these other gods, and the resulting sins, away from us. It is a commandment that we must obey not just once, but every day—even every minute of the day—as we continually go to war against our sinful nature to find or create other gods besides the one true God. But when we obey this commandment we will experience the true joy and satisfaction that we long for deep down within us, because it is only found in a relationship with God.

Exodus 20:3; Deuteronomy 5:7

Q. What is the second commandment?

A. The second commandment is not to make or worship idols.

People tend to need to see something, and perhaps even touch it, to know it is real. That is why Thomas said he would not believe Jesus had risen unless he was able to see and touch his wounds (John 20:25). Thomas needed that extra layer of evidence that Jesus had truly risen from the dead. And this is what drives idol worship—creating an object of worship that can be seen and touched. The second commandment clearly forbids all such idolatry and comes with a stern warning:

> Do not make an idol for yourself, whether in the shape of anything in the heavens above or on the earth below or in the waters under the earth. Do not bow in worship to them, and do not serve them; for I, the LORD your God, am a jealous God, punishing the children for the fathers' iniquity, to the third and fourth generations of those who hate me, but showing faithful love to a thousand generations of those who love me and keep my commands. (Exod. 20:4–6)

We are not to make any kind of idol fashioned after anything on earth, under the waters, under the earth, or in the heavens. That leaves nothing out including—God himself. We are not even to make an image of God to worship because he is Spirit (John 4:24) and there is no way to reflect his infinite character in a finite object. Any image of God lowers our view of him—it makes him small and limited—and harms our worship of who he truly is. Beyond that, it is foolish to make an idol of anything and worship it. Isaiah encouraged us to think about the absurdity of idolatry this way in Isaiah 44:

A man cuts down a tree and burns half of it to keep warm. Then he makes an idol out of the other half to worship. The same substance—part burned up, the other part worshiped. It makes no sense.

Paul pointed out the foolishness of idolatry too when he preached before a crowd in Athens. As Paul looked around and saw a number of idols in the city, he challenged the people to think about what they were doing. We see this story in Acts 17:24–25. God, who made everything in the world (including the substances from which the idols were made), cannot be made by the hands of a person. God isn't served by human hands either. God doesn't need to be dusted! He doesn't need to be fed!

Despite the foolishness of idolatry, the children of Israel would struggle with that sin for many generations, ultimately leading to God disciplining his people by sending two foreign armies to defeat them and take them away into captivity. That is why God added a strong warning to this commandment. He is jealous of the worship due him and will not watch his people give that worship to an idol. It dishonors him, but it also hurts the idol worshiper. God is the greatest good, and if we worship anything except from him, we are worshiping something that is not as good—something that will not satisfy us the way God does. Because of this, it is loving of God to discipline idol worshipers to draw them back to him.

God's statement about punishing children for three or four generations for their fathers' sin seems unjust, and it would be if God was saying that he punishes the innocent for the guilt of the prior generation. Thankfully, that is not what he means. God is warning us here that our sins often carry over from generation to generation. If we worship idols, there is a good chance our children will learn that behavior from us and commit the same exact sin as well. This is what God wants us to think carefully about here. Idol worship is not something someone does as an aside; it is a way of life that easily influences others. That is at the heart of God's warning.

But we also see God's merciful heart expressed at the very end of the warning. While our sins may carry over and impact three or four generations, God wants to show his faithful love to a thousand generations. His love is that much greater than our sin! And that is the love we experience when we obey him.

Exodus 20:4–6; Deuteronomy 5:8–10

18

Q. What is the third commandment?

A. The third commandment is not to misuse the Lord's name.

We tend to have a much different view of names today than God has. Most of us choose children's names based on what we like—what sounds good. A name for us is simply a way to identify someone. And that is OK, but it is not what names were meant to do in the Bible. Sure names helped identify someone, but they did more than that. Names reflected a person's character; they were a symbol of who a person was.

That is why God changed people's names in the Bible such as Abram to Abraham. Abram means "exalted father," but God changed his name to Abraham, which means "father of many" because he wanted to emphasize the nation Abraham would produce. God's value of names is also why he gave some parents the name they were to call their children, such as Mary and Joseph, who were to name their son Jesus. The name Jesus means "the Lord Saves," which revealed what he would do. But even more important is God's name—actually, his *names*. God has given us several different names that reflect something different about his character. God's most holy name is Yahweh, which is how he identified himself to Moses before the Exodus (Exod. 3:14).

It is for this reason—because names mean so much to God—that we read this in the third commandment:

> Do not misuse the name of the LORD your God, because the LORD will not leave anyone unpunished who misuses his name. (Exod. 20:7)

We often think that this commandment mainly forbids a person from using God's name in a profane way. That is certainly one way we should avoid misusing God's name, but it is not the only way, and perhaps not even the primary way God had in mind here.

Perhaps another way that we might be more likely to break this commandment is when we speak lightly of God and fail to speak of him with the reverence and honor due him. Yes, God is our loving Father whom we may call Abba—Daddy—but he is also the creator of the universe. He is holy and all-powerful. So we need to be careful not to speak of him in a trivial or light way, such as calling him the "big man upstairs."

A third way we can break this commandment is by misrepresenting God—by saying what he has not said. This is probably what the commandment mostly addresses. You may have heard someone say, "God is telling me to do XYZ" or someone else saying, "I promise as God as my witness!" We need to be very careful before telling someone else that God has told us to do or say something. Here is the warning directed toward a false prophet—someone in the Bible who claimed to receive an authoritative word from God to share with others:

> "But the prophet who presumes to speak a message in my name
> that I have not commanded him to speak, or who speaks in the
> name of other gods—that prophet must die." (Deut. 18:20)

Just as the Old Testament prophets were evaluated by their absolute faithfulness to God's word, we too need to be careful not to misrepresent God in any way. At the same time, we need to refrain from making promises based on God as our witness. God is not our witness in that way. We are his witnesses to the world. Jesus would later forbid anyone from using God's name in an oath (Matt. 5:33–37; 23:16–22) so it is best for us simply to make promises and follow through with integrity.

God's name matters. It is holy, and it is to be revered. If we always strive to honor God in all we say, then we will safeguard ourselves from breaking the third commandment.

Exodus 20:7; Deuteronomy 5:11

Q. What is the fourth commandment?

A. The fourth commandment is to remember the Sabbath to keep it holy.

To really understand God's intent for the Sabbath, it is helpful to look back just before this commandment was given when the people were hungry and in the wilderness without food. When the people grumbled that they were hungry, Moses asked God what he should do. God told Moses that he would provide manna from heaven and this bread would be given every day of the week except for one.

> Then the LORD said to Moses, "I am going to rain bread from heaven for you. The people are to go out each day and gather enough for that day. This way I will test them to see whether or not they will follow my instructions. On the sixth day, when they prepare what they bring in, it will be twice as much as they gather on other days." (Exod. 16:4–5)

God wanted to test his people to see if they trusted him to provide for their needs. Not surprisingly, the people failed this test because they could not bring themselves to believe God would provide. Trusting God is at the heart of the fourth commandment.

> Remember the Sabbath day, to keep it holy: You are to labor six days and do all your work, but the seventh day is a Sabbath to the LORD your God. You must not do any work—you, your son or daughter, your male or female servant, your livestock, or the resident alien who is within your city gates. For the LORD made the heavens and the earth, the sea, and everything in

them in six days; then he rested on the seventh day. Therefore the LORD blessed the Sabbath day and declared it holy. (Exod. 20:8–11)

The word *Sabbath* means "stopping." It is the day when God's people were to stop their normal work, rest, and worship God. For the children of Israel, the Sabbath was observed on Saturday, the last day of the week. For Christians, Sunday, the Lord's Day, has become the day for honoring the Sabbath through rest and worship.

So why does God want us to rest on the Sabbath? In part because we need it—God designed us for a rhythm of work and rest. Our need for sleep reminds us of this—we can only work, or even just be awake, for so long before we have to stop and rest.

But God's purpose of the Sabbath goes beyond that; being reminded every day of our weaknesses and our needs drives us to deeper dependence on God. We rest because it helps us remember that God is the One who truly provides. Just as God wanted the children of Israel to recognize that he was providing what they needed each day and to trust him, rest in him, and worship him because of his goodness, we are to do the same. Setting aside one day a week to rest and worship with our local church family humbles us and reminds us that it is not by our effort that we live each day, but by God's grace.

While people disagree on what honoring the Sabbath looks like for Christians today, it is clear that we are to obey this commandment as God leads us. Notice that it is rooted in God's creative work. God created the world in six days and rested on the seventh. For this reason, we too are to obey this command and rest and worship as part of our normal rhythm of life following the pattern that he gave us.

Exodus 20:8–11; Deuteronomy 5:12–15

Q. What is the fifth commandment?

A. The fifth commandment is to honor your father and mother.

The fifth commandment moves us to the second table of the Ten Commandments and shifts our attention to our relationships with others. The first horizontal commandment concerns one of our most important relationships, the one between parents and children.

> Honor your father and your mother so that you may have a long life in the land that the LORD your God is giving you. (Exod. 20:12)

This is the perfect commandment to bridge between the two tables because, while it mostly focuses on our relationship with our earthly parents, there is also a sense in which it applies to our relationship with God, our heavenly Father. We honor our earthly parents and we also honor our heavenly Father. Turning it around, parents also have the responsibility of representing God in so many ways to their children. A child's view of God is shaped largely by his or her relationship with his or her parents, namely the father. If a father is stern, his child will probably form a view of God as being stern. If a father is distant, the child will probably see God as distant. If a father is loving, his child will more likely see God as loving.

Getting back to the fifth commandment, it is important that we understand that it calls on children to honor their parents, not just obey them. Honoring is so much more than obeying. To obey is to do what you are told, but to honor is to love and respect and then to obey out of that love and respect. We can obey without honoring someone, but when we honor them, we will obey as well. We can see why God wants children to honor their parents—it parallels how we are to honor and obey him.

While this commandment is one-directional—a child honoring his or her parents—we see the other side of the equation elsewhere in the Bible:

> Fathers, don't stir up anger in your children, but bring them up
> in the training and instruction of the Lord. (Eph. 6:4)

Parents can help their children obey the fifth commandment by not provoking them to anger and by training and teaching them about God. And that is critical. When parents fail to point their children to the gospel, they withhold the greatest good from their children—the one thing for which we all long whether we realize it or not—God. But when parents disciple their children and point them to the beauty of the gospel each day, they give them the greatest gift they can give. All children are a blessing from God (Ps. 127:3), and parents have the amazing privilege of raising them in the Lord. Children in turn are to honor their parents. Families flourish when this happens in our homes, and when families flourish, our communities do as well. The fifth commandment has far more than just functional families in mind, then—it also positions God's people to expand the gospel to the nations.

Exodus 20:12; Deuteronomy 5:16

Q. What is the sixth commandment?

A. The sixth commandment is not to murder.

Life is a precious gift given to us by God, the Author of life, and for that reason we are not to take it lightly. We are to respect all life, and one of the best and simplest ways to do that is by not taking someone else's life from them, which is the sixth commandment:

Do not murder. (Exod. 20:13)

The King James Version of the Bible translated this commandment as "Thou shalt not kill," which has led to some confusion about what this commandment is about. The problem is that "kill" is not the best way to translate the Hebrew word here. "Murder," the wrongful and unjust taking of a life, is more accurate. That nuance is helpful to know because elsewhere in Scripture God commands capital punishment for certain sins and he also sends his people into battle, so the idea of all killing cannot be in mind in this commandment, but rather unjust killing.

With that said, this is perhaps the one commandment that most people think they have down pretty well. We've never murdered anyone, let alone killed anyone. But when we get to some of the other commandments, we have to acknowledge that we may not follow them as well. There are times when we have had other gods besides God. We do have idols in our lives, take God's name too lightly, and fail to remember the Sabbath as we should. We also don't honor our parents always or as well as we should. But when we get to "Do not murder," we tend to breathe a sigh of relief and think we finally got to one we can keep pretty easily.

But that's the problem—we cannot keep this one as easily as we think. In fact, when we consider what Jesus said about this commandment, we see that it is actually incredibly difficult to keep.

Early in the Sermon on the Mount, Jesus mentioned this commandment to the people gathered, but then he said that failing to keep this commandment begins in the heart (Matt. 5:21–26). Our concern should be not having hate in our hearts, not just not murdering anyone. So while most of us have never murdered anyone, we have all hated others, meaning we are all murderers in our hearts. And God sees and cares about what is in our hearts.

It is fitting that perhaps the easiest commandment to keep externally is also perhaps the hardest commandment to keep internally. It reminds us of how deeply sin has rotted us on the inside and how desperately we need heart transformation by the power of the gospel and forgiveness through Christ.

Exodus 20:13; Deuteronomy 5:17; Matthew 5:21–26

22

Q. What is the seventh commandment?

A. The seventh commandment is not to commit adultery.

The first marriage ceremony took place in Eden when Adam took Eve to be his wife as God looked on. We see this written about marriage:

> This is why a man leaves his father and mother and bonds with his wife, and they become one flesh. Both the man and his wife were naked, yet felt no shame. (Gen. 2:24–25)

The bonding in mind here is mostly through sexual intimacy; a primary way God designed two people to become one in marriage. Every time a married couple enjoys sexual intimacy, they are, in a sense, renewing their wedding vows and accepting one another once again. This is why God takes confining sexual intimacy within marriage seriously, as we see in the seventh commandment:

> Do not commit adultery. (Exod. 20:14)

While this commandment addresses a married person not having sexual relations with someone other than his or her spouse, elsewhere in the Law God clarifies that sexual intimacy is forbidden outside of marriage altogether.

That's a far cry from how our Western culture views sex today, isn't it? Sex is treated so casually in our society. We can be influenced by this so easily and begin to waver, falter, and rationalize why this commandment doesn't really mean that sex is only for marriage. But it most certainly does, and God takes adultery seriously—even going as far as to describe his people's idolatry as adultery (Jer. 3:8). Why? What is our culture missing, and what might we be tempted to move away from?

First, when sexual intimacy is reserved for marriage, marriages and families are stronger. God gives us this command to protect us in one of the most important and rewarding relationships we have with others. And because it is so meaningful, it also has greater potential to wound us if it goes wrong. Once again, we see God's commands are always for our best. Every single one of God's commands is for his glory and our good.

But the second and more important reason God is so serious about adultery is because the Bible often uses the marriage relationship as a picture of the church's relationship with Christ (see Eph. 5:22–33). Jesus is the Groom and the church is the bride. If we get marriage wrong and allow adultery, we tarnish the purity of this image of Christ and the church. Christ will always be faithful to his bride, the church, and we, in turn, should always be faithful to him. The church is not to commit adultery and join ourselves together as one with anything or anyone else besides Christ.

Being faithful, committed husbands and wives is good for us, good for our spouses, good for our children, and good for the world around us. That is why God takes adultery so seriously.

Exodus 20:14; Deuteronomy 5:18

Q. What is the eighth commandment?

A. The eighth commandment is not to steal.

Did you know that money is one of the most common topics in the Bible? It was even one of the things that Jesus talked about the most. God knows that money and possessions are easy for us to make into gods, and that is why he deals with them in the eighth commandment:

> Do not steal. (Exod. 20:15)

When we steal, three things happen. First, we wrong the person from whom we stole. We not only take something from the other person, but we also violate them as well. Stealing robs more than a possession; it robs a person's feeling of security. Many people who have had something stolen, such as a car, don't consider the loss of the possession as the worst part—what troubles them more is the feeling that they were violated.

Second, when we steal, we reveal a discontented heart. We steal because we value that item more than what God has given us. We aren't content with what we have been given and we want more, so we take it to make it ours. Stealing is the external sin that reveals the internal sins of discontentment and idolatry.

Third, and most important, when we steal we openly declare that we do not trust God to provide what we need and to know what is best for us. We sit in judgment of God and declare him guilty of failing to give us what we deserve.

This is why stealing cannot be taken lightly. It hurts others, reveals a heart issue within us, and shakes our angry fists in judgment of God. For many of us, though, not stealing is like not murdering. We don't rob banks, shoplift, or take things from our neighbors, so we think we are pretty good with this one as well. But when we think more deeply about what it means to steal, we may find that we break this commandment far more than we want to admit. From taking office supplies from work (who will miss a box of paperclips?), to not correcting a restaurant bill that left an item off, to downloading music that you didn't pay for, to surfing the Internet during your work day—there are a number of ways we steal in more "acceptable" ways. But taking something that is not ours—whether it is a bank vault full of gold or a single paperclip—is stealing, and is therefore a violation of the eighth commandment.

Exodus 20:15; Deuteronomy 5:19

24

Q. What is the ninth commandment?

A. The ninth commandment is not to give false testimony.

God is just, so it is important that we be a just people as well. That is what is in mind in the ninth commandment:

> Do not give false testimony against your neighbor. (Exod. 20:16)

Not giving false testimony has court testimony in mind. We are not to lie and pervert justice. But we know from the full counsel of Scripture that this principle carries over to lying in general. Just as God is just, he is also truth, so we should be people of truth too.

We see the importance of being people of truth very clearly in the account of Ananias and Sapphira in Acts 5. Ananias and Sapphira were part of the early church, and they surely watched as Barnabas sold some land and gave the proceeds to the church to help others in need (Acts 4:36–37). This couple apparently was jealous of the attention Barnabas was given, so they decided to do the same—they sold a piece of land and gave the money to the church. Only they didn't want to give all of the money to the church, so they decided to hold some of the proceeds of the sale back, while making it seem as if they were giving all of it to get attention and praise from others.

When Ananias brought the money, Peter saw through the charade with the Holy Spirit's power, and asked Ananias why he felt the need to lie to God. And at that, Ananias fell down dead. About three hours later, Sapphira came, and when she was asked about the price of the field, she lied too and fell down dead.

Now, this seems like an awfully harsh punishment for telling a lie, but we have to understand that this was at the start of the church and God was protecting it from sin entering and contaminating it from the start. Right after this happened we read that great fear came on the whole church (Acts 5:11), so it seemed to work at getting everyone's attention. But we also see how seriously God takes honesty. And that makes sense. How will people believe the gospel message if it comes from the lips of liars?

The ninth commandment calls for us to strive to live with absolute integrity. People should know that whatever we say is true, from the big things such as the gospel to the small things such as when you will be ready to leave the house, and everything in between.

Exodus 20:16; Deuteronomy 5:20

25

Q. What is the tenth commandment?

A. The tenth commandment is not to covet things that don't belong to us.

In the broadest sense, to covet is to yearn for something. So in many ways, it is right for us to covet. We should covet God. We should covet God's glory to be made known in the entire world. We should covet justice and an end to racism. We can even covet a family. Those are all good things for us to covet. As long as we don't make these good things we covet (such as a family) into an idol, there is nothing wrong with it. However, there are some things that we should never covet and that is what the tenth commandment addresses:

> Do not covet your neighbor's house. Do not covet your neighbor's wife, his male or female servant, his ox or donkey, or anything that belongs to your neighbor. (Exod. 20:17)

While this surely is not an exhaustive list of the wrong things to covet (and again, we can turn good things to covet into wrong things if we go too far and make them idols), it does give a pretty broad picture of coveting. We are not to covet someone else's house (which probably had more of the family in mind than the physical structure), their spouse, or their possessions.

To understand the seriousness of this commandment, we have to get to the heart of it as we have with the others. When we covet, we demonstrate a lack of trust in what God has given us—similar to stealing. But when we covet, we also fail to find joy for someone else, and that reveals a self-centeredness in our hearts that must be purged. If we love our neighbor as ourselves, we will be quick to celebrate with them when they are blessed by God, even when we are not in the same way. Finding joy in another person's joy is a mark of selflessness. And that is how God loves us in one sense. It pleases our Father to bless us. He finds joy in our joy. When we covet, we act contrary to the heart and nature of God. That is why we need to put aside all coveting, be grateful for what we have been given, and celebrate how God has blessed others.

Exodus 20:17; Deuteronomy 5:21

Q. Can anyone obey the Ten Commandments and the Law?

A. No, no one can obey the Ten Commandments and the Law because of our sin.

Can any of us say we have never coveted something that we shouldn't have? Honored our parents all the time? Never lied? Of course none of us can and those are the "easier" commandments from the second table! How about the more difficult commandments from the first table? Not making a god of anything? Resting and worshiping as a rhythm of life? Misusing God's name? We are all guilty of breaking the Ten Commandments—every single one of us—and when we really think about our inability to obey the Ten Commandments, we realize how sinful we really are. We cannot even keep those ten! What about the other 603 commandments in the Old Testament? What about the commands in the New Testament? This is why Ecclesiastes 7:20 tells us:

> There is certainly no one righteous on the earth
> who does good and never sins.

But that leads some to ask a follow-up question: If everyone sins and no one is righteous, won't God take that into account as he judges us? If some of us are better than others, won't God take that into consideration? Won't he focus on the good we are somehow able to do and not the bad that we are prone to do? In other words, won't God basically grade on a curve?

No, he will not. God is just and he will not look past sins, even if everyone commits them. Rebellion is rebellion and it is no less egregious to rebel against our creator God if everyone is doing it. God's standard is perfection, so if we were to break even just one single part of the Law, we would be guilty of breaking the entire thing because it is all held together by the One who gave it, as we read in James 2:10.

> For whoever keeps the entire law, and yet stumbles at one
> point, is guilty of breaking it all.

We are guilty of breaking the entire Law even if we were to break only a single commandment, because they are all held together by their Author. Any single violation is full rebellion against the Lawgiver who is holy and perfect in all his ways. Each command reflects God's heart and character, so to reject one is to reject his heart and character, from which the rest of the commands come.

And we haven't even talked about our hearts yet. It is far easier to pinpoint the external signs of sin, but how much more do we sin in our heart with selfish, hateful, unloving attitudes? Jesus told us that this is where all sin is born and this is where we lose the battle.

> "For from the heart come evil thoughts, murders, adulteries,
> sexual immoralities, thefts, false testimonies, slander. These
> are the things that defile a person." (Matt. 15:19–20a)

As we look at the Ten Commandments, we see how sinful we are. As we look at the rest of the commands in Scripture, we see our sin even more clearly. And then when we examine our hearts, we see that we cannot get away from the depth and pervasiveness of our sin. We are indeed sinners in need of a Savior.

1 John 1:8; Romans 3:23

27

Q. What is the main purpose of the Ten Commandments and the Old Testament Law?

A. The Ten Commandments and the Law show us God's standard of obedience and reveal our sin and need of grace.

If no one can obey the Ten Commandments and the Law, and God knows this, why did he give them? Why give commands we cannot keep, no matter how hard we try? Is he setting us up to fail? Well, actually, he is. But perhaps not for the reason you might think.

In one sense, God does expect us to obey all of the commandments. After all, they reflect his character, and he demands nothing short of perfect obedience. But in another sense, God expects us to fail because he knows we cannot be good enough. We cannot find salvation through our own righteousness. The Law, then, is God's standard for us, but it also reveals our sin and helplessness to do anything about it. This is what we find in Romans 3:20:

> For no one will be justified in his sight by the works of the law, because the knowledge of sin comes through the law.

So the Law primarily shows us how far short we fall of God's standard of perfection and why we deserve to be separated from him. Is the Law bad, then? Should we view the Law as something harmful? Paul anticipated this question, so he answered it a little later in Romans 7:7:

> What should we say then? Is the law sin? Absolutely not! On the contrary, I would not have known sin if it were not for the

law. For example, I would not have known what it is to covet if the law had not said, Do not covet.

So as painful as it is to be confronted by our sin and realize why we are condemned before Holy God, the Law is good because it forces us to face our sin problem. And once we are confronted by sin and realize we can do nothing about it, the door is open for us to finally grasp the hope of the gospel. We cannot overcome our sin problem, but God can through faith in Christ:

> But the Scripture imprisoned everything under sin's power, so that the promise might be given on the basis of faith in Jesus Christ to those who believe. Before this faith came, we were confined under the law, imprisoned until the coming faith was revealed. The law, then, was our guardian until Christ, so that we could be justified by faith. (Gal. 3:22–24)

In the kindness of God, he has given the Law to reveal our sin, but also to show us that we cannot bring about our own salvation; we need another way—a way outside of us—a way through Christ.

Romans 3:20; Galatians 3:22–24

28

Q. What did Jesus say is the greatest commandment?

A. Jesus said the greatest commandment is to love God.

Sometimes we just can't win. There are times in life when we want to do the right thing—we really do—but for us to do the right thing means that we might have to do something that is wrong as well. It's the quandary behind the proverbial question, "Is it right to steal a loaf of bread to feed your starving family?"

This is something the Jews wrestled with quite a bit. For generations, the children of Israel rebelled against God through idolatry. And generation after generation, God warned them that he takes sin seriously and they would be disciplined if they continued in their sin. But they didn't listen, so God followed through on his promise and sent foreign armies to defeat his people and take them into captivity.

God eventually brought his people back home into their land, and from that point forward, they didn't rebel through blatant idol worship again. They had learned that lesson. Instead they turned their attention toward obeying God's commands to the letter of the law. They did not want to experience God's discipline again.

The problem was that they learned the lesson too well and not well enough at the same time. They began to trust in their own obedience as the way to be right with God. This was the origin of the extreme religiosity of the Pharisees. Absolute obedience is what God demanded and so absolute obedience is what they would give him. But as we know, absolute obedience is not possible.

The Pharisees and other Jewish leaders such as the Sadducees learned this pretty quickly. There were 613 commands in the Old Testament—365 negative commands of what God's people could not do, and 248 positive commands of what they were supposed to do. The problem was that there might be times when obeying one command meant you had to break another. This was especially likely on the Sabbath when you were not supposed to work. But what happened if a friend's ox fell into a ditch on the Sabbath? According to Deuteronomy 22:4, you would have to help him get it out of the ditch. But that would mean working on the Sabbath (see Luke 14:1–6). And how do you define "work" anyway? Is walking work? Are you not supposed to walk? Well, that's not practical—we need to walk at least some—so how far is too far to walk on the Sabbath?

Different rabbis took on the task of answering these questions, and they provided a framework through which a person could know which commands were the more important ones (the heavy ones) and which were not as important (the light ones). This way, if two commands were in opposition to each other, you would know to obey the heavy command, not the light command.

This is what a Pharisee, an expert in the Law, was thinking when he approached Jesus to try to trick him. The Pharisee simply asked which was the greatest commandment. It was his way of asking how Jesus decided which were the heavier commands and which were the lighter ones. The Pharisee anticipated Jesus sharing which rabbinical school of thought he supported, and in doing so, would have exposed himself to criticism from those who followed different schools of thought. But Jesus wasn't One to do the expected:

> He said to him, "Love the Lord your God with all your heart, with all your soul, and with all your mind. This is the greatest and most important command." (Matt. 22:37–38)

Jesus quoted Deuteronomy 6:5, the beginning of the Shema, one of the most important Old Testament passages for the Jews. The Shema was valued pretty much universally by the Jews, so there was no way the Pharisee could find fault in Jesus' response, but more importantly, Jesus clarified the way we are to follow him—with love. The question is not which command is more or less important, the question is if we love God as much as we can and should. That is how we seek to obey God: with love.

Matthew 22:37–38; Deuteronomy 6:5

Q. What did Jesus say is the second greatest commandment?

A. Jesus said the second greatest commandment is to love others.

Jesus had answered the Pharisee's question. He had been asked what the greatest commandment was and he answered that it was loving God. It was a good answer—an answer that could not be argued. But Jesus didn't stop there. He also told the Pharisee what the second greatest commandment was—even if he hadn't been asked for it. Here is what he said:

> He said to him, "Love the Lord your God with all your heart, with all your soul, and with all your mind. This is the greatest and most important command. The second is like it: Love your neighbor as yourself. All the Law and the Prophets depend on these two commands." (Matt. 22:37–40)

Jesus directed the Pharisee to Leviticus 19:18 as the second greatest commandment—loving others. Love God and love people. Those are the first and second greatest commandments. And then he said something quite important. All of the rest of the commands depend on these two. These two commands are the way to interpret and obey every single one of the 613 commandments in the Old Testament, and all of the commands in the New Testament as well. If we get these two right, we will get all the rest right too.

Jesus didn't stop at the greatest commandment because he knew that his answer would be incomplete if he stopped there. That only gives half of the equation. But bringing in the second greatest commandment gives the full equation and truly answered the Pharisee's question. The way we follow God's commands is to always obey with a heart of love for God and for other people. If we do that, we won't go wrong.

The first and second greatest commandments are fused together. We cannot fully obey the first—loving God—without obeying the second—loving people whom he loves. In the same way, we cannot obey the second—loving people—apart from obeying the first—loving God—because our love is not adequate for other people; we need to love them through the love that God gives us.

Understanding these two commandments and how they work together gives us what we need to understand the Ten Commandments. The first table focuses on our love for God. The second table focuses on our love for others. For us to obey the Ten Commandments means we are fulfilling the two greatest commandments—we love God and we love people. Jesus was right. When we do that, all the rest falls into place.

Matthew 22:37–40; Leviticus 19:18

Q. How do the first and second greatest commandments help us live for God?

A. The first and second greatest commandments provide the purpose for all we do.

It has been said that if everything is important, then nothing is really important. Sometimes we might feel that way as we read the Bible or listen to sermons. One day we will interact with the importance of prayer—how vital it is for a Christian to be a person of prayer. And we will walk away thinking there is nothing more important for us to do than pray.

But then the next day we will interact with worship and how we were created for worship and that everything we do should be worship of God. So we will turn our attention to worship and commit to being people known for our genuine worship of God.

But then the next day we will hear about the importance of being part of a local church. And then the next day, the priority of evangelism. Then the next day our need to be in the Word of God.

It can be overwhelming and discouraging. There is so much we need to do—and it all makes sense and we want to do it—but we just can't do it all. So what do we do? What do we focus on? What is most important for us? Prayer? Worship? The church? Evangelism? Bible study? Something else still?

Do you see what we've become? Modern-day Pharisees trying to figure out which are the heavy activities for us as Christians and which are the light ones. If we have one hour, is it better to pray or evangelize? We take the same question to Jesus, just with a slight twist: "What is the greatest act of obedience?"

Jesus' reply would be the same. The greatest act of obedience is to love God. The second is to love others. Everything we do depends on those two. If we get these right, the rest will fall into place. Prayer matters because it is a way that we love God. But so is worship and reading the Bible. If you love God and want to express it in one of these ways in the moment, you will be doing what matters most no matter which you choose. Evangelism and gathering as part of the church are ways that we love others. If you love people and want to express it in one of these ways, you won't go wrong. The Holy Spirit will guide us to how we can best love God or love people in the moment, so if we just focus on loving God and loving people as our guardrails for living everyday, we will be fine.

Matthew 22:37–40

DISCIPLESHIP

Q. What is the purpose of our lives?

A. The purpose of our lives is to glorify God in all we do.

What is the meaning of life? That question is implanted deep down in the soul of every person. We all have a yearning to understand why we exist. Surely there is a bigger reason than just living for seventy, eighty, or even ninety years and then that's it. Surely there is more to life than just leaving the world a better place for the next generation who will just in turn do the same, but to what end? While the world continues to wrestle with this question, thankfully, those of us in Christ have the answer. We find it in 1 Corinthians 10:31.

> So, whether you eat or drink, or whatever you do, do everything for the glory of God.

Paul had been walking the church in Corinth through a disagreement of whether or not it was permissible for a Christian to eat meat from an animal that had been sacrificed to a false god as part of pagan worship. That was a real concern for the church in that time—this meat was sold in the marketplace and it might be tempting to purchase it, or you might be a guest in someone's home who serves it to you, so what should you do?

We don't have this issue today, but thankfully, the Holy Spirit guided Paul to expand his answer so it relates to us today. Paul counseled the church not intentionally to eat meat sacrificed to an idol not because it would be wrong to do it necessarily, but out of concern for the conscience of others (1 Cor. 10:28). And then Paul explained the heart behind this principle—the reason why we should abstain from something even if it is permissible is for

God's glory. But as he gave this summary, he expanded it to apply to much more than eating or drinking—he included everything we do. And this gives us, in a simple sentence of seventeen words, the key to the meaning of life. We exist to bring God glory.

To glorify God is to show his beauty and splendor to the world around us. So everything we do is to be done with that goal in mind—how we can make much of God through what we do. To the world, God seems distant at best, made up at worst. And that is where we come in. We are here to magnify God to the world around us so they can see him up close and see that he is very much real and very much glorious.

There are two ways you can magnify something. The first is by making something very small look bigger than it really is. That is what a microscope does. The second is by making something extremely large but far away so it appears small—such as a planet—look more as it truly is. That is what a telescope does. And that is how we magnify God. Everything we do is to show the unbelieving world around us God as he truly is. That is our purpose in life.

1 Corinthians 10:31

Q. Why should we glorify God?

A. We should glorify God because he made us, loves us, takes care of us, and is perfect in all his attributes.

Knowing that our purpose in life is to glorify God is one thing, but understanding why we should glorify him in everything we do is another. If we don't have the answer to that question implanted deep down in our hearts, it will be hard to live out this purpose in everyday life where there are so many distractions from our purpose, including our own sin.

One of the most basic reasons we should glorify God is quite simply because he made us. He is our creator and sustainer and therefore we owe everything to him. This was one of the reasons the twenty-four elders John saw in heaven glorified God:

> Our Lord and God,
> you are worthy to receive
> glory and honor and power,
> because you have created all things,
> and by your will
> they exist and were created. (Rev. 4:11)

God is our creator, and for that reason alone we should glorify him. We exist solely because of him. We wake up each day solely because of him. Everything we have is solely because of him. Had he not created it or given it to us, we wouldn't have it. It's that simple.

But that is just the starting point of why we should glorify God. We glorify him also because he loves us. More than we can ever grasp. Ever doubt

God loves you or the depth of his love for you? Here is God's response through what Paul wrote in Romans 5:8.

> But God proves his own love for us in that while we were still sinners, Christ died for us.

The greatest proof of God's love is that he provided Jesus to die for us. We weren't good people deserving such a gift; we were sinful, rebellious people fully deserving the death our sin had brought on us. God's gracious provision of Jesus is the greatest evidence of God's love for us, and because of it, we have good reason to glorify God in everything. In the book of 1 Peter, we read that angels long to see the gospel more clearly. That doesn't mean they lack the intellectual capacity to understand the gospel, but instead that they long to relate with us in one specific way—experiencing the gospel. Angels don't know what it is like—what it feels like—to have Jesus die for them. They don't know what forgiveness is like other than the concept. That is exactly what we have experienced in Christ and what we have the privilege of sharing with others to God's glory.

Another reason we should glorify God in all we do is because he cares for us. In the Sermon on the Mount, Jesus shared why there is no place for worry in the life of a believer—because God takes care of us (see Matt. 6:25–34). Jesus turned the listeners' attention to the birds God feeds and the wildflowers he causes to grow. They do nothing, yet God provides for them. How much more does God care about us, his children? The God of the universe knows us each by name and provides just what we need, just when we need it. That is a good reason to glorify him in all we do.

Yet another reason we glorify God is because of who he is—he is perfect in all his attributes. We don't just glorify God because of what he has done for us—that can lead us wrongly to see God as existing for us instead of us existing for him. So we also give God glory simply because of who he is.

> The Rock—his work is perfect;
> all his ways are just.
> A faithful God, without bias,
> he is righteous and true. (Deut. 32:4)

We could choose just one of his attributes—his omniscience, his justice, his grace, his omnipotence—and spend eternity glorifying him for that one attribute alone and yet still never fully exhaust giving him the glory he is due.

That's because he is eternal. His omniscience is infinite—we cannot praise him for all of it and reach the end!

That is our God. A God who is beyond our greatest expressions and abilities to give him glory, and yet for whom we find worthy of trying.

Revelation 4:11; Romans 5:8; Deuteronomy 32:4

3

Q. How can we glorify God?

A. We can glorify God by loving him, trusting him, and obeying him.

This is probably a good point to clear something up. When we say that we are to give God glory, we don't mean we give something to God that he lacks. The way we phrase it sounds like that, but of course that is not what is going on. God is perfect in all his ways, and he is perfectly glorious. He does not need us to give him glory as if he is missing it. Instead, what we mean is that we reveal God's glory to the world around us. Again, it is like the telescope—we show God more for who he truly is.

So how do we do that? How do we act like that telescope? Let's see what Jesus had to say about this:

> "My Father is glorified by this: that you produce much fruit and prove to be my disciples.
>
> "As the Father has loved me, I have also loved you. Remain in my love. If you keep my commands you will remain in my love, just as I have kept my Father's commands and remain in his love.
>
> "I have told you these things so that my joy may be in you and your joy may be complete." (John 15:8–11)

We have to appreciate it when Jesus is as clear as he was here. He told us point-blank what it looks like to glorify God: we produce fruit, remain in Christ's love, and keep his commands.

Let's start with love. One of the greatest ways we can glorify God in the world around us is by loving him. Have you ever been around someone who clearly loves his or her profession or perhaps a hobby? It's apparent, isn't it? It comes across as authentic, and even if you don't know much about their profession or hobby or care much about it, you still can often find yourself drawn in by their passion. Their love can be infectious. And that is what should happen with our love for God. The world doesn't need to see God's people obeying him and following him grudgingly or emotionlessly. That actually undermines the gospel. If God is as great as he is (and he is) and if salvation through Jesus is as beautiful as it is (and it is), it should show in God's people. We should wear our love for him on our sleeves.

It is this love for God that will compel us to obey him. We will want to follow him and bear the fruit of obedience. God will then take that obedience and use it for his purposes to bring more glory to himself, which is where trust comes into play. Sometimes it is easy for us to obey God, but there are plenty of times when it is challenging. There are times when God calls us to do something that is risky, difficult, or even painful. But our love for God and desire to obey him will bear themselves out in our trust of him—that he is good and faithful and that even if we suffer for him, he will use it for good. When we demonstrate that trust, the world notices and God is glorified. We can often shout God's glory to the world around us much more through our pain and adversity than through our abundance and pleasure.

Notice one last thing about how we glorify God. Jesus said that when we love God and obey him and bear fruit, we will find true joy. There is joy in obedience! As Christians we should be the most joyful people in the world. That doesn't mean we won't experience pain, sadness, and suffering or that we should always wear plastic smiles on our faces. But it does mean that we will experience genuine, lasting joy in our lives because we know we are God's and he is ours. And nothing will change that.

John 15:8–11; 1 Corinthians 10:31

Q. Why should we love God?

A. We should love God because he first loved us.

Love is fleeting in our culture, perhaps because it is conditional most of the time. People fall in love, but then the feelings fade, or they don't have their needs and desires met any longer, so the love goes away. With that in mind, what is our motivation for loving God? What will lead us to love him no matter what? We find the answer in 1 John 4:19.

We love because he first loved us.

It's that simple, and yet that important. We love because God loved us first. If it had not been for God loving us and reaching out to us by providing Jesus and bringing us into relationship with him, it would be impossible for us to love him. We would still be estranged from him—rebels and enemies. But because of God's initiating love and through the work of the Holy Spirit, we have the capacity and opportunity to love God.

But it is more than that. Because God loving us first is our motivation to love him, it makes our love steady. God's love is unconditional, faithful, and consistent; there is never a time when God does not love us, so there is never a time when we are not able to love in response to his love.

So how do we know we love God? It's an important question, especially since we tend to follow the world's definition of love based on our feelings. But feelings are fleeting and can betray us. Jesus gave us two signs that remind us that we do indeed love God.

The first is found in John 14:15.

"If you love me, you will keep my commands."

Obeying God's commands, albeit imperfectly, is one proof that we love God. We have to remember that the world is in rebellion against God. There is no desire on the world's part to obey God—the world wants to please itself. So when we strive to obey God, even in small ways and imperfectly at first, we know that God is changing our hearts and that we love him. It's important that we understand that this is what Jesus had in mind—it was not a challenge to his followers to prove their love by obeying him. It was the other way around—love is the means by which we can obey him. So if we are obeying, that means we do have love for him.

The second is found in John 13:35.

"By this everyone will know that you are my disciples, if you love one another."

Our love for other believers is another way we can know that we truly love God. Once again we see how our vertical and horizontal relationships are fused together. Love for God will lead to love for one another. And as we see here, the world notices our love for each other. One of the greatest ways we can declare the beauty of the gospel is when believers from every nation, tribe, and tongue join together as brothers and sisters—despite our numerous differences—and love one another. The world does not experience unity like that. It is beautifully peculiar. That is the power of our love for God, which leads us to obey Jesus and love others. It has the power to change other people's lives as well.

1 John 4:19; John 13:35

5

Q. Why should we trust God?

A. We should trust God because he is faithful and everything he does is for his glory and our good.

Everything God does is for his glory and our good, whether we see it or not, and whether it feels like it or not. That is the bedrock of our trust in God which comes from Romans 8:28.

> We know that all things work together for the good of those who love God, who are called according to his purpose.

It's easy for us to see the truthfulness of this verse in the midst of God's blessings—a new child, a raise at work, a growing church. But it can be quite challenging during times of pain, sorrow, and suffering. God can feel so distant and, if we can find the courage to admit it, unloving in those times. It is easy to question God's goodness in those moments, and our trust in him can waver so quickly. But it is in those times when we need to trust in God the most. It's in those times when we need to know that he is good no matter what, and that he will use what we are going through for his good, one way or another.

That doesn't mean the pain isn't real. It doesn't mean we cannot weep and ask God why we are going through such a difficult situation. God wants us to be real with him—and others. Walking around with a stiff upper lip and spouting bumper-sticker Christian platitudes is not trusting God—that's being inauthentic. If we are hurting, we need to be hurt. If we are struggling, we need to struggle. But we can hurt and struggle while trusting God—trusting that he will see us through and trusting that he can turn our pain into good and be glorified through it.

When our trust in that begins to falter, we can always return to the cross. Jesus' crucifixion was the greatest evil this world—the universe, indeed—has ever witnessed. The Son of God suffered and died, bearing the sins of the world on himself. And yet, as we know, the cross was also the greatest good the universe has ever experienced. It was the ultimate victory—the ultimate display of love from our God. If God can turn the greatest evil into the greatest good, he can certainly take our pain and suffering and bring good out of it.

God did that with Joseph. Joseph was betrayed by his own brothers and sold into slavery. He rose to a trusted position in his master's house, but when his master's wife lied about Joseph, he was thrown into prison. In prison he interpreted the dreams of two of Pharaohs' servants and asked one to remember him when he returned to Pharaohs' court, but he was forgotten. Joseph was certainly a man associated with hardships and suffering. And yet, this is what he said to his brothers later when he was second in command of Egypt:

> But Joseph said to them, "Don't be afraid. Am I in the place of God? You planned evil against me; God planned it for good to bring about the present result—the survival of many people." (Gen. 50:19–20)

What Joseph's brothers did was truly evil, and Joseph suffered greatly because of it. But God used that evil for the good of his people and for his glory, and he can do the same with our hardships.

Romans 8:28; Genesis 50:19–20; James 1:17

6

Q. Why should we obey God?

A. We should obey God because we love him and are thankful for who he is and what he has done.

You can make someone obey you if you try hard enough, but you cannot make someone love you, no matter how hard you try. Love, therefore, is greater than obedience. If we love, we will obey, but if we obey, we may or may not love.

The reason for our obedience of God has to be more than duty or obligation. While it is true in a sense that we need to obey God because he is our creator and our sovereign King, that cannot be our main reason for obeying him. That would mean that power is the currency of our relationship—we would still be God's servants. But we are not God's servants any longer. We are his friends (John 15:15), and more than that, we are his children (Rom. 8:15). Power does not hold friends together. Power does not hold family together. Love does.

In his Gospel, John didn't refer to himself by name, but instead as "the disciple whom Jesus loved." John was clearly in tune with love, which is why you see him address it so much in his writings—especially in 1 John. So it isn't surprising that John positions love as our primary motivator for obeying God:

> Love consists in this: not that we loved God, but that he loved us and sent his Son to be the atoning sacrifice for our sins. Dear friends, if God loved us in this way, we also must love one another. (1 John 4:10–11)

When we think about what God has done for us and who he is, we can't help but love him, and that love will translate to obedience. Just as we want our children to obey us because they love us, not merely because they have to, God wants our love for him to drive our obedience as well.

A second reason we obey, closely related to our love for God, is our gratitude to him:

> Give thanks to the LORD, for he is good.
> His faithful love endures forever. (Ps. 136:1)

God has done so much for us, but we don't have to move past providing salvation through Jesus to find an eternal reason for our deepest gratitude. Jesus gave us life. He brought us back from the dead and joined us into fellowship with God. How can we ever thank him enough for that? What could he ask us to do that would be too much for us to say yes—willingly and joyfully?

We obey God not because we have to, but because it is our privilege. The more we spend time pondering the gospel, the more we will find our love and gratitude growing, and the more we will eagerly obey God for his glory and our joy.

1 John 4:10–11; Psalm 136:1

Q. Will we fully obey God during our lifetime?

A. No, we will not fully obey God during our lifetime, but we should want to obey him more each day.

———————

While obedience is one fruit of our love for Christ (John 14:15), we cannot expect to fully obey God during our lifetime because of our ongoing struggle with sin. There will be many times when we want to obey Christ, but our sin quells our desire and we will fail to follow through. Then there will be times when we will be led by our selfish desires and we won't even want to obey. But as we grow in Christ, we should find our desire to obey and our follow through gradually increasing. This is part of the Holy Spirit's sanctification process we read about in Philippians 1:6.

> I am sure of this, that he who started a good work in you will
> carry it on to completion until the day of Christ Jesus.

Notice that this completion doesn't happen until the day of Christ Jesus—when he returns and we are changed and sin is finally done away with. But until then, the Holy Spirit will continue to grow us and change us on the foundation of the gospel, which he established in our hearts. As this positive growth takes place, we will also see sin gradually decrease in our lives. Our sinful desires and actions will diminish in an inverse function with obedience. But even though we will continue to sin, as Christians, our lives will look different than from before Christ because we will not deliberately sin as a way of life. This is how the writer of Hebrews put it:

> For if we deliberately go on sinning after receiving the knowl-
> edge of the truth, there no longer remains a sacrifice for sins.
> (Heb. 10:26)

Deliberate, unrepentant sin is a sign that a person has not trusted in Christ. Once we are in Christ, we will continue to sin, but our struggle with it, the conviction we sense because of it, and the gradual decline of it all serve as evidence that we are indeed in Christ. And as that sin declines, our obedience will grow—gradually and imperfectly, but grow all the same.

Philippians 1:6; Hebrews 10:26

Q. What helps us obey God more?

A. God helps us obey him more by giving us wisdom, the ability to make choices that glorify him.

Every day we choose dozens, even hundreds, of times whether we will obey God or not. Some of these decisions to obey are fairly easy—it is easier to obey God when what he tells us to do is pleasant or even beneficial for us. But there will be other times when obeying God is quite difficult and we will struggle with either obeying him or feeding our selfish desires. But then there will be still other times when we won't be able to tell how we should obey God. It won't be a matter of sinning or not. It won't be a matter of obeying a clear command in Scripture or not. It will be a matter of choosing between two or more options that each feel right. It is in these times when we will need wisdom—the ability to make the choice that most glorifies God. Here is how Paul put it in Ephesians 5:15–17.

> Pay careful attention, then, to how you live—not as unwise people but as wise—making the most of the time, because the days are evil. So don't be foolish, but understand what the Lord's will is.

Every decision we make matters, no matter how small it seems. Each decision can create ripples we cannot anticipate in the moment, or may just be a bigger decision than we think at the time. For this reason, we need to live with wisdom—to make the right decisions and make the most of our time—our lives.

But how do we get this wisdom? That's the amazing part—all we need to do is ask God for it.

Now if any of you lacks wisdom, he should ask God—who gives to all generously and ungrudgingly—and it will be given to him. (James 1:5)

When we ask God for wisdom, he will give it to us generously, and no matter how much we ask him for it, he will always give it to us without hesitation. God wants us to live in a way that glorifies him, and he wants us to experience abundant living. He delights when we come to him acknowledging that we need wisdom from him. That is why he gives it to us generously—for our good and his glory.

Ephesians 5:15–17; James 1:5

Q. Where does God's wisdom come from?

A. God's wisdom comes from him through his Word.

According to James 1:5, wisdom comes from God. That is important for us to remember because we desperately need God's wisdom—not the world's—to obey him. The wisdom of the world is in fact foolishness, as we read in 1 Corinthians 1:21.

> For since, in God's wisdom, the world did not know God through wisdom, God was pleased to save those who believe through the foolishness of what is preached.

Think about the world's "wisdom": We are here by random chance. Follow your heart. Do what feels right. Do what pleases you the most as long as it doesn't harm someone else. Once we die, that's it, so live for today. There is no such thing as absolute truth, everyone decides what is true for themselves.

All of this "wisdom" is contrary of God's wisdom. We are not here by chance, but because of God's will and for a purpose. We don't follow our hearts, because they are deceptive. We don't do what feels right, but what is right according to God's Word. We don't do what pleases us the most, but what glorifies God the most, no matter how difficult it may be. Everyone is eternal—it is just a matter of whether we will be with God or not. God is truth—we don't decide what is true, he is the one and only standard.

We can see why it is so important for us to put aside the world's wisdom and ask God for his wisdom. And when we do ask God, he will give us his wisdom through the work of the Holy Spirit:

> We also speak these things, not in words taught by human
> wisdom, but in those taught by the Spirit, explaining spiritual
> things to spiritual people. (1 Cor. 2:13)

Wisdom is taught to us by the Spirit first through the Word of God. It might be surprising—although it shouldn't be—how often we can find wisdom for any of life's situations simply by reading the Bible. Many times we will find God's will revealed directly to us so we will know what to do in the situations we encounter. But there will be other times when we will instead find principles that will guide us in making decisions. And that brings in the second way the Spirit gives us wisdom—through his ministry of guiding us. When Jesus ascended, he promised to send the Spirit and told us that it would be for our good. The reason is because the Spirit is always present with us and always guiding us to live in a way that glorifies God. All we need to do is listen and follow what he guides us to do. Between the Spirit's work in the Bible and the Spirit's work in guiding us, we can live with wisdom in any situation we face.

James 1:5; 1 Corinthians 2:13

Q. From where do all blessings come?

A. All blessings come from God.

We tend to live in the moment and that makes it hard for us to look at the bigger picture of what goes on around us every day. Take food, for example.

If we went into our kitchen pantries right now, most of us would probably find more food than many other people in the world would hope to have for several months, or longer. And yet, we take it for granted. We will often stare at a refrigerator full of food and sigh because we have "nothing to eat." Or we might get frustrated because we are missing an ingredient we need to make a meal and have to get in our cars and drive a full ten minutes to a grocery store to get what we need. And so we grumble as we walk down aisle after aisle overflowing with every food imaginable in dozens of varieties each.

And all the while we fail to appreciate with genuine humility and awe what God has provided for us. We fail to remember that the only reason we have the money to purchase any of the food we have is because God has provided it. Oh, we think we earned it through our jobs, but from where did our abilities to do that work come? And why did we get that job when there were so many other candidates?

And we fail to appreciate what God provided for the food even to be there to be purchased. We pull down one box of wheat flakes off of a shelf filled with them, and we don't even think how that box is only there because God provided the rain to grow the wheat. And God provided the wheat seed in the first place. And the soil. And the sun. And the air.

When we live like this—in the moment, taking all God does for granted—we deprive ourselves of seeing how deeply God loves us and all he does to provide for us. Every good thing we have is from God and gives us the opportunity to experience his love and worship him:

Every good and perfect gift is from above, coming down from
the Father of lights, who does not change like shifting shadows.
(James 1:17)

God's faithful provisions are designed to draw our hearts to him. When
we experience God's blessings and connect them to God instead of taking
them for granted, we will not only give God the worship he deserves but we
will enjoy them more. Eating a meal that you feel you earned isn't nearly as
gratifying as eating a meal you know is given to you by the kindness of our
good God. This is why we should be a grateful people for all of God's blessings, and this is also why we should be a people who enjoy life more fully than
all others—because we are receiving God's gracious blessings fully and enjoying them to the fullest, as he wants us to.

James 1:17; Philippians 4:19

Q. How has God blessed us?

A. God has blessed us with life, talents, possessions, and salvation through Jesus.

When we think about how God has blessed us, we probably think mostly of our possessions. And while it is true that everything we have—food, clothing, a home, furniture, vehicles, appliances, and so forth—are blessings given to us by God for which we should be deeply grateful, God's blessings go far beyond that. Many times we overlook some of the greatest blessings God gives to us—such as each new day to live. We are not owed a single day of life so each day we wake up is further evidence of God's kindness to us and is a blessing from him. But God doesn't just bless us by giving us a new day to live; he blesses us with life of the utmost quality.

> "A thief comes only to steal and kill and destroy. I have come so
> that they may have life and have it in abundance." (John 10:10)

Think about that. Jesus came to earth and lay down his life for us not just so that we would have life—as great as that would be—but so that we would have an *abundant* life—a full life. That is why God gives us family, friends, hobbies, a church family, meaningful work, and, most importantly, himself—so that we would experience abundant life each day.

In addition to possessions and life, God also blesses us with talents and abilities for our enjoyment and to be used for him. One of the best examples of this in the Bible is found in Exodus 35:30–33 during the construction of the tabernacle:

> Moses then said to the Israelites: "Look, the LORD has
> appointed by name Bezalel son of Uri, son of Hur, of the tribe

of Judah. He has filled him with God's Spirit, with wisdom, understanding, and ability in every kind of craft to design artistic works in gold, silver, and bronze, to cut gemstones for mounting, and to carve wood for work in every kind of artistic craft."

Just as God gave Bezalel talent in various kinds of crafts, he blesses each of us with talents and abilities like music, art, gardening, and athletics for our enjoyment and to be used for his glory.

But the greatest blessing we experience—even more than life—is salvation through Jesus:

> "For God loved the world in this way: He gave his one and only Son, so that everyone who believes in him will not perish but have eternal life." (John 3:16)

We don't deserve salvation; it is a free gift—a blessing—given to us by God. And just like the other blessings God has given us, he intends for us to enjoy the blessing of our salvation and also to share it with others so that they too might trust in Jesus and experience this greatest blessing imaginable.

John 10:10; Exodus 35:30–33; John 3:16

Q. Who owns all that we have?

A. God owns all that we have, and we are his stewards.

God is Creator of everything, which means he owns everything. The one who creates is the one who owns and has a right to do with what he creates as he wishes.

> The earth and everything in it,
> the world and its inhabitants,
> belong to the Lord. (Ps. 24:1)

Notice how broad that is. God owns the earth, everything on it, and all who live on it—including you and me. Everything belongs to God.

So what does that mean for our possessions? If they are not truly ours but God's, does that mean we aren't responsible for them? Actually, it is quite the opposite. While God owns all that we have been given by him, we are responsible for caring for all of it. We are to be faithful stewards, as we read in 1 Peter 4:10.

> Just as each one has received a gift, use it to serve others, as
> good stewards of the varied grace of God.

While Peter is referring directly to the spiritual gifts God gives, the principle carries over to everything else he has given as well. We are stewards of all of our possessions, our time, our talents, and even our salvation. As stewards, we are to care for these blessings and ensure that they are used wisely for God's glory.

Psalm 24:1; 1 Peter 4:10

Q. What is a steward?

A. A *steward* is a person who takes care of someone else's possessions.

A steward is a manager who takes care of something that belongs to someone else. Because all that we have is from God, we are to faithfully manage these resources with wisdom so that we can use them most effectively for God's glory.

> In this regard, it is required that managers be found faithful. (1 Cor. 4:2)

One of the many parables Jesus told, and one of the longer ones, focused on what it means to be a faithful steward. We find this parable in Matthew 25:14–30.

A man was about to go on a journey, so he gathered his servants and entrusted his possessions to them. He gave the first servant five talents—or about 100 years of wages. The next servant he gave two talents, and the last one a single talent. He then left on his journey.

The first servant put the five talents he had been given to work and he earned five more. The servant with two talents did the same and doubled what he had for his master as well. But the last servant buried his talent for safekeeping.

When the master returned from his trip, he called on his three servants to settle accounts. The first servant presented his ten talents to the master and the master praised him and told him he would be put in charge of more because he had proven to be faithful. The second servant presented his four talents to the master with the same response. But then the last servant returned the single talent and explained that he knew his master was harsh so he was afraid and hid the talent.

The master replied that the servant should have at least put the money into a bank and earned interest, so he took the talent from him and gave it to the first servant.

So what was Jesus' point of this parable? Why was the master so harsh toward the last servant? The servant gave his master back what was his in the first place, right? That's true, but if all the master was worried about was holding onto what he had, he could have done that himself. He could have buried the money himself or even taken it with him. But that wasn't his concern; he wanted his talents to be *used*—to be put to work. But this one wasn't. The servant didn't do anything with it. That is why the master was so upset, and that is what we are to learn from this parable.

Everything God gives us is to be used to demonstrate more of God's glory to the world (1 Cor. 10:31). God is not interested in us protecting his possessions and blessings—he wants us to put them to work. If we are going to be faithful stewards, we can't just focus on not losing what we have been given; we need to focus on using every single blessing to make God's glory known to all the nations. If we do this, we too will hear what the master said to the first two servants: "Well done, good and faithful servant! You were faithful over a few things; I will put you in charge of many things. Share your master's joy" (Matt. 25:21).

1 Corinthians 4:2; 1 Corinthians 10:31

14

Q. Why should we serve God as stewards?

A. We should serve God as stewards to glorify him and help others.

As with all else we do, we are to serve God as stewards with the goal of glorifying him. When it comes to stewarding the blessings God has given to us, we should seek to help others, which in turn glorifies God.

> Just as each one has received a gift, use it to serve others, as good stewards of the varied grace of God. (1 Pet. 4:10)

God has blessed us with possessions, time, and talents, not just for us to enjoy and worship him out of gratitude for what he has given, but also so that we might be able to help others. We see a beautiful picture of this in the very first days of the church:

> Now all the believers were together and held all things in common. They sold their possessions and property and distributed the proceeds to all, as any had need. (Acts 2:44–45)

The church holding all things in common did not mean that no one owned private property or possessions. We know that isn't the case, because right after these verses we read of the church selling possessions and property to help others when they had a need. Instead, what this means is that the church viewed their possessions and property as not just their own, but as blessings God had given them to help others as the need arose. Their perspective of what they had changed.

This is a wonderful example of being a good steward of what we have been given. Our love and concern for others should prompt us to eagerly give what we have as we can to help others. And in doing so, God will be glorified. Nearly two thousand years later we are still talking about the stewardship of the early church. May future generations talk about ours as well.

1 Peter 4:10; Acts 2:44–45

15

Q. How should we give of our time, talents, and possessions as stewards?

A. We should give of our time, talents, and possessions regularly, generously, and cheerfully.

Have you ever forced your child to share something he or she didn't want to share? It's not pretty, is it? Pouting. Crying. Anger. They may have shared, but they sure didn't do it in the right way.

That is exactly how we can be too if we aren't careful. We can reach the point of knowing that we are supposed to give our time, talents, and possessions to be faithful stewards, but do so grudgingly—just like a child forced to share a toy. But God doesn't just want us to be good stewards—he is not just focused on the end result—he wants us to be the kind of people who *want* to be good stewards. The condition of our hearts matters far more than what we are actually doing with God's blessings. Here is how Paul put it in 2 Corinthians 9:6–7.

> The point is this: The person who sows sparingly will also reap sparingly, and the person who sows generously will also reap generously. Each person should do as he has decided in his heart—not reluctantly or out of compulsion, since God loves a cheerful giver.

Paul hit on the heart behind our giving here when he shared that we are to give generously and cheerfully. To give generously means we don't give the minimum of what is expected of us. We don't try to figure out the least amount we can give away to be OK with God. Instead, we ask the opposite—how much *can* I give away? Our focus is not on what we keep, but what we give. That is what we are more concerned with.

To give cheerfully, of course, means that we give with joy and delight. We recognize that it is a privilege to give God's blessings to others and it is more fulfilling—often far more—than had we held onto what God had given.

When God creates a generous, cheerful heart within us, we will find that we give abundantly, as Jesus called for us to do in Luke 6:38.

> "Give, and it will be given to you; a good measure—pressed down, shaken together, and running over—will be poured into your lap. For with the measure you use, it will be measured back to you."

We have to be careful with this verse and ones like it. We could walk away with the wrong idea that God gave us a formula to get more possessions from him—by giving much away. While God may choose to bless us with more possessions when we give abundantly, there are other ways God may give to us in good measure—such as joy. But even if God does give us more possessions as a result of our giving, what would we do with those possessions? That's right! Because of our generous and cheerful hearts, we would seek to give the new possessions away abundantly too! If God is giving a formula here, it is not a formula designed to accumulate wealth; it is a formula designed to make us greater conduits through which his blessings flow to others around us.

And that takes us to the next way we are to give—sacrificially.

> Sitting across from the temple treasury, he watched how the crowd dropped money into the treasury. Many rich people were putting in large sums. Then a poor widow came and dropped in two tiny coins worth very little. Summoning his disciples, he said to them, "Truly I tell you, this poor widow has put more into the treasury than all the others. For they all gave out of their surplus, but she out of her poverty has put in everything she had—all she had to live on." (Mark 12:41–44)

In that day, the temple had these trumpet-shaped containers in which people would place the temple tax and gifts. As you can imagine, when a wealthy person dropped in a large number of coins, it was easy for people to notice. Surely many gave when crowds were around just to be noticed. As Jesus watched how people gave, he saw a poor widow drop two of the smallest coins—like our pennies—into one of the receptacles. Surely no one noticed but him. This woman made an impression on Jesus, so he called the disciples over and taught them something important. The depth of our giving is not measured by its quantity, but its quality. You can give large sums of money that you won't even miss, or you can give a small sum of money that will hurt. The latter is the more meaningful gift because it is sacrificial. And that is what God wants us to strive toward—sacrificial giving, no matter what quantity that might be.

2 Corinthians 9:6–7; Luke 6:38; Mark 12:41–44

Q. What is our mission as Christians?

A. Our mission as Christians is to make disciples of all nations by the power of the Holy Spirit.

———————

It's easy to fall into the trap of thinking everything is about us. After all, that is what companies market to us all the time—what we deserve, how we need to treat ourselves, and that our happiness is paramount.

But that thinking is contrary to the gospel, even though many of us carry it over into the gospel. We make the mistake of thinking that the gospel is about us. That God sent Jesus to save us—which he certainly did—but then we stop right there. We are saved, we are good with God, so now we can just enjoy a nice, quiet life as we await the day when we experience our ultimate reward. But that has never been God's intention. If it were, why wouldn't he just take us home to be with him the moment we are saved? Why leave us on earth? It sure would be a lot more loving, wouldn't it?

But God doesn't do that for a reason—a good one—we have a mission to fulfill on earth. Our salvation is not meant to stop with us; it is meant to move through us as we live on mission to share the gospel and make disciples of others.

As Jesus prepared to ascend to be with the Father, he made this mission crystal clear to his disciples. He was leaving them, but they weren't just supposed to wait for his return—there was work for them to do. Each Gospel ends with a commission where Jesus sent out his disciples, but the one recorded in Matthew, that we know as the Great Commission, is the most familiar:

> Jesus came near and said to them, "All authority has been
> given to me in heaven and on earth. Go, therefore, and make

disciples of all nations, baptizing them in the name of the Father and of the Son and of the Holy Spirit, teaching them to observe everything I have commanded you. And remember, I am with you always, to the end of the age." (Matt. 28:18–20)

Jesus began by reminding us of his authority. He wants to make it clear that what he is about to say is not a suggestion, but a command. Because Jesus has all authority, we are supposed to go. When we hear that word *go*, we often think of mission trips. We aren't going, but then one day the trip begins, so we "go." And then we come back and it is over. While mission trips are wonderful, that is not what Jesus had in mind here. The command could actually be translated "as you are going." Reading it that way helps because it reveals that this going is ongoing in nature. As you are living, or as part of your normal lifestyle, here is what you are supposed to do. That's important, because it reminds us that making disciples is not something we do at certain times or something that is above and beyond how we normally live—making disciples is supposed to be woven into what we do every single day.

So what are we supposed to do as a rhythm of normal life? Make disciples of all nations. A disciple is a learner, or a follower of Jesus. So we are to be followers who replicate ourselves. We want to make other disciples who in turn make still other disciples, and so on. Notice the extent of our disciple making—it is of all the nations. We tend to think of a "nation" as a political entity, but nations here is more of a people group who share a common culture. Depending on how you define them, there could be up to 24,000 people groups in the world today.[3] Our mission is to reach every single one with the gospel.

Jesus then shared what we are to do as we make disciples of all nations—we baptize and teach them. Teaching them makes sense—a learner needs to be taught something, and in this case it is what Jesus shared with us—the gospel. Baptism makes sense too when we understand what it is. The basic meaning of baptism is a new believer showing others the change that the gospel has made within them. That is quite important, but it is not the only meaning of baptism. Baptism is also a picture of joining—us to Jesus *and* us to his church. When we baptize new believers, they are connected to God's *global* church, so baptism assumes that we are helping them connect to a *local* church too. This is where they will continue to grow as they also carry out their part of making more disciples of the nations.

The last thing Jesus shared is critical—he will always be with us. It's comforting to know that our mission is not up to us—Christ is with us, empowering us every step of the way. And it is also comforting to connect this with what he said first—the One who has all authority will be with us! What do we have to fear? Failure? Rejection? There is no place for these fears when the all-powerful Son of God is with us!

Matthew 28:18–20; Mark 16:15; Luke 24:47; John 17:18

Q. Why should we seek to make disciples of Jesus?

A. We should seek to make disciples of Jesus because it is our duty and privilege, and so that others may come to experience the joy of salvation.

Being part of fulfilling the Great Commission is our responsibility as Christians. Remember that Jesus framed those instructions around his authority, so it is certainly true that we make disciples because we have to. But that should not be our main motivation. Once again, God is concerned with our hearts—why we do what we do—not just our obedience. For this reason, God wants us to see making disciples as a privilege he has given us. There is perhaps no better example of making disciples with this attitude than the most famous missionary ever—Paul. Here is what Paul wrote to the church at Rome in anticipation of visiting them:

> I am obligated both to Greeks and barbarians, both to the wise and the foolish. So I am eager to preach the gospel to you also who are in Rome. For I am not ashamed of the gospel, because it is the power of God for salvation to everyone who believes, first to the Jew, and also to the Greek. (Rom. 1:14–16)

Paul was quick to share that he was obligated to share the gospel with those in Rome, but that he was also eager to do it. Paul was excited about sharing the gospel and making disciples because he understood the power and beauty of the gospel. So for Paul, the obligation he felt was not one of God saying he had to share the gospel, but the internal burden on his heart. He had experienced the transforming power of the gospel himself, and he knew that so many others needed to experience it as well, so he could not sit still. He had to share it with others.

That is what God wants us to feel. He wants us to experience so much joy in knowing him through Jesus and care so deeply for others that the duty of sharing the gospel isn't our main motivation. We won't ask why we should share the gospel; we will instead ask how we could not share it. God could have chosen angels as his instruments of spreading the gospel. But he didn't. He chose us—not to burden us, but to bless us. We have the privilege of sharing the gospel with others and being part of seeing lives transformed all around us!

Of all the things we will do better in heaven, there is one major thing that we will not be able to do at all on that day—share the gospel with an unbeliever. That is why we need to do it as much as we can now, while we still can.

Matthew 28:18–20; Romans 1:14–16; Romans 10:14–15

Q. In what two ways do we make disciples?

A. We make disciples by telling others about Jesus and showing them the love of Jesus.

Making disciples requires that we tell them the gospel of Jesus Christ. There is no way around this. Some people think we can just demonstrate how the gospel has changed our lives, but that is like general revelation—there is no way for a person to understand how they can be forgiven of their sin through Jesus by just watching us. This is why Paul writes this in Romans 10:14–15.

> How, then, can they call on him they have not believed in? And how can they believe without hearing about him? And how can they hear without a preacher? And how can they preach unless they are sent? As it is written: How beautiful are the feet of those who bring good news.

Someone cannot call on God if they have not believed in the gospel, but they cannot believe in the gospel without hearing it first, and they cannot hear it without someone telling it to them. It starts with us verbalizing the gospel.

But this is where some people make the opposite mistake—they think that the only thing that matters is telling the gospel. While it is the most important thing, it is not the only thing. Making disciples also includes showing them the love of Jesus, which in turn works together with our telling the gospel. This twofold plan is what Jesus did:

> Jesus continued going around to all the towns and villages, teaching in their synagogues, preaching the good news of the kingdom, and healing every disease and every sickness. When

he saw the crowds, he felt compassion for them, because they were distressed and dejected, like sheep without a shepherd. (Matt. 9:35–36)

Jesus preached the gospel, but he also showed love for people by meeting their physical needs, and he cared about them. Jesus loved people, he didn't just preach *at* them. And that is what we need to do as well if we want to see the gospel take root in others. We strive to meet their physical and emotional needs as we share the gospel. When we do these together, the gospel we verbalize will be strengthened—people will know that there is power in the words we share because they have seen it in our love for them.

Matthew 9:35–38; Matthew 25:31–46; Romans 10:14-15

19

Q. How should we feel about people who have not trusted in Jesus?

A. We should love and have compassion for those who have not trusted in Jesus.

The church has this tendency to focus on the wrong enemy at times. Sometimes it is politicians. Sometimes it is people who practice certain sins. Sometimes it is people from other religions, or people who have no religion at all. Sometimes it is people in different countries. Sometimes it is just unbelievers in general.

The problem is that not a single one of these is our enemy. Not one. Our enemy is Satan and his forces of evil, not people (Eph. 6:12). Never people.

Even those who are in open hostility with the gospel are not our enemies to fight. It is just the opposite—they are the very people who should move our hearts the most. They are people under the sway of Satan, sin, and evil, and who are in desperate need of the deliverance only found through Jesus. And the only way they will hear about that deliverance is if we tell them. There is no place for resentment, anger, or disdain for unbelievers when God wants our hearts to be filled with love and compassion for them. It is like oil and vinegar; these emotions simply do not mix.

This was the lesson Jonah needed to learn. You remember Jonah—the Old Testament prophet whom God told to go to Nineveh, but who ran in the opposite direction until God caused a giant fish to swallow him and then spit him out in the right direction three days later. Yeah, that Jonah. In the end, Jonah went to Nineveh and preached, but pay attention to what happened at the end of the account. We often focus on the beginning as if that is the most important part. It's not. Here is what God really wants us to drill down on:

Jonah was greatly displeased and became furious. He prayed to the LORD: "Please, LORD, isn't this what I thought while I was still in my own country? That's why I fled toward Tarshish in the first place. I knew that you are a gracious and compassionate God, slow to anger, abounding in faithful love, and one who relents from sending disaster. And now, LORD, take my life from me, for it is better for me to die than to live." (Jonah 4:1–3)

Let's be clear what is going on here. Jonah was sent to Nineveh—the fierce enemy of God's people. That is why he didn't want to go in the first place—this was his enemy, right? But when he preached, the people actually responded! They began to repent, and God spared them from judgment. So what did Jonah do? Did he worship God and praise him for allowing him to be part of seeing the enemy of God's people repent? Not at all. He sat on a hillside and pouted. He pouted because he knew God was gracious and compassionate, slow to anger, and abounding in faithful love. That's right, he pouted about some of the most glorious aspects of God's character! He pouted for the reason that any of us are saved! But Jonah was so stuck in seeing another people as his enemy, he was bitter that God would show them kindness. So he sat on a hill pouting, trying to convince God to destroy the people of Nineveh despite their repentance.

We don't know if Jonah ever repented of his own sinful perception of other people. The book ends before telling us, probably for a good reason. Our concern should not be if Jonah repented and began to love people the way God does, but if we do. Do we love people and have compassion for them, wanting to see them respond to the gospel? Or are we like Jonah?

Luke 10:25–37; John 3:16; Romans 9:1–3

20

Q. How much of the world should we want to see reached for Jesus?

A. We should want all the world—people from every nation, language, and ethnic group—to trust in Christ.

God's plan all along was for men, women, and children from every people group to come to saving faith through his Son. We see this all the way back in the covenant he made with Abraham to form the nation of Israel:

> I will bless those who bless you,
> I will curse anyone who treats you with contempt,
> and all the peoples on earth
> will be blessed through you. (Gen. 12:3)

All of the peoples on the earth would be blessed through Abraham's descendants. But at some point, the children of Israel lost sight of this and thought that God was only concerned about saving them. By the time we reach the Gospels in the New Testament, Israel had fully fallen into the trap of believing that God was only for the Jews—Abraham's descendants—and all of the rest of the people, the Gentiles, were not his concern.

Unfortunately, we can fall into a similar trap. While we may not build relational walls between Jews and Gentiles, we often do when it comes to ethnicity, socio-economic status, nationality, and more. Any time we do this, to any degree, we think and act contrary to God's glorious gospel. God's heart is for all people, and as people who have been saved by his matchless grace, we should be the first not to look past the differences of people, but to celebrate them. God is most glorified when people of every tongue, tribe, and nation unite in celebration of our differences because we are one people of God. This is the beautiful scene that is in store in heaven as described in Revelation 7:9–10:

> After this I looked, and there was a vast multitude from every nation, tribe, people, and language, which no one could number, standing before the throne and before the Lamb. They were clothed in white robes with palm branches in their hands. And they cried out in a loud voice:
>
>> Salvation belongs to our God,
>> who is seated on the throne,
>> and to the Lamb!

That is a beautiful picture of our future hope in heaven and that is what should motivate us to share the gospel—joyfully—with all people everywhere.

Genesis 12:3; Revelation 7:9–10

Q. What is the kingdom of God?

A. The *kingdom of God* is God's general rule over all of creation and his direct rule over those who have trusted in Jesus.

———————

When we think of the kingdom of God, we often think of the church, but while they are related, they are not the same. The church is part of God's kingdom, but it is not the extent of it. God's kingdom certainly includes his direct rule over his people, but it also includes his general rule over all of creation. God is King over all whether everyone yields to his authority or not, even if everything is not presently as it should be:

> Sing a song of wisdom,
> for God is King of the whole earth.
> God reigns over the nations;
> God is seated on his holy throne. (Ps. 47:7–8)

God is on his throne reigning at all times, even if most of creation rebels against his rule. This reality is at the core of the kingdom of God. God always has, and always will, reign over his creation.

> Your kingdom is an everlasting kingdom;
> your rule is for all generations.
> The Lord is faithful in all his words
> and gracious in all his actions. (Ps. 145:13)

The difference for the church is that we have recognized God as our King and strive to yield to his authority in our lives. Our role as part of God's kingdom is to express what it looks like to live under God's sovereign rule. As kingdom citizens, we are called to reflect the values, priorities, and character of the King. This includes praying for and working toward the day when God's kingdom will come in fullness and all will submit to his authority. This is what Jesus had in mind when he was asked at his trials if he was a king:

> "My kingdom is not of this world," said Jesus. "If my kingdom were of this world, my servants would fight, so that I wouldn't be handed over to the Jews. But as it is, my kingdom is not from here." (John 18:36)

Jesus' point was that he is not a king in the way the religious leaders thought. They were thinking of an earthly political kingdom, but Christ's kingdom is far greater than that. It is not limited to one nation or even the entire earth. Christ's kingdom is over all creation—what is seen and what is unseen. One day when Christ returns, that kingdom will be made fully known to all.

Psalm 47:7–8; Psalm 145:13

22

Q. What should we pray for the kingdom?

A. We should pray for God's kingdom to come and God's will to be done.

As the people of God, we understand that Jesus is King of kings and Lord of lords. We know that God is sovereign over all, even if the world remains in open rebellion against his authority. But it is not enough for us to know this and keep it to ourselves; we should desire to see God's kingdom come in fullness and pray for that to happen.

When Jesus taught his disciples how to pray, this was one of the parts of the model prayer that he shared:

> Our Father in heaven,
> your name be honored as holy.
> Your kingdom come.
> Your will be done
> on earth as it is in heaven. (Matt. 6:9b–11a)

Jesus taught us first to acknowledge who God is—he is our heavenly Father who is holy and to be honored. And then our first petition to our Father is for his kingdom to come and his will to be done on earth as it is done in his throne room in heaven—perfectly. We are to pray that God's reign will be realized fully on earth—that he will rule visibly with all authority and for all rebellion against him to come to an end.

There is a day coming when this will happen. Every knee will bow to God as King, as we read in Romans 14:11.

> For it is written,
> As I live, says the Lord,

> every knee will bow to me,
> and every tongue will give praise to God.

Paul expounded on this in the book of Philippians when he wrote that every knee will bow and tongue will confess that Jesus Christ is Lord (Phil. 2:9–11). This will happen when Jesus returns, so when we pray for God's kingdom to come and his will to be done, we are specifically praying for the return of Jesus. On that day when Jesus returns as conquering King, he will put an end to all sin and rebellion and establish God's kingdom in its fullness, and all who have trusted in him will enjoy his loving rule forever.

Matthew 6:9–11; Romans 14:11

23

Q. How should we live in an unjust world?

A. We should live seeking to promote justice, defend the helpless, and oppose sin.

Things were not looking good for God's people in the mid-eighth century BC. The kingdom was split in two—the northern kingdom of Israel and the southern kingdom of Judah—and both nations were ruled by mostly wicked kings who plunged God's people deeper and deeper into idolatry. Of course God was not having any of that. So he sent prophet after prophet to warn the people—repent of your sin and turn back to God or else judgment is coming.

Not surprisingly, the hard-hearted people continued in sin and actually moved even further away from God's ways. The northern kingdom experienced a financial boom, but it occurred on the backs of the poor. The rich got richer by exploiting the poor, who got poorer.

And that is when Amos, a shepherd from Tekoa in Judah, showed up. The people of Israel were surely skeptical when Amos began to announce a message from God—after all, he was not one of them. But when the strange shepherd began to announce God's prophetic judgment against the enemy nations surrounding them, they found themselves nodding in agreement.

Aram. Philistia. Phoenicia. Edom. Ammon. Moab. One by one, Amos decried God's judgment on Israel's enemies. And then he announced judgment on Judah. Now, this was an interesting turn. Judah and Israel were two different nations, but they were of course family—estranged, but still family. Amos's message was starting to hit a little close to home. And then Amos sprung his trap and announced God's judgment on them—the people of Israel.

God was going to judge Israel for their sin—mostly idolatry, but that was not all. God was also going to judge them because they were exploiting the poor. God was fed up with the people's two-faced worship—they worshiped false gods but still tried to worship him too—and Amos shared God's revulsion to their hollow singing and sacrifices. The singing was a noisy racket; the sacrifices smelled foul to God. And then God told the people this through his prophet:

> But let justice flow like water,
> and righteousness, like an unfailing stream. (Amos 5:24)

It wasn't enough for the people to clean up their worship and ban idolatry. That was important, but even if they did that they would still be under God's judgment because they weren't loving each other. Idolatry and injustice go hand-in-hand; God's people needed to repent of both. They needed to pursue overflowing justice and righteousness in their land.

And that is what we, as God's people today, need to do as well. We are to take a stand against all forms of injustice that exist in our communities and oppose every form of sin—in our own lives, in our churches, and in our communities. This is exactly what another of God's prophets, Micah, would share with Israel around the same time as Amos:

> Mankind, he has told each of you what is good
> and what it is the LORD requires of you:
> to act justly,
> to love faithfulness,
> and to walk humbly with your God. (Micah 6:8)

It is telling that the first requirement God listed was justice. God's kingdom is marked by absolute justice, so it is fitting that as we pray for God's kingdom to come we promote this attribute of his kingdom today.

Amos 5:24; Micah 6:8; Isaiah 1:17

24

Q. Do Christians continue to sin?

A. Yes, Christians continue to sin, although all our sin is forgiven.

Christians are often accused of hypocrisy. While this certainly may be true of some Christians, the claim is usually made when Christians sin. The world seems to think that Christians are supposed to be perfect, but that is not the case at all. Christians are not perfect, and certainly not hypocrites for being imperfect. In fact, the Bible is clear that as Christians, we are not to claim to be without sin:

> If we say, "We have no sin," we are deceiving ourselves, and the truth is not in us. If we confess our sins, he is faithful and righteous to forgive us our sins and to cleanse us from all unrighteousness. If we say, "We have not sinned," we make him a liar, and his word is not in us. (1 John 1:8–10)

Christians are still sinners—only we are forgiven of our sin and are no longer defined by it. And that's the beautiful truth that we should seek to tell the world. Every single sin a Christian commits is forgiven in Christ. Every one. There is no sin too great and no sin too small to have been taken on the cross and paid for by Christ. Once we are in Christ, all of our sin—past, present, and future—is paid for and no longer held against us. We read of this in Psalm 103:12.

> As far as the east is from the west,
> so far has he removed
> our transgressions from us.

Some people have a hard time understanding how our future sins can be paid for by Christ when we place our trust in him. But when you think about it, when Jesus died on the cross, *all* of our sins were in the future! Forgiving future sins is no difficulty for an eternal God.

Knowing that we will continue to sin, but that each of those sins is forgiven, is freeing for us. We don't have to live in fear. We are forgiven and we have been given Jesus' righteousness. That is how God sees us, and that is how we need to see ourselves.

1 John 1:8–10; Psalm 103:12

25

Q. Do Christians have to sin?

A. No, Christians can resist sin.

It is helpful to think about our sins as Christians in two ways—positionally and experientially. To think of our sins positionally is to see them as God sees them, or through the lens of what our position is with God because of our sins. When we look at our sins through this lens, we are reminded that we are completely forgiven in Christ:

> Therefore, there is now no condemnation for those in Christ Jesus. (Rom. 8:1)

Our sins do not change our standing with God at all. We are able to stand with confidence as God's children because Christ has already paid for every sin we will ever commit and God has declared us righteous. Positionally, God sees us as completely pure.

But experientially, it is a different story. This is how we experience life, and when we sin as Christians, it does affect us in different ways. Again, our salvation is secure, but sins have consequences for us now on earth.

One of the main experiential impacts of our sin is strained, but not broken, fellowship with God. Our relationship is always secure, but our fellowship is not. When we sin, we tend to move away from God. You may have experienced this yourself. How much do you want to pray, read the Bible, evangelize, or worship with other believers when you have sinned? Probably not much. We tend to allow shame and guilt to creep in, and these feelings create a wedge between us and God. This is what John had in mind when he wrote:

If we say, "We have fellowship with him," and yet we walk in darkness, we are lying and are not practicing the truth. If we walk in the light as he himself is in the light, we have fellowship with one another, and the blood of Jesus his Son cleanses us from all sin. (1 John 1:6–7)

We cannot have fellowship with God and walk in darkness, but it is also hard to have fellowship with God even when we step into the darkness just for a moment. Our joy diminishes because we know we are not living as we should. But when we walk in the light—apart from sin—we are able to have the fellowship with God we desire deep down.

Another impact of our sins is that we open ourselves to God's discipline. Because God loves us, he will not allow us to step into the darkness and stay there. He will discipline us so that we repent of our sin and step back into the light:

"As many as I love, I rebuke and discipline. So be zealous and repent." (Rev. 3:19)

But the wonderful news is that we don't have to sin. That is really what Christian freedom is about. In Christ, we have the freedom to turn from sin and to please God. Apart from Christ we can do neither. This is what Paul tells us in Romans 6:11.

So, you too consider yourselves dead to sin and alive to God in Christ Jesus.

We are no longer slaves to sin. We have the ability to turn from sin, because its power is dead to us. But even when we sin, that sin is forgiven. That's great news. That's the gospel.

Romans 6:11; Romans 8:1; 1 John 1:6–7

26

Q. How can Christians resist sin?

A. Christians can resist sin through the power of the Holy Spirit, reading the Bible, and the encouragement of other Christians.

_____

As Christians, we know that we can resist sin because of verses like 1 Timothy 6:11, which follows Paul's description of the various sins money causes:

> But you, man of God, flee from these things, and pursue righteousness, godliness, faith, love, endurance, and gentleness.

If we could not resist sin, this verse would make no sense. How can you flee something you cannot get away from? But the beautiful truth is that we *can* resist sin, so we are commanded to flee from it. How do we do that though, especially when we remember that sin is born within us? How can we flee from ourselves?

And that's the answer. We can't flee on our own. We need help from outside of us. We need help from God, which means we actually do need help from within us after all. It's just the part that is not *us* within us; it is the Holy Spirit within us.

God has given us the Holy Spirit so that he can work in our hearts and give us the power to turn from sin and live victoriously. We will fail if we try to tough it out against sin on our own, so it is foolish to even try, as Paul told the Galatian church:

> Are you so foolish? After beginning by the Spirit, are you now finishing by the flesh? (Gal. 3:3)

It's foolish to know that we needed the Holy Spirit to bring us to saving faith in Christ, but then think we can live out that faith in our own power. The Holy Spirit stays with us for a reason—to empower us to live for Christ every day. But while the Holy Spirit is always present within us, we don't always yield control to him, which is why we find ourselves falling into sin instead of resisting it. It's a matter of who has control—us or the Holy Spirit. Giving the Holy Spirit control is called being filled with the Spirit, as we see in Ephesians 5:18:

> And don't get drunk with wine, which leads to reckless living,
> but be filled by the Spirit.

Paul uses a helpful word picture here. When someone is drunk with wine, the wine controls him; it's the same way when it comes to being filled with the Spirit. The idea is that the Spirit should control us like wine does, only in a good way of course. When we are filled with the Spirit, he will guard our minds and hearts to protect us from sin.

Related to being filled with the Spirit is spending time in God's Word. The more time we spend reading and meditating on the Bible, the more it too will fill our minds and hearts and protect us from sin, as we read in Psalm 119:11:

> I have treasured your word in my heart
> so that I may not sin against you.

There is a third way that we can resist sin—the church. God has given us the church to come alongside us and encourage us to follow God and turn from sin, as we read in Hebrews 3:13:

> But encourage each other daily, while it is still called today, so
> that none of you is hardened by sin's deception.

This is why it is so critical that we be part of a local church and that we establish meaningful relationships with other believers. We need to invite people into our lives so that they can help us fight against sin. That means we need to be appropriately transparent with one another. There is no place for masks among God's people. We all know we sin, and many of us share similar struggles. If we aren't honest with one another and invite others to tell us what we need to hear, even if it is difficult to hear, we rob ourselves of one of God's key ways for us to fight sin in our lives.

Galatians 3:3; Psalm 119:11; Hebrews 3:13

27

Q. How does the Holy Spirit help us when we are worried, afraid, or sad?

A. The Holy Spirit comforts us and gives us peace when we are worried, afraid, or sad.

One of the Greek words used in the New Testament for the Holy Spirit is *paraclete*. This is one of those Greek words that can be difficult to translate because it has several meanings including "helper," "advocate," "counselor," and "comforter," but as we can see they all have to do with the Holy Spirit coming alongside us and helping us. Proverbs 12:25 tells us that anxiety in our hearts weighs us down. We all experience many reasons for our hearts to be weighed down—worry, fear, and sadness. This is where the Holy Spirit ministers to us as *paraclete*. He comes alongside us and gives us peace whenever we need it.

When the Bible speaks of peace, it can mean one of three things. First, there is **peace with God** (Rom. 5:1). Apart from Christ, we are enemies of God in hostility with him. We are rebelling against God, and because of our sin, we are under his wrath. But when we trust in Christ, we experience peace with God. The hostilities are ended, and we move from being enemies of God to become his children.

The second peace is **peace with others** (Rom. 12:18). Again, because of sin, we experience tensions and fractures in our relationships with others. But when we are guided by the Holy Spirit, he helps us experience peace with other people.

The third kind of peace is **peace within.** This is the inner peace that is needed when we are afraid, worried, or sad. This is the comfort of God we receive through the Spirit that reminds us that he is in control and that everything will be all right. This is the peace that reminds us of eternity—that our worries and fears will not last and one day it will all be behind us. And this is the peace that comes from knowing deep down that we are beloved children of God, as we see in Romans 8:16:

> The Spirit himself testifies together with our spirit that we are God's children.

No matter what problems in life we experience, no matter how painful they might be, we know that the Holy Spirit is always there to give us the comfort we need.

Romans 5:1; Romans 12:18; Romans 8:16

28

Q. How does the Holy Spirit help us when we sin?

A. The Holy Spirit helps us when we sin by convicting our hearts and helping us to repent and turn back to God.

———————————

Jeremiah had it right when he wrote:

> The heart is more deceitful than anything else, and incurable—who can understand it? (Jer. 17:9)

Even when we have trusted in Christ, our hearts still deceive us all the time. Sin is rooted deep down in our hearts, and it wants to continually feed our flesh. The world around us only adds fuel to this fire. Because of this, there are times when we will sin and not even know it (see Lev. 5:17) or our hearts will resist admitting our sin. This is where the Holy Spirit helps us by convicting us of our sin and leading us toward repentance.

When we think of the convicting work of the Holy Spirit, we have to understand two things. First, this is not the same as our conscience. While everyone has a conscience—an inner sense of what is right and wrong based largely on societal norms—conviction of the Holy Spirit is different. This is where the Holy Spirit reminds us of God's standards, not society's.

Second, the goal of the Holy Spirit's conviction is always for us to repent and enjoy restored fellowship with God. This is one of the Holy Spirit's main ministries Jesus told us about:

> "When he comes, he will convict the world about sin, righteousness, and judgment: About sin, because they do not believe in

me; about righteousness, because I am going to the Father and
you will no longer see me; and about judgment, because the
ruler of this world has been judged." (John 16:8–11)

While experiencing the Holy Spirit's conviction is not pleasant, we know
that God uses it for our good. Without this ministry of the Holy Spirit, our
hearts would continue to deceive us and drive us further into sin and farther
away from God. It is because of the kindness of God that he gives us the Holy
Spirit to convict us of our sin and bring us back to him.

Jeremiah 17:9; John 16:8–11

29

Q. How does the Holy Spirit change us?

A. The Holy Spirit changes us by reminding us of the truth of the gospel and making us to be more like Christ.

When we trust in Christ, we are instantly and completely changed in many profound ways. We move from being dead in sin to being alive in Christ. We move from being enemies of God to being his children. We move from being under God's wrath to being recipients of Christ's righteousness. All of these are immediate and total changes.

But not all of the changes we experience are immediate or complete. We still need to grow in our relationship with Christ and be changed more in his image each day. This process is called sanctification, and it occurs, in part, by the Holy Spirit reminding us of the truth of the gospel over and over again each day as we let it sink deeper into our hearts so that it works its way through us to make us more like Jesus. This is what Jesus promised in John 14:26.

> But the Counselor, the Holy Spirit, whom the Father will send in my name, will teach you all things and remind you of everything I have told you.

The Holy Spirit continues to teach us and remind us of what Jesus taught—the gospel. While this is a gradual process in many ways, there are times when we can experience explosive and rapid growth in Christ. Perhaps one of the best examples of this occurred at Pentecost in Acts 2.

When you read through the Gospels, you will see that Jesus' disciples were rather . . . slow . . . at times. They just didn't seem to get it. One minute they might demonstrate great faith in Jesus, and the next minute they would do something utterly foolish. Peter is probably best known for this. He always had this way of putting his foot in his mouth.

But then we get to Pentecost and we see these same disciples—just a few weeks after the arrest and crucifixion of Jesus—boldly proclaiming Christ to Jews in Jerusalem. And it worked. More than five thousand people trusted in Jesus that day! What happened to these men? How were they able to be so faithful and effective at Pentecost when they had failed so often before? The answer is the Holy Spirit. Jesus had promised that he would send the Holy Spirit, and that when he came, they would receive power (Acts 1:8). And sure enough, that is what happened:

> Then they were all filled with the Holy Spirit and began to speak in different tongues, as the Spirit enabled them. (Acts 2:4)

The Holy Spirit enabled the disciples to preach in languages they had not spoken before, which made quite an impact on the crowd gathered in Jerusalem. But the Holy Spirit also gave the disciples courage and the right words to share. Pentecost shows us the power of the Holy Spirit to change us and use us in potent ways. Some change will be gradual, but some may be just as fast and impressive as that day two thousand years ago.

John 14:26; 1 Corinthians 6:11

Q. How does the Holy Spirit help us live for God?

A. The Holy Spirit helps us to pray, read, and understand the Bible, and to obey God.

The first time you read John 16:7, it is jarring:

> "Nevertheless, I am telling you the truth. It is for your benefit that I go away, because if I don't go away the Counselor will not come to you. If I go, I will send him to you."

Surely Jesus didn't mean that it was good for us for him to leave, right? There has to be a nuance we're missing here. Nope. We're not. He said it and he meant it. While it feels wrong for Jesus to say that, the more we learn about the Holy Spirit's ministry to us, the more we see just what Jesus meant.

As we have seen, the Holy Spirit helps us to resist sin, comforts us, convicts us of sin to bring us back to God, and changes us to be more like Jesus. We could stop here and probably understand how Jesus was right, but that is not all the Holy Spirit does. He does so much more, such as helping us to pray, understand the Bible, and obey God.

Let's start with prayer. How hard can prayer be, right? Why do we need the Spirit's help? Here is what Paul said about this in Romans 8:26:

> In the same way the Spirit also helps us in our weakness, because we do not know what to pray for as we should, but the Spirit himself intercedes for us with unspoken groanings.

We need help because we don't know for what we should pray. Oh, sure we know what we *want* to pray for, but that is not always what we *should* pray for. We might want to pray for a promotion at work, but the truth is that it might not be good for us. When we pray for that promotion, the Holy Spirit intercedes for us to the Father. He takes our prayers that are limited by our perspective and hindered by our sin and he prays on our behalf for what we truly need. In this case, it might not be the promotion, but patience as we need to wait for something else God has planned for us.

The Spirit helps us in a similar manner when it comes to reading the Bible. The Bible is God's Word given to us to reveal who he is and his will for our lives, but we need God's help to understand him and his ways. This is where the Holy Spirit steps in once again:

> Now God has revealed these things to us by the Spirit, since
> the Spirit searches everything, even the depths of God. (1 Cor.
> 2:10)

The Spirit is able to search the depths of God and reveal the mind of God to us because he is God himself. There are times when we read Scripture and God's truth leaps off the page at us in fresh and powerful ways. This is the Holy Spirit at work in us.

And that takes us to the Holy Spirit helping us obey. As we pray and read God's Word, we should respond by living differently—in fuller obedience to God. But once again, we cannot obey in our own power; we need the Holy Spirit:

> I say then, walk by the Spirit and you will certainly not carry
> out the desire of the flesh. (Gal. 5:16)

Walking by the power of the Holy Spirit is what enables us to put our desires of the flesh away and obey God instead. One way we obey God is by praying and reading the Bible more, which in turn leads to obeying God more. And so the upward spiral continues as the Holy Spirit changes us to be more like Jesus. It was good for Jesus to go because through his provision of the Holy Spirit we can grow to be more like him.

Romans 8:26; 1 Corinthians 2:10; Galatians 5:16

31

Q. Is the Holy Spirit a Person?

A. Yes, the Holy Spirit is a Person just like God the Father and God the Son.

The Holy Spirit is a Person just like the Father and the Son because he too possesses will, intellect, and emotion. We see the Holy Spirit's will in 1 Corinthians 12:11.

> One and the same Spirit is active in all these, distributing to each person as he wills.

Paul is speaking of spiritual gifts in this passage. Spiritual gifts are given to believers not randomly, but with purpose based on the Holy Spirit's will. The Spirit has a will for *who* receives *what* spiritual gift.

We see the Holy Spirit's intellect in Romans 8:27.

> And he who searches our hearts knows the mind of the Spirit, because he intercedes for the saints according to the will of God.

Here we see that the Spirit has a mind—he has thoughts and intellect. Finally, we see the Holy Spirit's emotion in Ephesians 4:30.

> And don't grieve God's Holy Spirit. You were sealed by him for the day of redemption.

We can grieve the Spirit, or cause him anguish, by not following him.

It is important that we understand that the Holy Spirit is a Person because he is God. If the Holy Spirit were just a divine force, and not a person, that would impact our understanding of the Father and the Son as well.

But because he is a Person, our understanding of all three Persons of God is strengthened. Each has will, intellect, and emotion, but all three Persons are completely unified as our One God.

1 Corinthians 12:11; Romans 8:27; Ephesians 4:30

Q. Where is the Holy Spirit?

A. The Holy Spirit lives in all Christians.

The instant we trust in Christ and are saved, we receive the Holy Spirit, who dwells within us from that day forward. We see this in Romans 5:5.

> This hope will not disappoint us, because God's love has been poured out in our hearts through the Holy Spirit who was given to us.

The Holy Spirit is not given to unbelievers, just believers. While he works in unbelievers to draw them to repentance and faith in Christ, he does not indwell them as he does believers. And as we have examined the Spirit's ministry, we have seen that the Spirit's permanent indwelling is truly an amazing gift from God.

But as wonderful as his ministry is, there is another reason the Spirit is given to us permanently—he seals us in Christ:

> Now the one who prepared us for this very purpose is God, who gave us the Spirit as a down payment. (2 Cor. 5:5)

The Holy Spirit is a seal, or down payment, guaranteeing that we belong to God and also that God is not done with us yet. Christ will return for us one day! And when Christ returns, we will receive new glorified bodies that are no longer stained by sin and the curse. The proof that Christ will do this is the Holy Spirit within us. God has given the Spirit to us, and there is no way he will forfeit his deposit. He will make good on his promises.

While the Spirit has been given to us permanently, that does not mean we are always controlled by him. We continue to struggle with our flesh, and there are times when we refuse to give the Holy Spirit control of our lives, something the Bible calls filling:

> And don't get drunk with wine, which leads to reckless living,
> but be filled by the Spirit. (Eph. 5:18)

This filling is not permanent but is something we need to do repeatedly throughout our lives—even day by day. When we are filled by the Spirit, he controls our minds, hearts, and behavior so that we live more like Christ, and he produces his fruit in us (Gal. 5:22–23).

Romans 5:5; Ephesians 5:18

Q. What is prayer?

A. *Prayer* is talking with God.

The simplest way to think of prayer is that it is talking with God. Notice that it is talking *with* God, not talking *to* God. That's because prayer is a two-way conversation where we speak to God but where we also listen for him to speak to us. That is critical for us to remember. God wants to speak to us, not with an audible voice, but through the Holy Spirit bringing God's truths to our minds and stirring our hearts to follow him. When we pray as if it were a monologue, we miss out on some of the real power of prayer!

Thinking of prayer simply as a two-way conversation also helps us to remember how essential it is in our relationship with God. Think about the meaningful relationships that you have. How healthy would they be if you and the other person never talked? Not very healthy, right? The same is true of prayer. If we want to grow closer to God, we will need to talk with him—often—but it shouldn't be seen as a chore. Praying should be the natural desire of our hearts. This is what we see the disciples demonstrate in the Gospels:

> He was praying in a certain place, and when he finished, one of his disciples said to him, "Lord, teach us to pray, just as John also taught his disciples." (Luke 11:1)

This disciple, surely representing the group by his request for Jesus to teach "us" to pray, had a natural desire from a gospel-transformed heart to understand how to communicate with God better. The reason why many of us struggle with praying and see it as a chore is perhaps because we think prayer is a formulaic, structured requirement instead of a life-giving part of our relationship. While there are several helpful models for prayer, such as

A.C.T.S.—adoration, confession, thanksgiving, supplication—we can't lose sight that at its core, prayer is just having a conversation. Our conversations with people tend to be more organic—more natural—not highly structured. If they were, we'd probably talk less with other people too! So while the elements of A.C.T.S. are certainly helpful and Jesus himself even gave us some principles for praying in answer to this request, we would be wise to always remind ourselves of the simple nature of prayer.

Although prayer is just a conversation, we have to be careful not to treat it too lightly. When we pray, we are told we are to pray in faith.

> Is anyone among you suffering? He should pray. Is anyone cheerful? He should sing praises. Is anyone among you sick? He should call for the elders of the church, and they are to pray over him, anointing him with oil in the name of the Lord. The prayer of faith will save the sick person, and the Lord will raise him up; if he has committed sins, he will be forgiven. (James 5:13–15)

This means that we pray believing that God is listening to us and that he is speaking to us as well. We pray also believing that God cares and that he is sovereign—that he is in control of whatever we are praying for. When we pray in faith like this, we will see how powerful prayer can be. That is not to say that prayer is a magic formula or that God is bound to do whatever we ask him to do when we pray, but it is to say that when we are in close fellowship with God, our hearts will be closely aligned with his so we will find ourselves praying not for our desires, but for his. This is what Jesus had in mind when he told us this:

> "In that day you will not ask me anything. Truly I tell you, anything you ask the Father in my name, he will give you." (John 16:23)

To pray in Jesus' name does not mean we have to tack that phrase on at the end of our prayer. It means that we pray in his power according to his will and character.

At the same time as we need to be careful not to take prayer too lightly, we also cannot use prayer as a way to show others how spiritual we are. This is what Jesus warned us about in the Sermon on the Mount:

"But when you pray, go into your private room, shut your door, and pray to your Father who is in secret. And your Father who sees in secret will reward you. When you pray, don't babble like the Gentiles, since they imagine they'll be heard for their many words." (Matt. 6:6–7)

This doesn't mean that we can never pray in public—Jesus himself did—but it does mean that we should not use prayer as a way to make ourselves look more spiritual to others. Praying with fancy words and for a long time does not please God unless our hearts are sincere in how we are praying. God is pleased more in a simple, short, heartfelt prayer than he is in a theological diatribe. It makes sense when we remember the basics. Prayer is simply having a conversation with God, and conversations are when you talk *with* someone, not *at* them.

John 16:23; James 5:13–15

34

Q. When do we pray?

A. We are to pray always.

Does God really want us to pray always? He sure does! Here is one place where we see this in the Bible:

> Rejoice always, pray constantly, give thanks in everything; for
> this is God's will for you in Christ Jesus. (1 Thess. 5:16–18)

Not only do we see that we are to pray constantly, but that doing so is part of God's revealed will for us. We sometimes struggle to know God's will, but there are times, like here, where it is crystal clear. God's will is for us to pray at all times.

But wait a minute. Those verses seem to say that we are to pray when we are joyful—when we have something for which to thank God. So maybe God only wants us to pray at all times when we are happy. Fair enough, but let's look at another passage where we are commanded to pray always:

> Don't worry about anything, but in everything, through prayer
> and petition with thanksgiving, present your requests to God.
> (Phil. 4:6)

So here we see we are to pray always—when we are worried or when we have a need or when we are thankful. We are to pray when we are joyful, when we are worried, and all in between.

OK, so how does that work? How can we close our eyes and pray all the time? Thankfully, we don't have to! While there is nothing wrong with closing our eyes when we pray to help us focus, we can certainly pray with our eyes open. When we remember that prayer is simply having a conversation with God—speaking and listening—we understand how we can pray always. There will be times when we are talking to God, but there will be plenty more times when we are listening instead. We can be in prayer throughout the day by always listening for God to lead us. Remember, we aren't the only ones who can initiate a conversation. God can too. From the time our eyes open in the morning until the time we drift off to sleep at night, we can be in a constant state of prayer with God—speaking and listening—as he guides us throughout the day.

1 Thessalonians 5:16–18; Philippians 4:6

35

Q. What are some of the things we share with God as we pray?

A. As we pray, we praise God, share our desires with him, and confess our sins to him.

When we pray, we are not bothering God. We have to keep that in mind. Some of us may feel that way—we are, after all, talking to the creator God, right? It is easy to see how some people would feel that God doesn't have time for them—or at least not for the little things they might want to share with him. So when we pray, it better be important, right?

But this is the exact opposite of God's heart for us. He wants us to talk with him. He wants to hear from us—the big things and the little things and everything in between. He wants to hear these things because he loves us and he wants us to enjoy fellowship with him.

So what are some basic things God wants us to share? First, he wants to hear our praises and how we are thankful for him:

> Rejoice always, pray constantly, give thanks in everything; for this is God's will for you in Christ Jesus. (1 Thess. 5:16–18)

Part of what we talk with God about should be focused on who he is and what he has done for us. Now, that may seem like it is self-serving on God's part, but it really is not. We have to remember that God wired us to worship and he is absolutely worthy of worship. God is the greatest good, so when we focus on how good he is, it actually benefits us. God deserves our praise, he commands our praise, but we benefit greatly when we give it.

Second, God also wants us to share our requests with him:

"So I say to you, ask, and it will be given to you. Seek, and you will find. Knock, and the door will be opened to you." (Luke 11:9)

We are to share our needs with him and even our desires. We have to remember that God is our loving Father—he delights in blessing us. However, we also have to remember that he is sovereign King and as such he knows that some of the things for which we ask are not good for us. In God's love, he will not give us anything that is not good for us, so one of God's most gracious answers to our prayers is sometimes "no."

But it isn't just our needs and desires for which we should ask—we should also ask for things on behalf of others:

First of all, then, I urge that petitions, prayers, intercessions, and thanksgivings be made for everyone. (1 Tim. 2:1)

Intercession is so important for us because it helps keep our selfishness in check, but also because it mirrors the heart of God. When we were in our most desperate need because of our sin, God provided Jesus, who interceded on our behalf and paid our sin penalty. And Jesus continually intercedes for us with the Father, so when we intercede for others, we are following in the footsteps of Christ.

Third, we are to confess our sins to God:

If we confess our sins, he is faithful and righteous to forgive us our sins and to cleanse us from all unrighteousness. (1 John 1:9)

All of our sins are forgiven in Christ, but that doesn't mean that they don't impact us. One way they do is by hindering our relationship with God. When we sin, we don't feel close to him (because we have moved from him, not him from us), and the way that we can come back to God is through confession of our sin. Confession can be thought of as agreeing with God about our sin. So when we confess, we agree with God that we were wrong and that we sinned against him. When we do this, we will be reminded of his matchless grace for us and that will drive us back to worship him—our amazing God who has forgiven us so greatly.

1 Thessalonians 5:16–18; Luke 11:9; 1 John 1:9

36

Q. What should our desire be when we pray?

A. As we pray, our desire should be to know and submit to God's will for our lives.

Suppose that a friend of yours wasn't feeling well, so he asked you to take him to see a doctor. After examining your friend, the doctor tells him that she knows what is wrong with him. She shares the diagnosis and then hands him a bottle and tells him he needs to take the medicine in it or he will not get well. Your friend hands the medicine back to the doctor and begins trying to convince her that he needs a different course of treatment. He then turns to you and asks you to help him convince the doctor.

What would you do? Probably not help your friend, right? It is foolish of him to believe he knows better than his doctor. He should listen to her wise counsel and follow her instructions.

But this is exactly how many people approach prayer—they see prayer as the way to convince God to give them what they want and do what they say. And that is completely backwards. Prayer is not about us changing God; it is about God changing us. How much more foolish are we when we approach God—our all-knowing, all-powerful Creator—with the goal of convincing him that we know better than him and that he should get on board with our plans? It is only when we remember that we pray so that God can reveal his will to us and change us to follow his perfect plans that prayer will be powerful in our lives.

The greatest example of praying for God's will, not our own, is Jesus himself when he prayed in the garden of Gethsemane:

> "Father, if you are willing, take this cup away from me—nevertheless, not my will, but yours, be done." (Luke 22:42)

Jesus was anticipating the cross. He prayed for that "cup" to be taken from him. We know this "cup" referred to God's wrath. Perhaps Jesus was focusing on the physical suffering this would entail; or maybe he was considering the separation from the Father he would experience. It is helpful for us to see what he said next: "Not my will, but yours, be done." Even Jesus submitted to the Father's will, and so should we.

Another helpful example comes from Paul. In 2 Corinthians, Paul shared how he had been given a "thorn in the flesh." While he doesn't say what the thorn was—perhaps a physical ailment such as poor vision or perhaps persecution that he faced—he shares that he prayed for God to remove it. But here is what he said happened:

> Concerning this, I pleaded with the Lord three times that it would leave me. But he said to me, "My grace is sufficient for you, for my power is perfected in weakness."
>
> Therefore, I will most gladly boast all the more about my weaknesses, so that Christ's power may reside in me. So I take pleasure in weaknesses, insults, hardships, persecutions, and in difficulties, for the sake of Christ. For when I am weak, then I am strong. (2 Cor. 12:8–10)

Paul's will was for God to remove the thorn, but when God revealed his will was for the thorn to remain, Paul not only accepted God's will but praised God for it. Paul understood that God's will is always better than ours, so even if God's will was difficult at times, it was worth celebrating. And that is the attitude we need to strive to have as we pray and seek to know God's will for our lives and submit to it—not grudgingly, but with joy.

Luke 22:42; 2 Corinthians 12:8–10

37

Q. What should our attitude be as we submit to God's will?

A. We should submit to God's will with joy.

Submitting to God's will is similar to obeying God, only obedience is always active, while submitting to God's will may be passive as well. God's will doesn't just involve us, but those around us too. Sometimes we are called on to submit passively to his plans in the lives of others. While there may be a subtle difference between obeying God and submitting to his will, our attitude should be the same—we obey and submit with joy. Just as God doesn't want us to obey heartlessly or grudgingly, he doesn't want us to submit to his will that way either. Philippians 4:4 tells us:

> Rejoice in the Lord always. I will say it again: Rejoice!

Saying it one time wasn't enough for Paul. He just had to say it twice. We are to rejoice in the Lord all the time, in everything. Joy, then, is what should saturate our submission to his will. Proverbs 17:22 explains why:

> A joyful heart is good medicine,
> but a broken spirit dries up the bones.

Joy protects our hearts and our souls. When we lack joy, we open ourselves to a variety of heart ailments such as frustration, bitterness, anger, and selfishness, just to name a few. But joy is the medicine we need for all of these. Joy pushes these away and keeps us submitting to God with a pure heart that trusts him and delights in his ways.

Once again, we turn to Jesus for the best example of this. Just after walking through what is commonly called the "Hall of Faith," the writer of Hebrew summarizes this way:

> Therefore, since we also have such a large cloud of witnesses surrounding us, let us lay aside every hindrance and the sin that so easily ensnares us. Let us run with endurance the race that lies before us, keeping our eyes on Jesus, the source and perfecter of our faith. For the joy that lay before him, he endured the cross, despising the shame, and sat down at the right hand of the throne of God. (Heb. 12:1–2)

We are to find encouragement from the Old Testament saints who have gone before us so that we persevere as we follow God too. But as good of examples as they were, they were not the ideal example—Jesus is. Jesus went to the cross—an instrument of horrible suffering—knowing that he would bear the weight of the world's sins on him and be separated from the Father, but he went with joy. His joy was anchored in submitting to the Father's will and bringing him glory. He knew that as difficult as the cross would be, God would use it to bring about the greatest good imaginable. And that is why he endured it with joy. That is also why we should submit to God's will with joy—because we know that all God does is for his glory and our good.

Philippians 4:4; Hebrews 12:1–2

38

Q. What is worship?

A. *Worship* is declaring and celebrating the great worth of God.

We are all worshipers at our core. We are wired to worship, and worship we must. The problem is that God designed us to long for worship of him, but because of our sin, we will often worship something—anything—else. We see this all around us as well as within us and within our kids. Sports. Movie stars. Musicians. Money. Possessions. Hobbies. Power. Popularity. Success. A spouse. Ourselves. The list goes on and on. We can worship just about anything—even worship itself.

But all of those things that we worship, apart from God, will fail us. None will satisfy our hearts. None are worthy of worship. Sure, many can be good gifts from God, but when we worship the gift instead of the Giver of the gift, we will find out how empty our idols truly are.

That's because only God is worthy of our worship. He alone is God. He alone is good. So God invites us to worship him simply for who he is:

> Ascribe to the Lord the glory due his name;
> worship the Lord
> in the splendor of his holiness. (Ps. 29:2)

We are to worship God because of his name—or his identity and character. The more time we spend getting to know who God is and his attributes, the more we will see how worthy of praise he truly is. We could worship God forever for his love and never run out of reasons to continue worshiping him *just* for that attribute, because he is infinite in all his ways.

But God also calls on us to worship him for what he has done:

> Come, let us worship and bow down;
> let us kneel before the LORD our Maker.
> For he is our God,
> and we are the people of his pasture,
> the sheep under his care. (Ps. 95:6–7)

There is so much God has done that is worthy of our worship. From what we read in God's Word to what we have experienced in our lives and in the lives of those around us, we find ample reason to celebrate God. Everything we have is due to his provision. Every gift is due to his goodness. God is at once our glorious Creator *and* our loving Father who is deserving of our eternal worship.

And that takes us to the last point about worship. True worship comes from the overflow of our hearts. When the Samaritan woman at the well asked Jesus about where the proper place to worship God was, this is part of what he told her:

> "God is spirit, and those who worship him must worship in Spirit and in truth." (John 4:24)

To worship God in Spirit and truth means that we are genuine in our worship—that it is produced in our hearts and that it is not artificial. A heart that loves God and is reminded of the gospel will be a heart that drives us toward genuine worship—the worship Jesus described. That is true worship.

Psalm 29:2; Psalm 95:6–7

39

Q. When should we worship God?

A. We should worship God at all times in all we do.

_____

If worship is declaring God's worth, it makes sense that we would always be in a posture of worship—just as we are always to be in prayer. There is never a time when we lack a reason to worship. Every single breath we take is evidence of God's love and provision in our lives and a reason to worship him! Here is how the writer of Hebrews put it after marveling at Jesus' sacrifice for us and our future hope in him:

> Therefore, through him let us continually offer up to God a sacrifice of praise, that is, the fruit of lips that confess his name. (Heb. 13:15)

Just as each breath is grounds for worship every second of the day, so is the truth of the gospel. Every time we think of what Jesus has done for us and what is in store for us for eternity, we can't help but be in awe of God's kindness to us and be driven to worship him. That is the key to worshiping continually—to have our minds and hearts set on the gospel.

At the end of Paul's detailed explanation of the gospel in the book of Romans, he interacts with the profound mystery of Israel's rejection of Jesus. The children of Israel, God's own people, rejected Jesus and crucified him, which resulted in the gospel going out to the Gentiles. The mystery is that Israel's rejection was used by God for good and that God isn't done with Israel yet. Their rejection is not complete. As Paul wrote this and considered the depth of God's ways, he was moved to worship. And so he did:

> Oh, the depth of the riches
> both of the wisdom and of the knowledge of God!

How unsearchable his judgments
and untraceable his ways!
For who has known the mind of the Lord?
Or who has been his counselor?
And who has ever given to God,
that he should be repaid?
For from him and through him
and to him are all things.
To him be the glory forever. Amen. (Rom. 11:33–36)

That is what it looks like to worship always, even in the middle of writing Scripture under the inspiration of the Holy Spirit. And that is what we should strive to do as well—to worship God day by day and minute by minute as we experience his goodness in our lives and as he uses us to impact others around us.

Hebrews 13:15; Romans 11:33–36

40

Q. How do we worship God?

A. We worship God by ourselves and with other believers as part of a church.

When we think of worship, especially if we have been part of a church for a while, we probably think of worship mostly as what happens when God's people gather. While that is an important part of worship, that is not all of what worship is. Worship is also something we do on our own. After diving deeply into the gospel for eleven chapters in his letter to the church at Rome, this is how Paul transitioned to how the gospel should make a difference in our lives:

> Therefore, brothers and sisters, in view of the mercies of God,
> I urge you to present your bodies as a living sacrifice, holy and
> pleasing to God; this is your true worship. (Rom. 12:1)

The gospel should compel us to live completely sacrificed to God. That is far more than what we do once or twice a week—this describes a way of life for us, and Paul calls it our true worship. That makes sense because if we truly understand God's great worth, we cannot contain our worship to just a few hours—it will change how we live moment by moment. We will find opportunities to worship God all around us as we take in a sunset, eat a good meal, hold a child, enjoy a hobby, or even sit quietly. We will see the fingerprints of God's beauty and majesty all around us and be prompted to worship. Now, these activities aren't worship in themselves. We can certainly eat a good meal without worshiping God. But when we connect what we are doing to God's gracious provision of it, we position ourselves to worship.

If that is true, do we need to gather for worship, then? Can't we just worship on our own? Here is the answer we find in Hebrews 10:24–25:

And let us watch out for one another to provoke love and good works, not neglecting to gather together, as some are in the habit of doing, but encouraging each other, and all the more as you see the day approaching.

We are not to neglect gathering together as a people of God so that we can encourage one another and provoke love and good works in each other. That is the key to why we need to gather with others for worship. It isn't just for us; we gather for others as well. God is relational and intends for us to be relational too—for our benefit and the benefit of others.

Notice the final phrase in that passage. We are to gather all the more as the day is approaching. That day is Christ's return—a day of celebration for us in Christ, but a day of judgment for those who have not trusted in him. And that is another reason why we gather—because the good works and love are not just for others in the church, but for our world as well. We gather to remember the gospel—what it has done for us, and the need of others to experience it as well. This passage was written almost two thousand years ago. That day is that much closer. Time is short, which is why we should gather to worship together with even more passion and urgency than ever before. Every week is more urgent than the last. Every week's worship as a church may be the last before Christ returns. That is why we gather.

Romans 12:1; 1 Corinthians 10:31

THE CHURCH AND THE LAST THINGS

Q. What is the church?

A. The *church* is a local community of Christians who are committed to one another and gather together regularly.

_____

When we think of *church*, we often think of a building, and that's understandable because we say things like, "It's time to leave for church" or "I missed you at church last week." But the church is not really a building or even an activity—it's a group of people who have trusted in Jesus.

In its broadest sense, the church is all those who have trusted in Jesus since his ministry on earth. This includes Christians all around the world throughout the centuries and is known as the universal church. We can think of this as *the* church. Here is how the Bible describes the church in Ephesians 1:22–23.

> And he subjected everything under his feet and appointed him
> as head over everything for the church, which is his body, the
> fullness of the one who fills all things in every way.

The church is the body of Christ, with him as the head. That picture is helpful because it reminds us of how interconnected the church is supposed to be. Each part of the human body is important and works together with the other parts for a person to function fully. And this takes us to how we think of the church most of the time—as a local group of Christians who gather together on a regular basis for worship, discipleship, fellowship, and more. We can think of this as *a* church. Because the church is a body, and we are each part of it, every Christian is called to be deeply committed to a local church to help it function fully. A Christian who is not part of a local church is disconnected from Christ's body and is not helping the church fulfill its mission of making disciples of the nations. So it is vital that every Christian be part of a church.

Not only is it vital that every Christian be part of a local church, it is also essential that each church be unified in spirit and purpose. This is why Christians should not just be part of a church, but be committed deeply to it and be willing to work through any differences that may arise, setting aside personal preferences for the good of the church as a whole and for the glory of God. Notice how Paul emphasized this unity when he wrote this about the church:

> There is one body and one Spirit — just as you were called to one hope at your calling, one Lord, one faith, one baptism, one God and Father of all, who is above all and through all and in all. (Eph. 4:4–6)

The word *one* appears seven times out of the forty words in those verses. Paul wanted to be clear how critical unity is. When the church is united around the gospel, it is an unstoppable force in our world.

Ephesians 1:22–23; Ephesians 4:4–6

Q. When did the church begin?

A. The church began at Pentecost, shortly after Jesus ascended into heaven.

It's somewhat of a surprise that Jesus hardly mentioned the church in the Gospels. He only mentions the church, *ekklesia* which means "called-out ones," "an assembly," or "a gathering," twice—in Matthew 16:18 and Matthew 18:17. But don't take how little Jesus talked about the church to mean he didn't value it. He does—greatly—because the church is his bride. Both times he talked about it, he spoke of the church as having great value. There is a reason he didn't talk about the church more, and we see it in Matthew 16:18.

> And I also say to you that you are Peter, and on this rock I will build my church, and the gates of Hades will not overpower it.

Notice the verb tense Jesus used—the future tense. He *would* build his church on faith like Peter's, not he *was building* his church on it. This means the church hadn't been formed at this point late in Jesus' ministry. If we jump ahead to the New Testament epistles, they speak of the church as already existing, such as 1 Corinthians 12:13:

> For we were all baptized by one Spirit into one body—whether Jews or Greeks, whether slaves or free—and we were all given one Spirit to drink.

Paul says that the Corinthians and he were all baptized into one body, the church, before he wrote to them. This means the church began at some point between the end of Jesus' ministry and when the epistles were being written, roughly twenty to thirty years later.

We can pinpoint the exact beginning of the church when we think a little more on what Paul said there. Baptism into the church coincided with being given the Holy Spirit, which makes sense because the indwelling of the Holy Spirit is a sign of a true believer. The church, then, began at Pentecost, roughly around AD 33, as it is recorded in Acts 2:1–4.

> When the day of Pentecost had arrived, they were all together in one place. Suddenly a sound like that of a violent rushing wind came from heaven, and it filled the whole house where they were staying. They saw tongues like flames of fire that separated and rested on each one of them. Then they were all filled with the Holy Spirit and began to speak in different tongues, as the Spirit enabled them.

This event marked the fulfillment of Jesus' promise to send the Holy Spirit to indwell his followers and also marked the official beginning of the church.

Matthew 16:18; 1 Corinthians 12:13; Acts 2:1–4

3

Q. Who is head of the church?

A. Jesus is the head, or leader, of the church.

Imagine if each part of the body did whatever it wanted. One leg might decide to go one direction and the other leg in a different direction. One arm might go up, while the other arm chooses to go down. One eye would choose to be closed while the other eye decides to blink rapidly. That wouldn't work very well, would it?

The reason this doesn't happen is because the head controls the body. The brain sends signals to the legs to have them work in unison to walk in the direction the head wants the body to go. The head tells the arms when to swing in stride with the legs' movements as it tells the eyes to stay open and focus in the correct direction. The body functions only because of the head. Without it, the body would not work at all or would be in chaos.

When it comes to the church body, we could experience even worse chaos if each part of the body chose what it wanted to do on its own. Each person in a church could go in a different direction with different goals and values if it weren't for the head of the church—Jesus—leading and controlling it. Jesus is the head, our leader, who keeps each part of the church working together as one. This is what Paul had in mind in Colossians 1:18 when he wrote this of Jesus:

> He is also the head of the body, the church;
> he is the beginning,
> the firstborn from the dead,
> so that he might come to have
> first place in everything.

The church belongs to Jesus. It is his body—his bride—and as its head he provides the leadership, vision, and purpose of the church. Ultimately then, every person in the church is accountable to him:

> And he subjected everything under his feet and appointed him as head over everything for the church, which is his body, the fullness of the one who fills all things in every way. (Eph. 1:22–23)

Our goal in the local church is to follow Jesus' guidance for his church. Everything we do should be done faithfully following Christ's will for his glory. He is the head; we are the body. Just as a leg doesn't tell the body what to do, neither do we tell Christ's body what to do—that is Jesus' right and privilege given to him by the Father.

Colossians 1:18; Ephesians 1:22–23

4

Q. What leaders has Jesus given the church under him?

A. Jesus has given pastors, elders, and deacons to lead the church under him.

———————

While Jesus is the head of the church, he has given the church pastors, elders, and deacons to provide leadership under his authority. Jesus has given these church leaders the responsibility of preaching and teaching the gospel, and nurturing, equipping, caring for, and guiding the church. One of the first times we see these leaders in action is at the Jerusalem Council recorded in Acts 15.

As the gospel was expanding out from Jerusalem, Gentiles began to trust in Jesus and enter into the church. But the question quickly arose if these Gentiles needed to first follow parts of the Old Testament Law—namely, circumcision. The church leaders gathered in Jerusalem to address this question, and when they reached a decision that Gentiles did not need to follow the Law first, they wrote a letter to send to the churches where the question first arose. When it came time to send the letter, the leaders needed to choose who would deliver it. Here is how it was decided in Acts 15:22.

> Then the apostles and the elders, with the whole church, decided to select men who were among them and to send them to Antioch with Paul and Barnabas: Judas, called Barsabbas, and Silas, both leading men among the brothers.

We see the apostles—those who had been with Jesus—work with the elders as well as the church as a whole to select the men to carry the letter to the churches. This gives a wonderful example of how church leadership is designed by God—with leaders guiding the church to act, but in concert with the church as a whole, not in isolation from it.

Pastors are also referred to as overseers, shepherds, and elders in the New Testament (1 Tim. 3:1–7; Titus 1:5–9). Pastors are charged with the primary responsibility of preaching the gospel and equipping the church.

While many consider elders a synonym for pastors, others believe that pastors are a subset of elders. All pastors are elders, but not all elders are pastors. In this view, elders are those who are responsible for guiding the church and protecting the doctrines of the church. Pastors, then, are elders who also preach and teach and who equip the church (Eph. 4:11–16).

Deacons are servants in the church who are called to help the pastors primarily by caring for those in the church (Acts 6:1–6; 1 Tim. 3:8–13). This is seen in what is most likely the calling of the first deacons in the church in Acts 6, although the title is not used in that passage. When a disagreement arose in the church about widows being cared for equally, the apostles led the church to select men to handle this problem so that they could continue focusing on preaching the gospel. This provides the model for the function of pastors and deacons in the church.

Whether Jesus has appointed pastors, elders, and deacons or pastors/ elders and deacons, these leaders are a gift from him to the local church, and they deserve our love, appreciation, and gratitude. One of the best ways the church can be united and fulfill its purpose is by submitting to the godly leaders Christ has given the church and praying for them as they bear the weight of leading the body of Christ under his authority.

1 Timothy 3:1–13; Titus 1:5–9

5

Q. Why does the church exist?

A. The church exists to glorify God by worshiping together, growing together, and taking the gospel to all the world.

While the early church in the book of Acts was not perfect and we are not required to do everything the way they did it, we can learn quite a bit from them. Right away at its formation at Pentecost, we see this great summary of what the church was doing:

> They devoted themselves to the apostles' teaching, to the fellowship, to the breaking of bread, and to prayer. (Acts 2:42)

Put simply, the church was devoted to worshiping and growing together. They were serious about it, and it showed in how rapidly the early church grew. The same is true of the church today. When God's people are devoted to worshiping and growing as part of a local church, the church flourishes. When the church flourishes, it reaches out and shares the gospel in its community and to the ends of the earth as Jesus commanded it to do in Matthew 28:18–20.

> Jesus came near and said to them, "All authority has been given to me in heaven and on earth. Go, therefore, and make disciples of all nations, baptizing them in the name of the Father and of the Son and of the Holy Spirit, teaching them to observe everything I have commanded you. And remember, I am with you always, to the end of the age."

These three activities—worship, growth, and evangelism—are tightly intertwined. Worship focuses on the greatness of God and fuels evangelism. Evangelism leads to new believers coming into the church and the need to help them grow in their faith. This growth, in turn, fosters worship, which repeats and deepens the cycle all over again.

For a church to be healthy and fulfill its purpose, it needs to maintain a healthy balance between focusing on helping the people in the church grow, caring for one another, and reaching out into the community to advance the gospel. A church can easily turn inward and fail to reach out and not fulfill the mission given by Christ. But at the same time, a church can turn outward and reach people for Christ but fail to nurture and grow those in the church and not fulfill its mission in a different way. A church that keeps these in balance is a church that positions itself to be used by God to bring him glory.

Acts 2:42; Matthew 28:18–20; 1 Corinthians 10:31

Q. What unites a church?

A. The gospel of Jesus Christ unites a church.

Sometimes it doesn't take much for people to connect. People who are different in nearly every way can be brought together because they cheer for the same sports team, grew up in the same area, went to the same school, share the same social cause, or just enjoy the same television show. The same thing can happen in a church. People in churches can be joined together for just as many reasons, but there is just one main reason a church *should* be joined together—the gospel.

The church in Galatia had fallen into the trap of thinking that it was up to them to preserve their salvation—they had to work to keep it. Paul wrote his epistle to the church to remind them of the critical truth that the gospel is what saves us and it is also what preserves us—our salvation from start to finish in glory one day hinges on what Christ has done for us, not what we can do for him. This is what he wrote as he began addressing the church's wrong thinking:

> I am amazed that you are so quickly turning away from him who called you by the grace of Christ and are turning to a different gospel—not that there is another gospel, but there are some who are troubling you and want to distort the gospel of Christ. (Gal. 1:6–7)

Paul would go on to write that the gospel isn't just the beginning of our relationship with Christ; it is the foundation of living in Christ as well. We are to live out our faith in Christ always remembering the gospel and recalling how much we have been forgiven in Christ as we rest in the righteousness Christ has given us.

This is why the gospel is the one thing that should unite a church. It is what we need to focus on, what we need to share, and what we have in common that matters most. Anything else that unites a church is fleeting and doesn't connect people as deeply—even seemingly good things. Interests change. Passions change. Reasons to divide can pop up quickly and can overshadow even the strongest reason to unite, unless that reason is the gospel.

When a church is united by the gospel, it can weather any storm and remain one body of Christ to fulfill its mission of taking that gospel to the rest of the world. This is so important that Jesus prayed for it right before his arrest and crucifixion:

> "I pray not only for these, but also for those who believe in me through their word. May they all be one, as you, Father, are in me and I am in you. May they also be in us, so that the world may believe you sent me." (John 17:20–21)

Did you know that Jesus prayed for us? We are the ones he mentions here—the ones who have believed in him through the words of his first disciples. And what does Jesus pray for us? Unity. Unity that reflects the perfect unity within the Trinity and unity that is so powerful that the world believes in Christ. This is unity that can be found only in the gospel.

Galatians 1:6–7; John 17:20–21

Q. What is the gospel?

A. The *gospel* is the good news of how God has provided forgiveness of sin through Jesus and how Jesus will restore all things one day.

The word *gospel* means "good news," which at its core refers to the message of salvation through Jesus Christ. This is how Paul summarized the gospel in 1 Corinthians 15:1–4.

> Now I want to make clear for you, brothers and sisters, the gospel I preached to you, which you received, on which you have taken your stand and by which you are being saved, if you hold to the message I preached to you—unless you believed in vain. For I passed on to you as most important what I also received: that Christ died for our sins according to the Scriptures, that he was buried, that he was raised on the third day according to the Scriptures.

The first thing to notice about Paul's definition of the gospel is what is most important. Think of three concentric circles. This gospel message would be in the center—the bull's eye—of what we believe. These are the essentials. The next ring out would be other doctrines from Scripture—convictions based on God's Word. These doctrines are very important in their own right, but they are not *most* important. We can unite while disagreeing on these doctrines, but we cannot unite if we don't believe in the same gospel. The outermost ring would be opinions and other beliefs. If we care about people, we will value these, but these are held very loosely in a church and should never divide us.

The second thing to notice is that the gospel is rooted in the Scriptures. Paul is careful to connect his summary of the gospel back to the Bible. It was important that the Corinthian church understood that Paul did not make this gospel up. It was given to us in Scripture from God.

The third thing to notice is that the gospel has the power to save. We trust in the gospel at first to be saved from our sin, but we also continue to trust in it as we live each day with the hope that our salvation will be completely fulfilled at Christ's return. Salvation is past, present, and future for us. We are saved, we are being saved, and we will be saved.

The fourth thing to notice is the core message of the gospel. Christ died for our sins, was buried, and was raised again. When we think about each of these three points, we realize that they are summaries of the gospel message—not the fullness of the gospel message. To properly understand these three points, we really need to understand much more, such as Jesus being the Son of God and living a sinless life, what sin is and the penalty of sin, and how a person needs to trust in Jesus to be forgiven and receive Jesus' righteousness.

And that takes us to the broader definition of the gospel. The gospel is best understood as the good news of all God has done to provide forgiveness through Jesus from day one all the way through eternity. The gospel is the big story of the Bible. We see the gospel in the Old Testament as we encounter how devastating sin is and how futile man's attempts were to be right with God apart from Christ. We also see the gospel in the Old Testament as God lavished grace and mercy on his people and delayed judgment, giving time for Christ to come. We see the gospel in the four Gospels as Jesus taught about God's kingdom and forgiveness through him and verified his identity through miracles and signs. We see the gospel in the death and resurrection of Jesus and then in the book of Acts and the epistles in how the church was being built on the foundation of the gospel and advancing it into the world. And finally, we see the gospel in Revelation and other eschatological prophecies telling how Jesus will return one day and make everything right again. Jesus will put an end to sin and death once and for all, all of creation will be renewed, and we will all be changed to live with God for eternity.

That is the gospel—the good news of what Jesus has done, is doing, and will do one day.

1 Corinthians 15:1–4; John 3:16

Q. What two ordinances has Jesus given the church?

A. Jesus has given the church the ordinances of baptism and the Lord's Supper.

An ordinance is an act given to the church by Christ that pictures the truth of the gospel to its participants and its observers. Jesus has given the church two ordinances—baptism and the Lord's Supper.

In Matthew 28:19, Jesus commanded the church to baptize:

> "Go, therefore, and make disciples of all nations, baptizing them in the name of the Father and of the Son and of the Holy Spirit."

The ordinance of baptism occurs then as often as new disciples are made. Jesus' giving of the second ordinance, the Lord's Supper or Communion, is described in 1 Corinthians 11:23–26.

> For I received from the Lord what I also passed on to you: On the night when he was betrayed, the Lord Jesus took bread, and when he had given thanks, broke it, and said, "This is my body, which is for you. Do this in remembrance of me."
>
> In the same way also he took the cup, after supper, and said, "This cup is the new covenant in my blood. Do this, as often as you drink it, in remembrance of me." For as often as you eat this bread and drink the cup, you proclaim the Lord's death until he comes.

The frequency of the ordinance of the Lord's Supper isn't clearly defined and is open to how a local church defines "as often." Some churches will conduct the Lord's Supper at every weekly gathering, while others may conduct it once a month, once a quarter, or even less frequently.

Matthew 28:18–20; 1 Corinthians 11:23–26

Q. Why did Jesus give these two ordinances?

A. Jesus gave these two ordinances to help us remember what he has done and that we belong to him.

Christ knows two things about us—we tend to be quite forgetful and pictures and images connect with us more deeply than words. This is why he gave us the two ordinances of baptism and the Lord's Supper—to help us remember what he has done for us and who we are as his church.

Baptism pictures both of these truths through the image of burial and resurrection. When a person is baptized, he or she is lowered under the water, picturing death of the old self, and then raised up out of the water, picturing resurrected new life in Christ. This picture of the death of the old self and new life also reminds us of how it was made possible through Christ's death and resurrection.

Baptism also pictures our identity by the name in which we are baptized:

> "Go, therefore, and make disciples of all nations, baptizing them in the name of the Father and of the Son and of the Holy Spirit." (Matt. 28:19)

We are baptized in the name of the Father, Son, and Holy Spirit, signifying God's power and full authority over us. When we are baptized, we are confessing that we recognize and submit to God's absolute authority in our lives.

The second ordinance of the Lord's Supper reminds us of what Jesus has done for us on the cross to secure our salvation as we read in 1 Corinthians 11:23–26.

> For I received from the Lord what I also passed on to you: On the night when he was betrayed, the Lord Jesus took bread, and

when he had given thanks, broke it, and said, "This is my body,
which is for you. Do this in remembrance of me."

In the same way also he took the cup, after supper, and said,
"This cup is the new covenant in my blood. Do this, as often
as you drink it, in remembrance of me." For as often as you eat
this bread and drink the cup, you proclaim the Lord's death
until he comes.

The bread and the cup represent the broken body and shed blood of Jesus
to provide our forgiveness of sin. That is what we proclaim to one another and
all who observe when we participate in the Lord's Supper. Each individual
taking the bread and cup declares that he or she has trusted in what Jesus has
done on the cross. This is why only believers should participate in the Lord's
Supper.

The Lord's Supper also pictures our identity in Christ by how we consume the bread and drink of the cup. In a very real way, what we eat and drink
becomes part of us. While there is nothing special about what we consume,
it is a powerful picture of how Christ has come into our lives and changed us
forevermore.

Matthew 28:18–20; 1 Corinthians 11:23–26

Q. What is the Lord's Supper?

A. The *Lord's Supper* is eating the bread and drinking of the cup to remember the life, death, and resurrection of Jesus as we also look forward to his coming kingdom.

When the children of Israel called out to God for deliverance from bondage in Egypt, he heard their cries and answered them. God sent Moses to tell Pharaoh to let his people go, but Pharaoh refused. So God sent ten plagues on the land to show Egypt and his own people that he is the one true God whom Pharaoh should obey. The final plague was the death of each firstborn son throughout the land, but God was gracious to provide a way for his people to escape death through the Passover.

The Passover is recorded in Exodus 12 and featured every family taking a spotless lamb, sacrificing it, placing some of its blood on the sides and top of their doors, and then eating the lamb as part of a meal. Then when the Lord went through the land striking down the firstborn son in homes, he would pass over the homes with blood around its doorframes.

God established the Passover meal to be celebrated every year to remember how he had delivered his people from Egypt. This was the meal Jesus and his disciples were celebrating when Jesus instituted the Lord's Supper:

> As they were eating, he took bread, blessed and broke it, gave it to them, and said, "Take it; this is my body." Then he took a cup, and after giving thanks, he gave it to them, and they all drank from it. He said to them, "This is my blood of the covenant, which is poured out for many." (Mark 14:22–24)

Just as God's people in Egypt were spared from death by the blood of a lamb, we too are spared from death by the blood of the Lamb who was slain (John 1:29; Rev. 5:6). While the disciples probably didn't understand how Jesus was adding to the meaning of the Passover during that first Lord's Supper, they would soon after. Later that night, Jesus was betrayed and arrested and then the next day he was crucified, and they would see his body broken and blood shed for the forgiveness of sin.

When we partake of the Lord's Supper today, we look back on what Christ has done to provide the forgiveness of our sin—his perfect life, perfect sacrifice, and bodily resurrection—as we also look forward to the day when Jesus said we would eat of this meal with him in the fullness of God's kingdom in the future (Matt. 26:29).

Because of what the Lord's Supper represents, only those who have trusted in Jesus should participate. But even those who have trusted in Jesus should examine their hearts beforehand to determine whether there are any unconfessed sins or strained relationships that should be addressed first:

> So then, whoever eats the bread or drinks the cup of the Lord
> in an unworthy manner will be guilty of sin against the body
> and blood of the Lord. Let a person examine himself; in this
> way let him eat the bread and drink from the cup. (1 Cor.
> 11:27–28)

Once any sins are confessed and relationships are restored, believers can partake of the Lord's Supper in an attitude of both sobriety, remembering the suffering and sacrifice of Christ, and also joy, recognizing that sin and death have been defeated by the Lamb of God.

Mark 14:22–24; 1 Corinthians 10:16–17; 1 Corinthians 11:23–29

11

Q. What does the bread represent?

A. The bread represents the body of Jesus that was broken on the cross.

The bread used during the Passover meal was a flatbread baked without leaven because the meal was to be prepared and eaten quickly (Exod. 12:15–20). God commanded his people to celebrate the Festival of Unleavened Bread during the week leading up to Passover every year after. Before this festival began, families had to remove all leaven from their homes and only unleavened bread could be eaten during the week. Leaven, in this case, symbolized sin and the great effort of cleaning an entire house of every single morsel of leaven was to remind God's people of the hopelessness of them trying to remove their sin on their own.

The bread dough was made without leaven and holes were poked in the bread, and then it was roasted over a fire resulting in a striped pattern from the flames. The appearance of the bread reminds us of what Isaiah wrote about the Messiah in Isaiah 53:5.

> But he was pierced because of our rebellion,
> crushed because of our iniquities;
> punishment for our peace was on him,
> and we are healed by his wounds.

Jesus was pierced because of our sins, and by his wounds ("stripes" in the King James Version) we are healed. This imagery of the bread was why Jesus used it to picture his body:

> As they were eating, Jesus took bread, blessed and broke it,
> gave it to the disciples, and said, "Take and eat it; this is my
> body." (Matt. 26:26)

Jesus was our sinless sacrifice on the cross, who was striped with a whip and pierced through his hands, feet, and side for our sins. When we eat the bread during the Lord's Supper, God is inviting us to reflect on what Christ did for us on the cross—his suffering and death—so that we could be forgiven of our sin. Our forgiveness is free for us, but it came at a great cost paid by Jesus.

Isaiah 53:5; Matthew 26:26; 1 Corinthians 11:24

12

Q. What does the cup represent?

A. The cup represents the blood of Jesus that was shed on the cross for the forgiveness of sin.

Without the shedding of blood, there can be no forgiveness of sin (Heb. 9:22). Because the penalty of sin is death, blood must be shed and life must be given up. This is the picture God gave us in the Old Testament with the sacrificial system. Each animal that was sacrificed reminded God's people that their sin had to be paid for in blood—but that the blood of animals was not sufficient (Heb. 10:4). The sacrifice of one animal wasn't sufficient. Animals had to be sacrificed year after year.

All of this pointed to Jesus—who is the perfect, one-time-for-all sacrifice (Heb. 10:14). The blood Jesus shed on the cross as our perfect sacrifice is what is represented by the cup:

> Then he took a cup, and after giving thanks, he gave it to them and said, "Drink from it, all of you. For this is my blood of the covenant, which is poured out for many for the forgiveness of sins." (Matt. 26:27–28)

Jesus' blood shed on the cross provided forgiveness of sin for those who trust in him and also initiated a new covenant between God and people. In the Old Testament, God entered into a covenant with his people through Moses (see Exod. 19–24)—a covenant that was conditioned on the people's obedience and a covenant they failed to uphold through their disobedience. But then later, God spoke through the prophet Jeremiah and promised that a new covenant was coming—a covenant that would not be based on obedience, but on God changing the hearts of his people:

"Look, the days are coming"—this is the LORD's declaration—
"when I will make a new covenant with the house of Israel and
with the house of Judah. This one will not be like the covenant
I made with their ancestors on the day I took them by the hand
to lead them out of the land of Egypt—my covenant that they
broke even though I am their master"—the LORD's declaration. "Instead, this is the covenant I will make with the house
of Israel after those days"—the LORD's declaration. "I will put
my teaching within them and write it on their hearts. I will be
their God, and they will be my people. No longer will one teach
his neighbor or his brother, saying, 'Know the LORD,' for they
will all know me, from the least to the greatest of them"—this
is the LORD's declaration. "For I will forgive their iniquity and
never again remember their sin." (Jer. 31:31–34)

This covenant, known as the New Covenant, is what began with the
shedding of Jesus' blood. When we trust in Christ, our hearts are changed by
the Holy Spirit so that we have the ability for the first time truly to love God
and want to obey him. At the same time, our relationship with God is not
based on our obedience, but on our adoption as God's children, meaning that
it is always completely secure. God is our God and we are his people no matter what. All of our sin is removed from us and Christ's righteousness is given
in its place. This is what we remember and celebrate when we take of the cup
during the Lord's Supper.

Hebrews 9:22; Matthew 26:27–28; Jeremiah 31:31–34

13

Q. What is baptism?

A. *Baptism* is a symbol of how God has given us new life in Christ and joined us with him and the church.

Baptize is a Greek word that doesn't translate well into English so we just kept the original word. *Baptize* means to "immerse" or "sink" and is used outside of the Bible to describe a ship sinking. When we baptize a person, we immerse him under water to picture how he has died to himself, and then we bring him up out of the water to show how he has been given new life in Christ.

While Christ has commanded that believers are to be baptized as one of their first acts of obedience to him (Matt. 28:18–20), baptism does not save a person. We know that salvation is by grace through faith alone and nothing we can do (Eph. 2:8–9), so the act of baptism cannot be part of salvation. Baptism is an outward act demonstrating what God has done through Christ in us already.

One proof that we are saved apart from baptism is found during Jesus' crucifixion itself. When Jesus was crucified, a criminal flanked him on each side. One of the criminals mocked Jesus, but the other demonstrated faith in Jesus and asked him to remember him. Here is how Jesus replied in Luke 23:43.

> And he said to him, "Truly I tell you, today you will be with me in paradise."

Jesus promised the criminal that he would be with Christ in paradise— the place of the dead for those who had been forgiven by God. But the thief was not baptized, proving that baptism is not part of salvation, but instead an act of obedience that follows salvation.

While baptism is not necessary for salvation, that does not mean it isn't important. There is a good reason why Jesus commands it—because it not only pictures what God has done in each of us as individuals, but also how he has joined us to him and with others as a part of the church:

> Or are you unaware that all of us who were baptized into Christ Jesus were baptized into his death? Therefore we were buried with him by baptism into death, in order that, just as Christ was raised from the dead by the glory of the Father, so we too may walk in newness of life. For if we have been united with him in the likeness of his death, we will certainly also be in the likeness of his resurrection. (Rom. 6:3–5)

Notice that Paul begins by reminding the church that we all were baptized in Christ. He is not speaking necessarily of water baptism here, but more of the imagery of joining together which water baptism portrays. We each have been joined with Christ in salvation, and we have been joined together as one body as well. This is why water baptism is so important—it reminds us as individuals and as the church of this truth. God cares about both of these perspectives. Our faith is personal, but we are not in faith with him alone—we are part of the church and are to be joined together with it. Baptism pictures both of these beautiful truths together.

Matthew 28:18–20; Romans 6:3–5

Q. What is the hope of the church?

A. The hope of the church is the return of Jesus when he will make all things new.

When the Bible speaks of hope, it means something different from how we usually speak of hope today. We might say things like, "I hope it doesn't rain this weekend," or "I hope I get a new shirt for my birthday," or "I hope we have steak for dinner." In each of these cases, when we say we hope for something, we are not sure if it will happen or not, but we would sure like for it to.

But that's not how the Bible speaks of hope. When the Bible talks about hope, it means trusting in God and that what he has promised to do will happen one day. This definition is what is in mind in verses like Jeremiah 14:22, where God is described as our hope, and Psalm 39:7.

> "Now, Lord, what do I wait for?
> My hope is in you."

We are to wait on God with expectant hope—not with wishful thinking. We hope with confident certainty, not with wishy-washy uncertainty.

So what is the hope of the church? What do we confidently wait on with certainty? Paul tells us in Romans 8:22–25.

> For we know that the whole creation has been groaning together with labor pains until now. Not only that, but we ourselves who have the Spirit as the firstfruits—we also groan within ourselves, eagerly waiting for adoption, the redemption of our bodies. Now in this hope we were saved, but hope that is seen is not hope, because who hopes for what he sees? Now

if we hope for what we do not see, we eagerly wait for it with patience.

Our hope is in the return of Christ when we will finally experience the fullness of our salvation. On that day, we will finally be rid of sin, death, and all the results of the Fall, and our position in Christ and what we experience will finally and fully align. Our perfection in Christ will match how we think, feel, and live once and for all.

But our hope is even greater than that! When Christ returns he will make all things new again—those of us who have trusted in him as well as all of his creation. Just as we long for that day and we groan as if in labor anticipating when we will experience the fullness of our new birth, so does creation. Christ will renew all of creation, which is now under the curse, and we will once again have a perfect world and universe around us to enjoy and steward as part of our eternal worship of God.

Psalm 39:7; Romans 8:22–25

15

Q. When will Jesus return?

A. Jesus will return in God's perfect timing.

The church hopes in the return of Jesus because he made this promise to us—that he was going away but he would return one day for us:

> "If I go away and prepare a place for you, I will come again and take you to myself, so that where I am you may be also." (John 14:3)

Jesus first came as the Suffering Servant (Isa. 52–53), but he will return as the Conquering King (Rev. 19). We know this is true and we place our hope on it, but we don't know when it will happen. Just before Jesus ascended to return to his place of glory with the Father, the disciples asked him if he was about to establish the long-awaited kingdom of God. Here is how he responded to them:

> "It is not for you to know times or periods that the Father has set by his own authority." (Acts 1:7)

Timing shouldn't be our concern. God has set a time, but we cannot do anything about it and we don't need to know that part of his plan. All we need to know is what we are to do, and right after this, Jesus told his disciples that they would be his witnesses throughout the entire world. We are to do the same. We are to eagerly wait for Jesus' return (Phil. 3:20), but we don't wait idly. We take the gospel into the world as we wait for the day Jesus returns, knowing that it could happen at any time:

> About the times and the seasons: Brothers and sisters, you do not need anything to be written to you. For you yourselves

know very well that the day of the Lord will come just like a
thief in the night. (1 Thess. 5:1–2)

Jesus coming like a thief in the night doesn't mean that he will come
deceptively or secretly. It means that he can return at any time. His return is
imminent. That is great news for the church, but it is also a sobering reminder
that on that day anyone who has not trusted in Jesus will be judged for his or
her sin (2 Thess. 1:7–10). Our hope in Christ is also a powerful motivator for
us to share the gospel with all those around us—our families, friends, cowork-
ers, neighbors, and even strangers—knowing that this could be their last day
to hear and respond to the gospel.

John 14:3; Acts 1:7; 1 Thess. 5:1–2

16

Q. How will Jesus return?

A. Jesus will return in glory in his resurrected body for all the world to see.

We would have probably stood there and stared as well. That's what you tend to do when you experience something extraordinary. You stand there with your mouth hanging open in stunned silence. And that is exactly what the disciples did when Jesus ascended into heaven. Can you imagine what that was like? One minute Jesus is talking with you—on the ground—and the next minute, he just lifts off the ground and goes into the sky. Higher and higher until he disappears from sight into the clouds. It's no wonder the disciples stood there looking up.

But that is when two men in white clothes appeared to them—angels, no doubt—and said this to them:

> They said, "Men of Galilee, why do you stand looking up into heaven? This same Jesus, who has been taken from you into heaven, will come in the same way that you have seen him going into heaven." (Acts 1:11)

While this account is somewhat humorous, it also reveals something very important to us—that Jesus will return the same way he ascended. One day when Jesus returns, he will return in bodily form, just as he ascended, for all the world to see. Revelation 1:7 makes it clear that Christ's return will not be in secret—it will be known around the world:

> Look, he is coming with the clouds,
> and every eye will see him,
> even those who pierced him.

And all the tribes of the earth
will mourn over him.
So it is to be. Amen.

There will be one critical difference between Christ's ascension and return though. Jesus left as the Suffering Servant, but he will return as the Conquering King. Here is how his return is depicted in Revelation 19:11–16.

Then I saw heaven opened, and there was a white horse. Its rider is called Faithful and True, and he judges and makes war with justice. His eyes were like a fiery flame, and many crowns were on his head. He had a name written that no one knows except himself. He wore a robe dipped in blood, and his name is called the Word of God. The armies that were in heaven followed him on white horses, wearing pure white linen. A sharp sword came from his mouth, so that he might strike the nations with it. He will rule them with an iron rod. He will also trample the winepress of the fierce anger of God, the Almighty. And he has a name written on his robe and on his thigh: KING OF KINGS AND LORD OF LORDS.

When Jesus returns, he will return in power and glory and bring justice to the world—judgment for those who have rejected him and reward for those who have trusted in him. The donkey of a humble servant will be replaced with the regal white horse of a King. A crown of thorns will be replaced with a royal crown of absolute authority. The return of Jesus will be a great day for those who have trusted in him and a terrible day for all those who have opposed him.

Revelation 1:7; Revelation 19:11–16; 2 Thessalonians 1:7–10

17

Q. When Jesus returns, what will happen to all the people who have died?

A. All the dead will be raised again when Jesus returns.

Most of us know that when Jesus returns, those who have believed in Christ will be resurrected from the dead, but the Bible says that they won't be the only ones resurrected. All of the dead will be raised again. This is what Jesus said about the future resurrection of all people:

> "Do not be amazed at this, because a time is coming when all who are in the graves will hear his voice and come out—those who have done good things, to the resurrection of life, but those who have done wicked things, to the resurrection of condemnation." (John 5:28–29)

All who have done good things—believed in him—will be resurrected to life, but all who have done wicked things—rejected him—will be resurrected to eternal condemnation. Paul echoed this in his trial before Felix when he said:

> I have a hope in God, which these men themselves also accept, that there will be a resurrection, both of the righteous and the unrighteous. (Acts 24:15)

Both the righteous and unrighteous will be resurrected. Everyone has eternal life; it is just a matter of whether that eternal life is outside of relationship with God and apart from anything that is good, or in relationship with God enjoying all that is good.

While the resurrection of those who have rejected Christ will lead to their eternal judgment, the resurrection of those who have trusted in Christ gives us great hope for ourselves and our brothers and sisters in Christ. Death is not final! One day we will be raised in new life and be given new resurrected bodies. The church at Thessalonica had heard a rumor that Jesus had returned, and they believed it and thought they had missed it, which of course greatly concerned them. So Paul wrote to this church to remind them that Jesus would not come without them knowing and to encourage them in knowing what will happen when Jesus does return:

> We do not want you to be uninformed, brothers and sisters, concerning those who are asleep, so that you will not grieve like the rest, who have no hope. For if we believe that Jesus died and rose again, in the same way, through Jesus, God will bring with him those who have fallen asleep. For we say this to you by a word from the Lord: We who are still alive at the Lord's coming will certainly not precede those who have fallen asleep. For the Lord himself will descend from heaven with a shout, with the archangel's voice, and with the trumpet of God, and the dead in Christ will rise first. Then we who are still alive, who are left, will be caught up together with them in the clouds to meet the Lord in the air, and so we will always be with the Lord. (1 Thess. 4:13–17)

Because of our future resurrection, we grieve the death of a believer differently than the world grieves. We grieve with hope! One day, Jesus will return and all the dead in Christ will be raised first, and then those believers who are alive on that day will rise after and we will all be with Christ. If Jesus doesn't return in our lifetime, that is good news. We will be resurrected and be joined with him first! But if he does return in our lifetime, that is good news too. We will see all those in Christ whom we love and who have died be raised first and then we will join them and Christ together forevermore!

John 5:28–29; Acts 24:15

18

Q. What will happen to everyone who has not believed in Jesus when he returns?

A. Everyone who has not believed in Jesus will be judged for his or her sins and be separated from God forever.

Despite the many differences between people, there is really only one way to separate people: everyone is either righteous because of his or her faith in Christ, or unrighteous because of his or her sin. It's that simple. Everyone is either a believer or an unbeliever. When Jesus explained this, he used the image of sheep and goats (Matt. 25:31–46). The sheep are all those who have trusted in him and demonstrated their faith by their good works on earth. The goats are all those who have not trusted in him and demonstrated their lack of faith by their evil works. When Jesus returns, he will separate the sheep and the goats, with the sheep on his right and the goats on his left. Here is what he said will happen to the goats:

> "Then he will also say to those on the left, 'Depart from me, you who are cursed, into the eternal fire prepared for the devil and his angels!'" (Matt. 25:41)

And shortly after, Jesus added this:

> "And they will go away into eternal punishment, but the righteous into eternal life." (Matt. 25:46)

This tells us two important things about what is in store for unbelievers. First, they will be thrown into the lake of fire along with Satan and the demons, for whom it was prepared. While we aren't sure if this will be a place of literal fire, that isn't quite as important as understanding that it will be a place of punishment and anguish. Even if fire is figurative here, it is used to express an idea of great suffering—suffering brought on by sin against a perfectly holy and righteous God. James 1:17 says that God is the source of all that is good, so unbelievers will spend eternity in a place devoid of anything good—primarily a relationship with God himself.

And that takes us to the second thing we learn here—unbelievers will be punished for all eternity. There are some who believe that unbelievers will only be punished for a time and then they will cease to exist. This is called annihilationism—God will annihilate, or wipe out, those who reject him. The problem with this view is that Jesus compared eternal life with eternal punishment. If we believe, rightly so, that we will spend eternity with God, then we must accept that unbelievers will spend eternity apart from him. Paul also spoke of eternal punishment when he wrote this of Christ's return:

> When he takes vengeance with flaming fire on those who don't know God and on those who don't obey the gospel of our Lord Jesus. They will pay the penalty of eternal destruction from the Lord's presence and from his glorious strength. (2 Thess. 1:8–9)

But before unbelievers are cast away from God's presence for eternity, they will stand before him in judgment at an event sometimes called the Great White Throne Judgment. Every single person who has rebelled against God and who failed to repent of their sin and turn to Christ will see the evidence of God's righteousness and why they have been condemned by their own works:

> Then I saw a great white throne and one seated on it. Earth and heaven fled from his presence, and no place was found for them. I also saw the dead, the great and the small, standing before the throne, and books were opened. Another book was opened, which is the book of life, and the dead were judged according to their works by what was written in the books. Then the sea gave up the dead that were in it, and death and Hades gave up the dead that were in them; each one was judged according to their works. Death and Hades were thrown into the lake of fire. This is the second death, the lake of fire. And

anyone whose name was not found written in the book of life was thrown into the lake of fire. (Rev. 20:11–15)

This is also the likely time for God's promise that every knee will bow and tongue will confess that Jesus is Lord (Rom. 14:11; Phil. 2:10). No one will be able to refute his or her condemnation or God's justice on that day. Every unbeliever will acknowledge what he refused to acknowledge during his life—that God alone is sovereign King—as he is sent into the place of eternal punishment.

Matthew 25:46; 2 Thessalonians 1:8–9; Revelation 20:11–15

19

Q. What will happen to everyone who has believed in Jesus when he returns?

A. Everyone who has believed in Jesus will be rewarded for his or her faithfulness and be with God forevermore.

Our bodies are broken vessels containing a priceless treasure in Christ (2 Cor. 4:7). Even though Christ is within us, we have been declared righteous by God, and forgiven of all our sin, while we remain on earth and until Jesus returns, we continue to live in bodies ravaged by the Fall. Our bodies break down and wear out, but most significantly, they are prone to sin. But one day when Jesus returns, these broken vessels will be replaced:

> Listen, I am telling you a mystery: We will not all fall asleep, but we will all be changed, in a moment, in the twinkling of an eye, at the last trumpet. For the trumpet will sound, and the dead will be raised incorruptible, and we will be changed. (1 Cor. 15:51–52)

On that glorious day, the dead in Christ will be resurrected from the dead and all who remain alive will be changed instantly and we will all enjoy new, incorruptible, imperishable bodies for eternity. We will finally be rid of sin and we will be with Christ forevermore (1 Thess. 4:16–17). This is the ultimate reward in store for us, but it isn't the only reward. In God's kindness and graciousness, he has promised additional rewards based on our faithfulness to him. These rewards will be given at what is called the judgment seat of Christ:

> For we must all appear before the judgment seat of Christ,
> so that each may be repaid for what he has done in the body,
> whether good or evil. (2 Cor. 5:10)

Now when we first look at that, our eyebrow should rise. How can we be judged for doing evil? Aren't all of our sins paid for by Christ? Hasn't he been judged for our evil in our place? Then how can we be judged for it as well?

It's an important question. It is true that our sins have been judged already with Jesus paying their full punishment. So we know that cannot be in mind here. So what will this judgment of believers look like? Paul gave us a glimpse elsewhere when he wrote:

> For no one can lay any other foundation than what has been
> laid down. That foundation is Jesus Christ. If anyone builds
> on the foundation with gold, silver, costly stones, wood, hay,
> or straw, each one's work will become obvious. For the day
> will disclose it, because it will be revealed by fire; the fire will
> test the quality of each one's work. If anyone's work that he
> has built survives, he will receive a reward. If anyone's work
> is burned up, he will experience loss, but he himself will be
> saved—but only as through fire. (1 Cor. 3:11–15)

Paul begins by talking about the foundation we all share—the gospel—a foundation which is solid. But then Paul focuses on what each of us have built on that foundation—how have we lived our lives in light of the gospel? Some of the work is made of gold, silver, and costly stones. This is when we serve God faithfully with the right motives. But some of the work is made of wood, hay, and straw. This is when we fail to serve God or we do it with the wrong motives. The judgment seat of Christ will reveal what we have built, and we will be rewarded for the ways we have been faithful and we will lose reward for the ways we were not faithful. So this judgment is not one of salvation or condemnation—it is one of reward and loss of reward. Notice Paul concluded by saying that everyone who stands before the judgment seat of Christ will be saved.

Having received our resurrected bodies and any additional rewards for our faithfulness in life, we will enter into eternal fellowship with God:

> Then I saw a new heaven and a new earth; for the first heaven
> and the first earth had passed away, and the sea was no more.

> I also saw the holy city, the new Jerusalem, coming down out of heaven from God, prepared like a bride adorned for her husband.
>
> Then I heard a loud voice from the throne: Look, God's dwelling is with humanity, and he will live with them. They will be his peoples, and God himself will be with them and will be their God. He will wipe away every tear from their eyes. Death will be no more; grief, crying, and pain will be no more, because the previous things have passed away. (Rev. 21:1–4)

From this point forward for all of eternity, we will experience the abundant life God intended when he created us. Sin, death, pain, and suffering will all be done away with, and we will finally be able to serve and worship God perfectly on the new earth. Just as Adam and Eve had been given work to do for God's glory and were supposed to enjoy relationship with one another, we too will worship God through what we do and through enjoying being with our friends, family, and all others who have trusted in Jesus for eternity.

1 Corinthians 15:51–52; Revelation 21:1–4

20

Q. What will happen to the world when Jesus returns?

A. When Jesus returns, the world will be made right once again and God's kingdom will come in fullness.

There were two trees named in the garden of Eden—the tree of knowledge of good and evil, which Adam and Eve were forbidden from eating of, and the Tree of Life, which they were welcome to partake of. At least until they rebelled against God.

After Adam and Eve were judged for their sin, God removed them from the garden. But it wasn't as much a punishment as it was a provision, as we read in Genesis 3:22.

> The Lord God said, "Since the man has become like one of us, knowing good and evil, he must not reach out, take from the tree of life, eat, and live forever."

God did not want Adam and Eve to eat of that tree and live forever in their current condition. By removing them and then guarding access to that tree, he prevented them from eating of the tree and provided them with the opportunity to live forever in a different way—a better way—through repentance of sin and faith in him.

And then just like that, the Tree of Life isn't mentioned again. It isn't in the rest of the Pentateuch written by Moses. It isn't in any of the books of history in the Old Testament. It isn't in any of the writings or prophets either. (Proverbs mentions "a tree of life" several times which is different from the Tree of Life.) As you turn to the New Testament, it is still curiously absent.

Jesus doesn't mention it in the Gospels, and Paul doesn't even write about it in any of his epistles.

But then as we turn to the final book of the Bible—Revelation—we see it again. Twice. First, Jesus mentions it as the reward awaiting those who conquer as part of his letter to the church in Ephesus (Rev. 2:7). And then we see it near the very end of the book after the return of Jesus:

> Then he showed me the river of the water of life, clear as crystal, flowing from the throne of God and of the Lamb down the middle of the city's main street. The tree of life was on each side of the river, bearing twelve kinds of fruit, producing its fruit every month. The leaves of the tree are for healing the nations, and there will no longer be any curse. The throne of God and of the Lamb will be in the city, and his servants will worship him. (Rev. 22:1–3)

The Tree of Life is described as having a central place and purpose in the new creation. It straddles a river of living water and produces fruit year-round for the enjoyment of the people of God. Why is this so significant? Because God is making something crystal clear through the Tree of Life.

When Adam and Eve sinned, they did not fall alone. Creation fell with them, which was immediately evidenced by the thorns and thistles that made Adam's work difficult (Gen. 3:18). Just as those who have trusted in Jesus yearn for redemption, so does creation (Rom. 8:22). When Jesus returns, all of creation will be changed and made new and the curse will be removed from the universe completely as he says in Revelation 21:5.

> Then the one seated on the throne said, "Look, I am making everything new."

This is why the Tree of Life in the new creation is so important. It is an exclamation mark of God's victory. Sin and death have been defeated! What Satan tried to destroy still stands—even better than before! The Tree of Life declares to us that God's purposes cannot be thwarted. God will indeed reign over his kingdom forevermore, and his people he purchased through the blood of his Son will be with him forever, enjoying what he intended from day one—abundant life with him in his perfect creation.

Revelation 22:1–3; Revelation 21:5; 2 Peter 3:10–13

Notes

1. In case you are curious, the hypostatic union is how Jesus' full humanity and full deity relate to each other, and the peccability of Jesus is a question of whether or not Jesus could have sinned on earth.

2. http://www.space.com/26078-how-many-stars-are-there.html.

3. https://joshuaproject.net/resources/articles/how_many_people_groups _are_there.

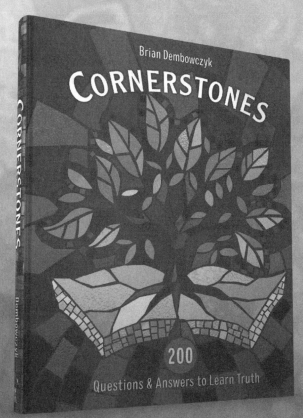